GROWING UP
ARMY

The story of a soldier, his loving wife,
and their nine adventurous Army Brats
traveling the world in service to our country

ROBERT R. HEATH SR.

ISBN: 978-1-960146-54-0 (hard cover)
       978-1-960146-55-7 (soft cover)

Edited by: Erika Nein

Book jacket concept by Robert R. Heath Sr.
Photographs and stories by members of the Heath family;
used with permission.

Warren
publishing

Published by Warren Publishing
Charlotte, NC
www.warrenpublishing.net
Printed in the United States

Growing Up Army *is dedicated to our parents—Sergeant Major Richard*
Heath and Virginia Mae Heath,
who took us around the world
in service to the country they loved—
and to my eight wonderful Army Brat siblings:
Dan, Dave, Mike, Rachel, Jim, Steve, Rick, and Pat.
You were my best friends, no matter where
on the planet we lived,
and remain so today and forever.

We Are Army Brats

My hometown is the world,
My friends are where I am today.
Home is where our hearts and family are,
With no house to be called home.

Here today, in another country tomorrow, is our life.
Wherever we are, we are curious about the differences
we see around us.
They are not like us, and we are not like them.
Yet, we see our differences as opportunities to explore and grow.

Across the Pacific and Atlantic Oceans,
From East Coast to West Coast of America, and back again.
Asia, Europe, North, South, East, and West in our country,
The world *is* our home.

"It's time to move, kids" means saying goodbye,
Then saying hello in our newest place in the world.
Yes, we have said goodbye to our friends,
But wherever we were, we always had us.

We find new friends quickly,
Always with the knowledge that friendships are temporary.
Will we see each other again at our next assignment?
Or the next?

Through it all, we love our family and country,
We respect and honor those who serve and protect our freedom.
We honor and love our parents who created our lives
And the many paths our lives traveled,
Growing Up Army!

FOREWORD

By Jim Heath, sixth of nine

I loved growing up Army. I knew at an early age I was getting to experience the world in a way very few people ever do, unless they are military Brats. Through all our lives, as Army Brats, we had to deal with the heartbreak of constant separation from good friends due to the normal rotation of Dad's assignments. Then occasionally we had the great joy of meeting them again a few years down the road at another base.

Growing up Army means never having roots to any one "hometown." Although I know I was born in Carlisle, Pennsylvania, I have always felt odd telling people that was my hometown. Truly, the most normal-feeling response I have ever given to the question, "Hey, where are you from, Heath?" has been: "I'm from planet Earth."

I have seen the beauty of the Grand Tetons and the amazing grandeur of the Austrian Alps, and though I don't remember much of it, I have been to Asia. I have eaten Chinese ants because Bob said that was what we were having for dinner. You may not ever see anything that compares to a swarm of termites in Taiwan, but I have. I flew over the entire expanse of both the Pacific and Atlantic Oceans by the time I was nine years old. I am certain there is nothing on this planet I would take in trade for growing up Army.

I joke sometimes about the Army owing all of us Brats a pension for all we did, but I really know the debt is the other way around. I believe my life has been a wonderful gift. The package includes eight siblings, all whom I love, and parents who taught me all I could ever need to be a success. I never had to find a "best friend"—I lived with eight of them; and with a brother ten years older than I was, I had a window to the future. I could always look at Dan and know what it would be like to be twenty or thirty or fifty years old, and I loved that. When the time came to marry and raise children of my own, I was fully equipped to handle this greatest of life's responsibilities, and I am very proud of the two young adults Sandy and I raised. They honor their grandparents with the way they live; with their character, integrity, and their personalities. I love that they are "old school." They would have made great Army Brats ... just like the eight with whom I grew up.

The most important part of growing up Army was the perspective it gave me of the world in which I live, especially compared to that of the kids I knew who were not military Brats. For instance, I never heard and therefore never knew the "N word" before we were stationed at Fort Jackson near Columbia, South Carolina. I had no comprehension of the value or purpose of prejudice. I still hold to the truth that there is no value or purpose in prejudice, but I spent the last few years of high school in the South where I was totally out of sync with the normal attitudes of those times. It was the sixties, and the race issues were really starting to boil. School integration and busing had just begun, and our country was going through some very trying times.

It was hard to be an Army Brat in the South. The formative years of seventh, eighth, and ninth grades were trying years for me; a real struggle to fit into a culture of which I did not have any understanding. We had grown up roaming freely among so many different types of people, most of whom spoke languages other than English, and had become comfortable with "different" being the norm.

I have adapted to the Southern culture; more than that, I have come to love much of it. Some things I will never understand, such as formal living and dining rooms you never use, and linens in the bathrooms you never use, both upon penalty of death, or at least the loss of your girlfriend for being so crude. Then the other side of the story is the beauty and respect delivered through Southern manners; even though my lack of training with "yes, ma'am" and "no, sir" got me thrown out of class a few times in high school, I am so glad my children grew up here in the South and have these simple portraits of respect built into their nature.

Most of the friends I had in high school had never been any farther from home than Myrtle Beach, South Carolina, or the North Carolina mountains for vacation. They had no clue most of the human beings on this planet did not think the way they did about the world and the other people in it. I can remember asking girls out for dates and being turned down because "my parents won't let me date Army kids." Or, heck, maybe it was just me, and that was a convenient excuse.

I ended up marrying an Army Brat—go figure. She is just perfect for me, and a Southern beauty at that. I believe with my global perspective, and having seen girls from all over the world, that they don't come any better than Southern. She has a heart big enough to make me feel at home in the vast world I was acquainted with as a child.

No, I'm not from around these parts. I grew up Army.

INTRODUCTION

This is the story of the life and adventures of Jinny and Dick Heath and their nine children as they traveled to various parts of the world and the United States, following the Army assignments and reassignments of a soldier. Jinny married Dick after a two-year courtship, not long after he entered the United States Army. His enlistment began shortly after the Japanese attack on Pearl Harbor—the impetus that launched the United States into World War II. Once married, Jinny and Dick wasted no time in getting their family started, and with nearly every move, one or two new Army Brats arrived. The oldest, Dan, was born in Manitowoc, Wisconsin, in May of 1943 after Dick joined the war effort in Tunisia. Dan didn't meet his daddy until he was two years old. Pat, the last of the Heath Army Brat Platoon, came along twenty years later in Heidelberg, Germany, in November of 1963. The rest of us joined in different places around the world in those two decades between Dan and Pat.

Almost always, Dick was at his new post assignment for a while before the rest of us followed, leaving organizing the moves to Jinny, which she always did calmly and smoothly. Nearly every duty station to which Dick was assigned was during or shortly following significantly historic times for those countries and ours. For example, our first duty station overseas as a family was Yokohama, Japan. We arrived there less than two years after the nuclear bombing of

Hiroshima and Nagasaki, which ended the war with Japan. The historic events and their impacts on the Heath Platoon will be further explored as we reach each new duty station throughout the book. Each of the nine Brats of the Heath Platoon has contributed stories of his or her adventures and memories growing up around the world during these interesting times.

Part of the history includes the courtship and correspondence between Jinny and Dick, particularly in the early chapters. Quotes from their letters are just as they were written to maintain the authenticity of what and how they wrote to one another.

While growing up in the Army, I always envisioned ours as a family of good soldiers: obedient, short haircuts, home for dinner at five, well-disciplined, and so forth. You can judge the accuracy of that vision as you read these stories. Perhaps there really is something to the term *Army Brat*. Perhaps we created the true meaning of the term. I can only say that, as Army Brats go, we set the bar high for those who followed.

ACKNOWLEDGMENTS

Twenty years before the writing of this book, I was talking with some of my siblings at our annual Thanksgiving gathering and we began sharing crazy, fun, scary stories about growing up in different parts of the world. We all had stories, and Mom's eightieth birthday was happening in a few months. I asked each of my fellow Brats to bring the scariest and/or funniest story they could remember to her birthday, especially crazy stories we didn't think she knew anything about.

We gathered around her before the birthday song and one by one told our stories. She did not know about any of them and kept shaking her head, saying, "I should have been paying more attention!" That was so much fun, I asked each of them to write down as many of their stories as they could remember and send them to me. For the few who don't care much for writing, I sat down with them, and they told me their stories.

These anecdotes were all compiled into a small book I created and printed, and everyone, including Mom and Dad, got a copy. About a year later, Mom decided to write her own story, which she sent to me, and it was made into a small book with copies for everyone.

Because Dad passed away before I began to pull all this together, I inquired with the National Archives to find what I could get regarding what he was doing during the war. He never spoke of it, and, sadly, we never thought to ask. I felt so fortunate to receive from the National Archives the daily Morning Reports for Dad's Army unit, detailing the specific movements of the 431st AAA AW Headquarters Battalion beginning with Dad's entry into the war zone in North Africa in March 1943, right up to the air attack from which he was wounded in Mutzig, France, on December 30, 1944.

I am incredibly thankful and excited that *Growing Up Army* pulls all the stories from me and my siblings—Dan, Dave, Mike, Rachel, Jim, Steve, Rick, Pat—our Mom, Dad (derived from letters), the National Archives, and interesting historical information about each of Dad's duty stations, and puts it together in an historical, fun, nonfiction work about how we grew up. More than anything else, it is my hope that all of us will get great enjoyment in reading about Dad and our adventures around the world, and this will be passed down to future generations.

PART I:

BECOMING ARMY

CHAPTER 1
THE BEGINNING, DICK AND JINNY

To most people, especially those who didn't grow up in a military family, the term *brat* refers to a child who misbehaves badly. That term and its definition have been around for centuries. To any child who grew up in the military traveling to many countries around the globe, the term refers to them. They are referred to as military Brats generally, and Army, Navy, Marine, or Air Force Brats more specifically. According to an article entitled "'Military Brat:' Do You Know Where the Term Comes From?" some believe the term came to be applied to military children sometime in the 1930s from British military offspring, referred to as British Regiment Attached Traveler (BRAT), but research casts doubt on that origin story.[1]

In a way, it is fitting that the use of *brat* to describe a military child does not have a definitive origin. One might even say it's almost poetic: if you ask a military kid, "Where are you from?" he or she will likely give you a blank look, blink a few times, then say something like, "I'm from the world." It is difficult to come up with a specific answer for both the origin of the term and the origin of the kid.

Brat isn't used to describe negative behavior necessarily, and many folks might make the assumption that a child who grew up in a military family would likely be well behaved due to "military style" parenting. Those who grew up this way would possibly substitute the word *adventurous* for *well behaved*, or even for *poorly behaved*. These kids follow their military parents wherever they are assigned and reassigned, often moving to different places ten or more times, frequently every one to three years. It isn't uncommon for a military kid to attend eight to ten schools while growing up; some are military dependents' schools in foreign countries while others are civilian schools, mostly in the States.

Friends are always temporary, which may explain why the children of Dick and Jinny all remain personally close decades after their military travels ended. We were the friends we always had, regardless of where we were. Not only are Brats' friends temporary, but we didn't have close relationships with extended family—something that would have been difficult to do when our cousins lived in Wisconsin or Illinois and we were in Japan, Virginia, Germany, Tacoma, or Taiwan. We only saw our grandparents and sometimes a few aunts, uncles, and cousins when we returned from overseas and Dad had some leave time between assignments. A few times, he would be off to his next duty station and Mom and us kids would spend a month or two with Mom's folks, Grampa Archie and Gramma Peggy. Those times were always fun, but it's difficult to establish close, extended family ties under those brief and rare circumstances. Still, we Brats had each other and our parents.

Before There Was Us, There Was Dick and Jinny

Richard "Dick" Heath was nine years old when the Great Depression hit the United States. He came into the world in Streator, Illinois, in January of 1920, the second of nine children of Charles and Helen Heath.

Dick's dad was the only male in his family who did not fight in World War I. This was due to his missing index finger —also known as the "trigger" finger —which was burned off when his glove got caught in a molten glass form at the bottle factory in Streator. Charles was an early advocate for the organization of the common workers, and it is believed he was fired from the bottle factory for engaging in union-organizing activities.

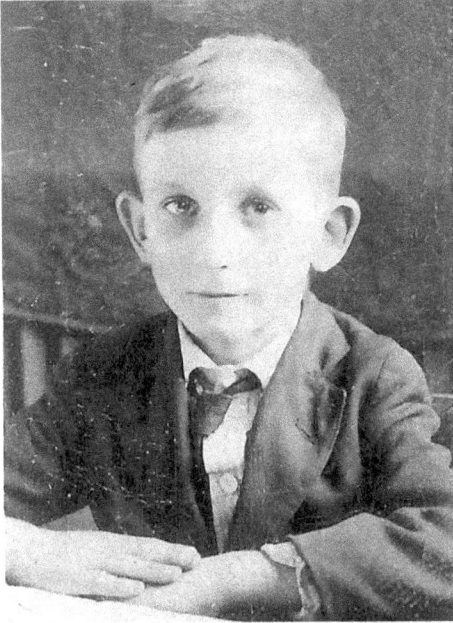

Dick, 1927

In 1933, Charles went to work at a glass production plant in Ottawa, Illinois, where he later served as president of the local union, as a member of the local branch of the National Labor Relations Board, and then as president of the Federation of Flat Glass and Ceramic Workers Union. The move from Streator to Ottawa in '33 was brought on primarily because he and Helen had lost their home to the Depression.

From my studies in American history, I know that without work, many people were unable to make their monthly mortgage payments or pay their property taxes. Hence, many homes were repossessed, and families had to find other places to live or became homeless. There were many times during the 1930s when Charles was not working due to plant closures and subsequent layoffs. When there was no work, there was no income. When there was no money, Charles and Helen were in deep desperation to provide for their ever-growing family.

Dick's mother, Helen (Nell) was a devout Catholic who followed the rules and rituals of the Catholic Church to the letter. She was also very much considered a lady with a lot of class, who dressed very properly and taught her children proper manners. She was said to be able to stretch a penny farther than anyone and was an excellent cook. Oatmeal, which was bought in twenty-five-pound bags, was breakfast every day, along with a couple slices of homemade bread. Nell made three loaves of homemade bread three times every week. The family grew vegetables behind the house, including potatoes, tomatoes, beans, carrots, peas, and corn—much of which was canned and stored to be eaten through the winter months. During the Depression, meat was scarce, but fortunately, Dick was an excellent marksman. He would often go into the woods and come home with some wild game to be prepared for dinner.

Nell Heath was a kind person who could not stand to see anyone suffer if there was anything she could do about it. On a day when it was very cold and snowing outside, Nell was looking out the front window of the house watching the children walking through the snow on their way to school. She saw a young girl with no boots or gloves, who looked like she was freezing. Nell ran to the door and called the girl to the house, then ran to her daughters' bedroom and came back with a fur muff, which she gave the girl to keep her hands warm.

Jinny and Gordon, 1928

Funny enough, Dick and Jinny were born with the same last name! Virginia "Jinny" Heath was born in May of 1922 in a farmhouse near Neillsville, Wisconsin, where her parents were homesteading. She was the older of two children. Her father, Archie Heath, was the eighth of eight children, born in Pittsville, Wisconsin, in 1896. Jinny's mother, Leone Sweetland, was the seventh of eleven children, born in 1901 in Neillsville, Wisconsin.

When Jinny was about a year old, they moved to Park Falls, Wisconsin, to help Archie's widowed mother on her small farm. The farm was only a few acres of land and had a couple cows and horses and some pigs and chickens. Jinny learned to hate chickens when she was very young when a rooster was chasing her and she fell—and the rooster pecked her on the head until her mom rescued her. Mr. Rooster was very much enjoyed for dinner that night! In addition to learning about roosters while they lived on the farm, Jinny learned how to sew on a treadle sewing machine. Though she had to stand up to reach the pedal that powered the sewing machine, this began one of Jinny's lifelong joys.

About a year after moving to the farm, the second child in the family, Gordon, was born. A few years later Archie's brother Frank was able to help out at the farm, and the family moved back to Neillsville. There, Archie and Leone opened a small fast-food restaurant, and they lived in an apartment in the back of the restaurant. Jinny started kindergarten that year. Just a year after starting the restaurant, Archie decided to return to the carpentry business, and the family moved to an apartment, then to a small house near a stockyard. Jinny and Gordon loved to go to the stockyard and watch the animals come off the train. They would get chummy with a calf and ask the man herding it if they could have it; he would tell them, "Someday," with a little smirk on his face.

In 1929, the beginning of the Great Depression, Jinny started second grade in a one-room schoolhouse; the school was for kindergarten through eighth grade. All the kids in a one-room schoolhouse were taught in the same room by one teacher. She walked to school, which in the Wisconsin winter was a very long, cold, snow-covered walk much of the time. During this time, Archie would occasionally bring home store-bought bread, which was a tremendous treat for the family.

From Neillsville, they would frequently go to visit the farm in Park Falls, always traveling in the wee hours of the morning when it was still dark. They could see the northern lights on clear, dark early mornings. Jinny and Gordon loved to sing, imagining themselves to be radio stars someday. Their favorite song was "A Little Grass Shack," and they sang it with great gusto! During one visit to the Park Falls farm, the family listened on the radio to President Franklin D. Roosevelt's Inaugural Address on March 4, 1933.

Archie was a builder and carpenter, and during the Depression there were very few building jobs, but he occasionally got small home repair work. Leone worked as a waitress and was able to bring home some income. Archie was also a hunter, so the family usually had meat. Thankfully, the law pretty much looked the other way when game was taken out of season during that time.

As a builder and carpenter, when Archie could acquire a piece of land and had the financial resources to do so, he would build a house from the ground up. The family would at times live in a tent until they could inhabit the house. Given the Wisconsin winters, he would have to hurry sometimes to get the house enclosed enough to keep them warm. After the house was built, they would live in it until Archie could sell it, and then they would move to an apartment until he could get another one built.

Jinny always loved to read—a trait she got from her mother—and reading led to her love of libraries. Once, when Jinny was a young girl of about ten years old, her mom asked her to go to the library to get a book. She said, "I want you to get me something deep to read." What book did young Jinny come home with? *20,000 Leagues Under the Sea*—they don't get much deeper than that! Jinny's love for reading also translated into her successes as a student in school.

She graduated from Waupaca High School in 1940 and was an excellent student. In the 1940 school yearbook, *The Crystal*, there were many written accolades about Jinny's scholarship.

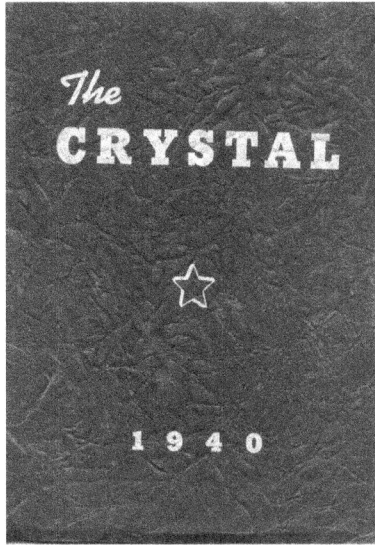

The Crystal Yearbook, 1940

"Dear Virginia, Will always remember you as the girl who always knew her English."

"Hi Jinny, Best of luck to a real geometry wizard."

"Dear Jinny, What would I have done in chemistry without you? Probably flunked it ... I think you have the makings of a very good teacher."

Jinny was also very active outside the classroom, as a member of the Glee Club, Social Dance Club, Drama Club, Sub-Deb Sorority, and Future Homemakers of America. What is most interesting is that her nine children never had any idea that she was a "geometry wizard" or was recognized as being particularly smart in chemistry or English, which is not to say we ever doubted her intelligence. When we learned that she had been a member of the Social Dance Club, we were all stunned, since she always professed to never being a good dancer—and wouldn't dance with Dick, who loved to dance!

How About a Date?
Dick always had a knack for fixing things, including an almost natural ability to repair automobiles. In early February of 1941, at the age of

twenty-one, Dick was working at Grey Warner's Service Station on West Norris Drive in Ottawa, Illinois. One day around lunch time he went across the street to the café for a bite to eat and sat at the counter, a few seats down from another gentleman. Dick wasn't known to be shy, and when a beautiful waitress came over to take his order, he said, "Would you like to go out on a date with me?" The waitress seemed a little befuddled and glanced at the other man sitting at the counter. The gentleman looked over at Dick and said, "Son, that lady is my wife. We do have a daughter who is about your age, and she might be interested in going on a date with you." With that said, he wrote down Jinny's phone number and gave it to Dick.

Jinny, age nineteen, was living with her parents and working for a Swedish masseuse in Ottawa at the time. Dick wasted no time contacting her, and soon they were seeing each other. Many of their early times together involved roller skating around town, and they would occasionally go to a movie or get something to eat. Like her mother, Jinny was a beautiful young lady, and Dick was totally smitten.

In addition to working at the gas station, Dick was working toward his General Educational Development diploma. He had joined the Civilian Conservation Corps (CCC), serving in the Illinois cities of Havana and Elmwood in what would have been his high school graduation year. His time in the CCC—July 1937 through June 1938— came near the end of the Great Depression. Working for the CCC allowed Dick to provide some much-needed income for his family.

The CCC began in 1933 by President Franklin D. Roosevelt in response to the growing poverty created by the Great Depression; about 25 percent of the US labor force was unemployed by that time, and things were tough for families,[2] including Dick's. Young men could serve in the CCC for one year, and during the time Dick served, he was paid $40 per month—a very decent stipend at that time. Of that $40, Dick was required to send home approximately $33 to help his family. In addition to his monthly stipend, Dick received three meals a day, lodging, clothing, and even had access to free dental and medical care. There also was a recreation hall and academic instruction available in some camps.[3]

In the CCC, the young men wore World War I Army uniforms and were supervised by US Army soldiers. Their work was determined by the needs of the state in which the CCC camps were located. During the 1930s, millions of acres of land had been overly logged or wiped out by wildfires due to the severe droughts the country was experiencing.[4] Dick's work most likely involved the development of a state tree nursery to reforest barren land during his six months in Havana, then he was transferred to the camp at Elmwood, where workers were building dams on public land and on farms.

Many of the camps were very primitive, but Camp Elmwood was said to be one of the really nice ones, with landscaping, tennis courts, dancing lessons, and other amenities (elmwoodil.com). It's very possible that this is where Dick picked up his love for dancing.

Courtship

After Dick and Jinny had been seeing each other for three or four months, Jinny and her family went on vacation through the month of June with several of their extended family and friends at a cabin her father built near Wisconsin Rapids. The couple communicated frequently by letter throughout that month. All Dick's letters let Jinny know he was crazy about her and was hoping she felt the same. As the end of June was approaching, Dick wrote,

> Do you know about what time you are going to get here Saturday? If you will be here in the afternoon, I'll come down and we'll make plans for Sunday—A Big One! I have never been glad to see anyone's vacation end before, but now I am, or will be. My theme song, "Won't you, Can't you, please come home." I'm as lonesome as a lone cactus on a desert.
> Hurry home.
> Thy willing Servant,
> Dick

Jinny came back to Ottawa around the first of July, and on the Fourth of July, Dick proposed! After their betrothal, Dick and Jinny had only July together before they were again separated, as Dick had been drafted into the Army and had to report to Camp Grant Reception Center in South Rockford, Illinois, for basic training at the beginning of August 1941.

After Dick was off to basic training, Jinny's best friend, Dorothy, told her of an inexpensive one-room schoolhouse teachers' college. Wisconsin had one-room schoolhouses, which were designed to teach relatively small groups of children ranging from kindergarten through eighth grades all in one room. These schools were open until around 1970, and the teachers' college was designed to prepare teachers for those schools. The college was located in Wautoma, Wisconsin, which is about twenty-five miles from Waupaca where Jinny was living with her parents. Jinny had a little money saved up, which she was able to use to register for school and to pay for a few months' rent. At the end of August, Jinny and Dorothy were off to school, and their dads would take turns driving them there and picking them up when they wanted to come home for weekends.

At this time, World War II was in full gear in Europe and Asia, but the United States was still holding out as a neutral country. That changed on December 7, 1941, when Japan attacked Pearl Harbor, Hawaii. Congress formally declared war on Japan the next day; three days later, Germany and Italy declared war on the United States.[5]

On that fateful date, Private Dick Heath had finished basic training and was stationed at Fort Warren in Wyoming. During World War II, Fort Warren was the training center for up to 20,000 soldiers of the Quartermaster Corps; more than 280 wooden buildings were constructed without insulation or interior walls to temporarily house the increased number of troops.[6] In the harsh Wyoming winter, waking up in these barracks often meant shaking snow from one's blanket before heading for the just-as-cold communal showers. In spite of the intense weather, Dick made certain Jinny knew he loved her. In a letter to Jinny, dated December 7, 1941, he signed it:

> 'Tis neither You Nor I
> But WE
> Jinny Mae and Richard D.

Dick and Jinny, 1942

Every letter he wrote to her from that point on ended with that sweet signature.

The month before, in late November, Dick was able to come from Fort Warren to Waupaca on leave to spend time with Jinny during her Thanksgiving break from school. He was able to save up enough money to buy an engagement ring, which he happily put on her finger. They were able to enjoy being together through all Dick's leave. Shortly after returning to Fort Warren, he was transferred to Fort Crook, Nebraska, where he trained in auto mechanics.

Jinny's dad was driving her back to school after that extended Thanksgiving weekend, on December 8, 1941. Big snowflakes were falling, and they were listening to the radio. President Roosevelt was speaking of the Japanese attack on Pearl Harbor the day before, and described it as "a date which will live in infamy."[7]

Because she had taken a few extra days to spend with Dick, Jinny had a pile of school work to catch up on. Along with that, Jinny and Dorothy were meeting with a Catholic priest and were baptized in the Catholic faith. They were both betrothed to Catholic men, and the Catholic Church was highly insistent that Catholics marry Catholics —as was Dick's mom!

Wedding Bells

When the spring semester ended in early June of 1942, Jinny went to Toma, Wisconsin, to be with her parents and took on a housekeeping job. Not long after that, Dick called from Fort Crook to propose a wedding date. Knowing that Jinny planned to continue her schooling to be a teacher, he said, "I think we should get married soon, and I know you plan to keep going to school to be a teacher. If you'll quit school and marry me, I'll provide you with your own kindergarten!" Believe it or not, Jinny bought that line, and on July 16 she was on her way to Omaha to get married.

They got their marriage license, and Dick had contacted a priest to officiate the wedding. They went in to meet with him before the wedding, and he told them that he wasn't aware that both of their last names were "Heath" and there would have to be extensive research to establish that they weren't related. Jinny didn't know that Dick had already addressed this with the priest and they were playing a little joke on her. In fact, Jinny and Dick had met with both sets of parents and looked back as far as they were able and found no connections for at least three generations. What they didn't know at the time is that the nine children of the Heath Platoon would always and forever have to answer the question, "No, I need your mother's *maiden* name, not her name now; don't you know that the maiden name was your mother's last name *before* she married your dad?" That became very annoying to all of us.

Dick and Jinny were married on July 18, 1942, in the Fort Crook Army chapel. In attendance were some soldiers from Dick's unit. Jinny had been staying with a family in a house nearby, and the lady and her daughters who lived there also attended the wedding. The soldiers had taken up a collection, and Dick's Aunt Irma sent along a radio for their wedding gifts.

Dick and Jinny's wedding day, 1942

After the wedding they drove into Omaha, had their picture taken, then went to check out the hotel room Dick had reserved. It was a beautiful room, large and airy—but there was another couple in it! They didn't understand how this other couple got their room, but they were able to get another one—a private room, albeit much smaller and with no air-conditioning. Omaha hit one hundred degrees that day. It didn't matter; they were too much in love to pay any attention to the heat in the air.

That night, they went to hear a big-name band at the Dreamland Ballroom, which booked many of the famous bands of the day, including Duke Ellington, Count Basie, and Louis Armstrong.[8] The next day, they toured Omaha by bus and went to see and hear another big-name band that night. When the show was over, Dick and Jinny were headed back to their room, but the buses had stopped running. They couldn't afford a taxi to take them the six miles, so they walked, stopping frequently to kiss. Jinny's eyes have always glittered when she talked about those magical kisses, and Dick wasn't shy about providing them! The room was their honeymoon destination, and they had it for a week. They would sit in the back yard and talk about their future, when they would have a house, kids, and a back yard of their own. A few weeks later, on August 1, Dick graduated from Army auto mechanics school, was promoted to private first class, and shortly afterward received his new assignment to Camp Crowder in Neosho, Missouri. One thing to note is that when a soldier gets a promotion, it nearly always precludes a new assignment. They moved to Neosho and rented an efficiency apartment in a very large old house. After the first night Jinny noticed there had been rats in the kitchen, so they set a trap; it had to be emptied five times that night! They would just doze off, and *SNAP* went the trap. Being upstairs in the house, they had to go downstairs and outside to the back to dump each rat. The next day, they were both exhausted. Dick found where the rats were getting in and nailed a piece of tin over the hole. That took care of the problem.

Dick's basic pay was twenty-one dollars a month, plus a housing allowance. Jinny got a job at the Post Exchange (PX), and they both rode the bus to and from work. Dick's older brother, Gene, was stationed there at the same time, so they were able to spend a good bit of time visiting with him for the next few months. It was a brief stay in Neosho, and Dick was transferred to Fort Riley, Kansas, where they got a basement apartment in a private home. Jinny was already pregnant with their first child, and she will tell you that she didn't have "morning sickness"—her pregnancy sickness came at any time of the night or day! Their apartment shared the only bathroom with two older men on the second floor. Those poor old fellows would hear Jinny running up the stairs, and if one of them was in the bathroom, he vacated it as soon as possible.

In December they moved to a very small house, but it provided them with their very own bathroom! Private first class and Mrs. Heath had their first Christmas in that little house in Salina, Kansas. Jinny didn't get a job while they were there because of her pregnancy and its associated issues, and money had become very scarce. They were getting very desperate to the point that they went to the local priest to ask for help, but received none. Today, the military has a family relief fund, but back then they did not. Still desperate, they went to the Salvation Army and were very generously helped. The Salvation Army became one of their favorite charities from that point on.

Called to War

Shortly after that first Christmas together, Dick was promoted to staff sergeant in January 1943 and received orders to Company E, 309th Infantry in Camp Butner, North Carolina, to await transfer to the European war zone. That was Dick and Jinny's last Christmas together for three years.

The couple traveled to Kansas City together that January. From there, Dick's train left before Jinny's, and she immediately felt a tremendous sense of desolation watching that train leave as she waved goodbye. Those six months they were able to be together after their wedding were cherished memories that had to last both Dick and Jinny until his return from the war. While he was gone, Dick kept the letters coming, and he never stopped saying, "I love you." He wrote that phrase at the top and bottom of all pages of each and every letter.

After his train left for Camp Butner, Jinny caught a train back to Waupaca, and she and their puppy, Pepper, stayed for a week in the family's cedar log cabin on the Waupaca River, near the Waupaca Rapids. Aunt Myrtle and Uncle Roy lived in a cabin nearby, and Jinny had friends in the area. She was nearing five months into her pregnancy. Jinny and Dick had decided the child was a boy, and that his name was to be Danny. No thought that the child could be a girl ever crossed their minds.

A few weeks following her arrival at the cabin, she went to join her parents in Manitowoc. She went to the train station in Waupaca in the very early hours of the morning to start her eighty-five-mile journey. Along the way, she experienced hours of delays and arrived nine hours later—absolutely exhausted—at the café where her mom was working. Jinny got some breakfast, and her dad came and took her and Pepper to their one-room apartment where she slept for fourteen hours.

Although their separation had only been a little less than a month, Jinny was feeling very lonely for Dick, and she expressed that sentiment in a letter dated January 27.

> *Darling, I missed you so last night that the old flood just had to come again. Every time I look at your picture, it makes me feel like crying. Our life was too happy and it's dreadfully hard to get used to being alone again … From now on, I'm only going to write when I have something to say. Now all I have to say is that my love is all yours, Darling. Of course, you know it but it gives me satisfaction to tell you so again and again.*

★★★

In a letter Dick sent Jinny about a month after his arrival at Camp Butner, he wrote about his thoughts on parenting their coming child: "Darling, we won't spoil him. Here is what I want to do. *We* will take him on picnics, fishing, hunting, swimming and make a real pal out of him just as soon as he is big enough to want his parents for pals. We are going to devote as much time as possible to him and whoever comes after him."

For Jinny, the hours passed to days, the days to weeks, the weeks to months—and, eventually, the months to years. Fortunately, little Danny would arrive soon, and the loving support of both their families as well as a continuous stream of loving letters from Dick would lessen the concerns she had for him while he was overseas serving our country in World War II.

CHAPTER 2
NORTH AFRICA AND
WELCOMING BRAT ONE, 1943

On March 5, 1943, Dad was on a ship headed for North Africa. American soldiers had first arrived in North Africa four months earlier. Commanded by General Dwight Eisenhower, this military effort, code-named Operation Torch, included both American forces and the British 1st Army.[9]

Dad's ship arrived in Algeria on March 19. He was assigned to the 431st AAA AW Headquarters Battalion, Headquarters Battery. In addition to HQ Battery, the battalion had four other AAA AW (Anti-Aircraft Artillery Automatic Weapons) batteries. Each battery was assigned a different location to protect, including ports, airfields, and supply areas. As they were moved from one location to another, the batteries would be assigned to other US or British Army or Air Force units from time to time for specific protection tasks, particularly when it was determined that an attack may be forthcoming in a certain area.[10]

Dad was positioned at La Salamandre, Mostaganem, on the northwestern coast of Algeria, directly across the Mediterranean Sea from Spain. One of his responsibilities was driving trucks to transport men and equipment from place to place as they were repositioned throughout the war, which would take them from Algeria to Tunisia, then near the coast of Italy to Sicily, Sardinia, Corsica, and finally into France. Dad's unit was there to guard the Headquarters Battalion Command Post and the port of La Salamandre from German and Italian air and sea attacks.[11]

According to Colonel E. Paul Semmens, the use of rapidly mobile anti-aircraft artillery was very new to the US Army and had been the subject of disagreement among high-level Army officers in the early days of the war, but it was ultimately determined to be highly necessary given that the German Air Force, or Luftwaffe, ferociously controlled the airways and would frequently and effectively attack troops, tank battalions, and Allied airfields with bombs and strafing. As the United States entered the war, frantic construction of various AAA AW weapons was taking place, along with equally speedy training of the tens of thousands of officers and enlisted men to use them effectively. Even though the soldiers received training, the frequency with which Allied aircraft were being shot down by "friendly fire" was an issue brought to the fore in all the World War II theaters in which the United States was fighting. The term *friendly fire* means that our aircraft were accidentally being shot down by our own guns because of the difficulties related to identifying enemy versus friendly aircraft. Throughout the course of the war, this issue was slowly addressed.[12]

In "Tunisian Campaign," we learn that, following the many battles in which the relatively "green" US forces were engaged in North Africa, many other lessons were learned regarding the movement and placement of troops and batteries to effectively fight the large numbers of seasoned enemy troops, tanks, and their air support. This war had been ongoing in Europe since 1939, after all. These lessons came at a very high cost in terms of US casualties and loss of equipment, but battle after battle new tactics were put in place, and the United States became a force to be reckoned with. This was ultimately a bit of a surprise to the German commander, Rommel, who believed the rookie Americans weren't much of a threat.[13]

Dad's unit typically followed the major battlefronts by as much as a month and served as follow-up support from attacks that the enemy might bring to the rear echelon troops. Dad's role, in addition to driving trucks, included the important task of helping organize and monitor the loading of vehicles with all equipment, as well as ensuring that motorized equipment was in good working order. Organization was always an excellent strength of his.

Dick in Tunisia, 1943

These moves in the northeast of Algeria and Tunisia were organized with British and French forces to close in from the northeast on the German headquarters, which was based at Gabès, on the Tunisian eastern coast. In late March 1943, the Germans were driven out of Gabès north toward Tunis. Dad's position at that time near Subaytilah was 165 miles from Tunis and was part of a defensive line along which the Germans were amassed, attempting to prevent the Allied forces from moving in on Axis supply lines at Tunis.[14]

Also from "Tunisian Campaign," we find that the squeeze being placed on the Axis forces was intensifying, and the Germans had lost many tanks and men. Within two days, the Allied attacks from the south had driven the Axis forces to the northeast coast of Tunisia near Tunis, where they attempted to protect their supply lines. Allies were also actively destroying Axis supply aircraft and marine supply venues through a well-coordinated and executed plan. Large numbers of fighting aircraft were being moved into airfields in preparation for a wide-scale Allied attack toward the Tunis area. All the North African Allied forces were being reorganized into battle-ready positions.[15]

The battles for Tunis began on the morning of April 22, with forces moving in from all directions. They were bloody and costly.[16] In the midst of these intense battles, on Easter Sunday, April 25, well-attended open-air church services were held at several of the airfields guarded by the batteries of the 431st AAA AW Battalion.[17]

It is likely Sunday services were held most Sundays throughout the war in all American theaters of operations to provide soldiers with outlets for their faith and other needs. There is no doubt Dad would have been in attendance at one of these services, given his upbringing as a dedicated Catholic.

The final Allied assault began on May 6, and on May 7 British armored units entered Tunis, and American infantry entered Bizerte just to the north. Six days after Tunis and Bizerte fell to the Allies, on or around May 12, more than 230,000 German and Italian troops surrendered at the various battlefields throughout the area. Both Allied and Axis forces suffered many thousands of casualties who were killed, wounded, or captured throughout the campaign in North Africa.[18] Four days after the end of the North Africa campaign's defeat of the Axis forces, Danny was born.

Brat One: Danny
When Jinny went to the hospital to birth Danny on May 16, 1943, there weren't even any buds on the trees. When little Danny and his mommy went home ten days later, the trees were all leafed out. Back then, mothers were kept in bed in the hospital for eight days and were only allowed to walk to a nearby chair on the ninth day. A young lady who became a good friend shared the room. Jinny had a picture of Dick on a table by her bed. Flowers came to the room for her roommate and were put right in front of Dick's picture. Jinny didn't let those flowers stay in the way of his picture for long!

Dick was in Tunisia when Danny was born, and it would take a few weeks for the newly promoted Technical Sergeant (TSgt.) Heath to learn of his son's arrival. Mail delivery into the war zone wasn't a regular occurrence due, of course, to the constant movement of men and the ravages of the war itself. In a V-mail Dick sent to his Uncle Claude—from Sicily on August 22, 1943—he said:

> *I was sure on pins and needles till I heard that Danny had finally decided to come as he was reported to be here by the eighth of May and didn't show up till the sixteenth. When the war is over I think a good idea would be to have a family reunion and do a little showing off of my little family. I'm mighty proud of them and they are two of the swellest people to show off that I know of.*

Mom and Danny in Manitowoc, 1943

★★★

Jinny's mom, now Gramma Peggy, lost her heart the moment she saw Danny, and that never changed. He always returned her love. After a few months, Jinny and Danny found their own little apartment, less than a mile from Grampa Archie and Gramma Peggy. It was upstairs in a family home in a nice neighborhood. The family's eight-year-old daughter fell in love with little Danny.

Jinny, being a first-time mom, was still learning the ins and outs of motherhood. One lesson along this journey happened one day during

Danny's first summer, when Manitowoc's weather decided to change rather suddenly. Jinny had him in his carriage, and they went into a store. It was quite hot outside, and he was in a sun suit. When they came out, fog had moved into town, and it was really chilly. Jinny wasn't prepared for that extreme change in weather, and the little sheet she wrapped him in wasn't enough to keep Danny warm, so she put him under the baby buggy mattress. This was the first of many mommy lessons she would learn over the years to come.

Every few months Jinny took Danny to Ottawa so he and Dick's parents—Gramma Nell and Grampa Grump (so named by his grandchildren, and a name he enjoyed!)—could get acquainted. They always had a good time there. Danny had a little cousin, Jean Marie, who was six months younger than he, in Ottawa. Jean Marie was the daughter of Dick's older brother, Gene, who was also serving in the war in Europe. She and her mom, Mary, came to visit when Jinny and Danny were in town. Mary and Jinny socialized and comforted one another over their fears about the war.

Bidding North Africa Goodbye
Three days after the birth of his firstborn—though he didn't know it yet—on May 19, 1943, Dad and his unit were on their way to Manzil Hurr, a town east of Tunis on the Mediterranean coast. The AAA AW batteries and tank battalions were placed in strategic areas around Tunis to thwart any Axis reprisals that may have been forthcoming from their recent defeats.

> Many Officers and Enlisted Men had souvenirs such as rifles, bayonets, pistols, cameras, helmets and plenty of German and Italian ammunition. The morale of the organization was at a peak, for the first time, the men were permitted to see and handle enemy equipment. The roads leading to the various batteries were lined with destroyed tanks, cars and trucks.

US Army Morning Report

Due to the rise in enemy activity resulting from the movements of Allied forces, and as noted in the June 1, 1943, Morning Report: "On June 1 the 431st AAA AW Battalion was relieved from attachment to the British Air Support Command and re-attached to the US 2626th CA Brigade."[19] *Attached* means "under the command of."

Then, on June 3, Battery D of the 431st was assigned to Fard Jouna Airfield, which at that time was occupied by the 99th Fighter Squadron. This was the fighter squadron manned by the famous Tuskegee Airmen, the all-African American fighter squadron.[20] The day before, on June 2, the Airmen of the 99th had flown their first-ever combat missions against the island of Pantelleria, a small island between Sicily and Tunisia. This island and another, Lampedusa, were targeted by the Allies because they were Axis radar stations and had big military garrisons. The raids from the Tuskegee and other airmen were highly effective in shutting down these two islands from serving the needs of the Germans and Italians. These attacks also led to the surrender of 17,000 more Italian forces. From the base at Fard Jouna, Tunisia, the 99th also supported the invasion of Italy through its participation in the air battle against Sicily, launched in early May of 1943.[21] In the Morning Report, it was reported that the men of the 431st AAA AW Battery D found the Tuskegee Airmen to be "generous and helpful."[22]

Throughout June, the batteries of the 431st were frequently repositioned and set up for possible action. They were periodically alerted that Axis paratroopers were being dropped over the area, or occasionally an Allied vehicle would hit a mine, destroying the vehicle and killing or wounding its occupants, among other concerns. On July 18, the entire 431st was relieved of their various duty areas and brought back together as a whole battalion near Protville, Tunisia. They had been alerted for movement into a staging area, where all officers and enlisted men were called together and given a history of their efforts in North Africa, along with praises for their successes by the executive officers. They were soon to be moving to the Italian island of Sicily, but they would have some time to rest and receive passes to go on leave in nearby towns before their departure.[23]

Dad's tour of duty in North Africa was four months and three weeks long. During his time off, he and other soldiers in his unit were able to visit nearby cities of Bizerte and Tunis. Given that Dad grew up in Illinois and had very little experience other than his Army training stations, these opportunities to visit cities in North Africa had to have been of great curiosity and interest!

CHAPTER 3
ITALY, 1943–1944

From July 22 through August 7, 1943, the "Morning Reports" tell us that the various batteries of the 431st moved into staging areas north of Tunis, near Bizerte to prepare for embarkation to Sicily, a large island just off the "toe" of the Italian mainland. While preparing to leave, suddenly, at 3:30 in the morning, approximately thirty enemy aircraft began dropping flares on the area. Fortunately, no bombs were involved. The planes were flying at a very high altitude and could not be reached by the mounted machine guns, and after about forty-five minutes, it was over. For safe keeping, the battalion began mounting. 50-caliber machine guns and Bofors 40 mm anti-aircraft guns on each landing ship tank (LST)—ships created during World War II to allow tanks, trucks, anti-aircraft equipment, cargo, and men to be landed directly on the beach where there were no docks or piers. By 10:00 a.m., the men and equipment of the 431st were loaded on the LSTs and ready for the 250-mile trek across the Mediterranean Sea to Palermo, Sicily. The seas had been very rough throughout the day, and finally, at 5:30 p.m., it was determined that they had calmed enough to go. They pulled anchor and were on their way, arriving twelve hours later, after crossing what was still a very rough Mediterranean Sea.[24] Their arrival was two weeks and two days after the capture of Palermo, Sicily, by advanced American forces—and the Axis Luftwaffe was consistently bombing and strafing Palermo at this time.[25]

According to the Commonwealth War Graves Commission, the Germans and Italians had been of the belief that the Allies were going to attack somewhere in southern Europe, but did not know specifically where this would happen. The British, in hopes of instilling erroneous thoughts about where attacks might happen, created a plan to give them information that would cause them to build up their forces in the wrong areas. The Allies at that time were planning a strong attack on Sicily as well as the invasion at Normandy in northwest France.[26]

Sicily was seen as a stepping stone to Italy, and the German and Italian forces had fled there from North Africa. In order to misdirect the Axis forces, the British came up with an intricate, long-shot operation called Operation Mincemeat, in which they acquired the body of a dead homeless British citizen and created a full history of him with a fictitious name and rank in the British Royal Air Force. They dressed him in a British officer's uniform and filled a briefcase with false secret documents of upcoming attacks in Greece, Sardinia, and the Balkans. The body of "Major William Martin" along with his briefcase was dumped into the Mediterranean Sea on April 30, 1943, at a location where the tide was expected to push him onto the coast of Spain, which it did. The body was found by a fisherman on the south Spanish coast and turned over to Spanish authorities.[27]

Spain was a neutral country concerning the war, but there were active spies in the country from both German and British forces, mostly due to the close proximity of Spain to the various war zones. The British spies creatively maneuvered the Spanish into allowing German secret agents enough access to the documents in the briefcase to take photographs of all of them. The photos were then passed on to the Axis military powers, who apparently bought into the ruse and began building up defensive forces in those areas. This amazing plan likely turned the tide of the war in favor of the Allied forces. Interestingly, a young intelligence officer named Ian Fleming, who was later the author of the James Bond novels, was one of those who helped devise this plan.[28]

Following heavily increased bombing of Sicilian cities beginning in May 1943, the Allies launched their invasion, Operation Husky, on the south and southeast coastline of Sicily on the night of July 9, 1943, one month before Dad's unit arrived. They landed a half million soldiers, sailors, and airmen as well as a huge amount of fighting equipment. The Sicilian invasion was intended to begin an Allied takeover of Italy to remove it from contention in the war and to divert attention of the Axis forces from the impending D-day invasion at Normandy, planned for June 1944. The ultimate goal was to occupy the northeastern port city of Messina, which could be a launching area for Axis forces to jump across the Strait of Messina to the toe of Italy to escape advancing Allies. The British Army moved northeast toward Messina and met a great deal of resistance, primarily from German forces, while American forces moved northwest, meeting mostly minor resistance from the Italians.[29]

When Dad's unit arrived, Operation Husky only had about another week before it was over. The unit's Morning Reports note the following: On the same day as their arrival, the battalion was ordered seventy miles east to the port city of Marina di Caronia at 1:30 in the afternoon on August 10. Once there, they bivouacked for the night. (A bivouac is a temporary campsite used as a brief pause in moving troops and equipment.) They were then almost immediately ordered to backtrack thirty-five miles to the port town of Santo Stefano and instructed to provide AAA protection for the beachheads in the area.[30]

The men experienced some intense battle zone activity while they were there. One big issue they discovered while setting up the AAA AW batteries was that they had to deal with heavily mined areas in the beachheads where they were to set up. It took time to clear the mines, but in spite of that delay, they were able to get the batteries in place fairly quickly, which was critical.[31]

On the morning of August 13, beaches at Sant'Agata were attacked twice by bombs dropped from the southwest. Then, again that afternoon, nine Italian planes bombed and strafed the beach at Sant'Agata, approaching from the northeast, coming in out of the sun, and followed by more bombs dropped on the east end of the beach.

Although the anti-aircraft batteries fired their weapons at the aircraft, they didn't hit any of the planes, but they did suffer six casualties, one of which was fatal. Again, the next morning, four more bombs were dropped on the same beach. Anti-aircraft guns fired a lot of rounds at the planes, but again without hitting any of them. Thankfully, Dad was with HQ Battalion several miles away and not the target of this action.[32]

Three days later, on August 17 General Patton's 7th Army took the port city of Messina, arriving there a little late, as three divisions of German soldiers had already been evacuated to Italy earlier that day. After thirty-eight days of battle in Sicily, approximately 165,000 Axis personnel were dead, wounded, or missing, and 31,158 Allied personnel suffered the same fate. Importantly, the Germans had been driven out, and most of the Italians had surrendered.[33]

According to History.com, an important historical World War II detail, of which most folks may not be aware, is that most Italians were not favorable toward the Fascist rule of Benito Mussolini or being caught up in this war.[34] Around the time of the Allied defeat of Axis forces in Sicily, General Eisenhower was negotiating an armistice with Italian King Victor Emmanuel, who had put Italian Fascist Party leader Benito Mussolini in jail. On September 8, as Allied forces were moving into southern Italy, the king announced an armistice with the Allies, but made the announcement before letting his Italian troops know about it. So, for a short while, the Italians weren't sure who they were fighting for—or against! Meanwhile, the Germans suspected something of this nature was about to happen, rescued Mussolini from jail, and set him up in northern Italy where he established the Italian Social Republic, a puppet Fascist territory controlled and supported entirely by the Germans.[35]

Once the Germans fled Sicily, most Italian troops surrendered, and Fascist government officials vacated Sicilian towns as quickly as possible, fearing retaliation by local Sicilians, many of whom didn't like the Fascists at all. When they fled, the locals ransacked their homes and offices in many towns.[36] As a different order was being established in Sicily, Dad's unit set up their command post at San

Leone, on the southern coast of Sicily, and the other batteries were sent to various positions northwest to set up defenses along the shoreline and at airfields.[37]

In the meantime, most of the Axis bombing and strafing had stopped, and Dad and his comrades had lots of opportunities to visit local towns and cities in the area. Dad was somewhat appalled by the squalor in which he saw so many people living. "If Americans lived as dirty as these people do, we would all be dead inside of a month," he wrote in a V-mail to Uncle Claude. "Water and soap are both scarce, but I still can't see why they can't sweep the floor or go a little farther from the house for some businesses."

Of course, "some businesses" meant going to the bathroom. It's unlikely that Dad or most of his fellow soldiers had been aware that there was little running water, little or no electricity, and very little indoor plumbing at that time in those areas. Additionally, the country had been at war for four years, which very much led to much of the poverty they observed.

In the Morning Reports, we see that on September 8, when the armistice with Italy was announced, 431st Battalion Headquarters received instructions "not to fire on Italian planes unless hostile act committed. Fire on German planes in vicinity." This, of course, was due to the confusion running through the Italian air, naval, and ground forces as to just who they were now fighting for and against. But as they became aware that Italy was no longer associated with the Fascist rule of Mussolini, throughout September, Italian airmen, merchant marines, and soldiers came into the fields occupied by batteries of the 431st and other Allied forces and surrendered in large numbers. Dad's battalion was given the responsibility of holding these prisoners until other arrangements were made, which was very difficult, given the large numbers who surrendered.[38]

On November 22, the battalion was alerted that they were to move to the staging area near Palermo to prepare for transport to the island of Sardinia, which is about 290 miles across the Mediterranean Sea northwest of Sicily. The entire battalion was at the staging area the next morning and began preparations to load equipment and supplies onto the ships.[39]

Dad in Sardinia, 1943

Sardinia

After three months and three weeks in Sicily, some of that time with intense action, TSgt. Heath and the 431st AAA AW Battalion moved to Sardinia, where they had a pretty lengthy, uneventful stay of nine months and one week. They loaded on the ships on December 3, 1943, sailed overnight, docked at Cagliari, unloaded, and awaited movement orders.[40]

According to a Wikipedia article Cagliari, Sardinia, was of high strategic importance to Axis powers and had been where some of the most significant Axis air bases were located, in addition to a submarine port. This location had provided the Axis with the ability to attack the entire western Mediterranean area by air and sea as well as an excellent port through which to move supplies. In 1943, after the United States and British forces captured a number of airfields in Algeria and Tunisia, they launched a tremendous number of significant and destructive air raids on Cagliari and the surrounding airfields, creating an incredible amount of damage. Unfortunately, bombs also destroyed most of the city and killed hundreds of civilians.[41]

Over a three-month period, Allied aircraft dropped 773 tons of bombs on the city, port, and surrounding airfields. One reason for the intensification of these air raids in 1943, beyond eliminating Axis air and sea power, was to divert their attention from the upcoming invasion of Sicily. A little over a week after the armistice with Italy was signed, on September 17 Allied troops arrived at Cagliari. Through 1944, most of the inhabitants of the city of Cagliari returned and began rebuilding their city, a task that would take many years.[42]

On December 7, Dad, Headquarters and HQ Battery moved to Decimomannu Airfield and set up their command post. From these two airfields, many bombing raids were made on German positions in Italy as Allied forces continued their march north to France. [43]

On Christmas Eve, high-flying enemy aircraft dropped propaganda pamphlets, putting the battalion on alert. Nothing happened beyond the pamphlets, and the alert was lifted on Christmas Day. According to the Morning Report, "The Battalion resumed its normal duties, and Christmas Day was enjoyed by all."[44]

As 1944 began, the 431st had more than two thousand active Italian troops under its operational control and fighting with the Allies. The Italian troops were made up of anti-aircraft and machine gun batteries. The battalion was also working hard to set up gun positions on the two Sardinian airfields, which were on difficult, hard terrain and in constant downpours of rain.[45]

In a letter to Mom dated January 17, 1944, Dad wrote:

> *I see by this letter that Our Son has inherited my Wife's temperament. I only hope that he learns to control it half as well as his Mom can control hers ... You do a beautiful job of it, Darling ... Darling, I have yet to see a bombed church. That is a fact. I just stopped to think about it and I can't remember ever seeing one in Africa, Sicily, or Sardinia. There might be one here but I haven't been around enough to see it. These churches are beautiful, Darling. I've seen them as old as 500 BC Lady, that's old.*

In February, Dad and the other men of the 431st were given Battle Stars for their service in the conflicts in Algeria, Tunisia, and Sicily, and then the battalion began creating what seemed like a permanent residence in Sardinia. The batteries laid brick and concrete floors for their tents and began building facilities to heat water to clean mess gear—all while heavy wind and rain continued. Building efforts continued throughout their time on Sardinia, including the construction of houses for the battery sections and medical detachments. The area began to look like a new subdivision. Unfortunately, during this time they became aware of a serious malaria issue in the area and began training key members of the battalion on controlling mosquitos and other malaria safety measures. At this time in Sardinia, little if any combat was taking place, so malaria was the biggest threat to their well-being and became a big problem.[46]

The 431st opened a rest camp near Cagliari, and groups of men were sent to the camp for a period of seven days at a time. Additionally, the American Red Cross opened a Beach Club near the camp, so those at the rest camp could take advantage of the Beach Club to swim, watch movies, bathe in the sun, and even enjoy going to dances. This kind of recreation in the midst of the war was a very new and welcome experience for these fighting men.[47]

On June 6, 1944, the battalion was notified that Rome had been captured by Allied forces two days earlier, and the men were ecstatic. They were not aware this was also the day their counterparts in France were involved in the D-day invasion on the beaches at Normandy.[48]

A little over two months later, on August 14 the men were informed of the D-day invasion. Following that news, they had a great treat when World Heavyweight Boxing Champion Joe Louis put on several exhibition bouts with men from various branches of the US Army, Navy, and Italian forces. These were held at the Red Cross Club at Cagliari and were no doubt well-attended. Dad, being an avid boxing fan, would surely have been there if his work permitted![49]

All the building, resting, and fun came to an end on August 26, 1944, when the unit was attached to the Mediterranean Theater of Operations, United States Army (MTOUSA) for administration and relieved of operational control of the Decimomannu and Villacidro Airfields and went into bivouac. Three days later, they received movement orders and began packing for their next move, which was the island directly north across the twelve and a half miles strait to Corsica. By the first of September, the battalion was packed and ready to move, but rough seas made crossing the strait very difficult and dangerous.[50]

CHAPTER 4
FRANCE, 1944–1945

On September 6, 1944, the battalion traveled through heavy rain the two hundred miles to the very northern tip of Sardinia. Arriving that evening, the seas were still too rough to cross the strait, and they had to wait several more days. On September 10, they were finally able to cross over to Bonifacio, Corsica, on the southernmost tip of this French island. They then moved north and went into bivouac for infantry training. They were scheduled for extensive training in infantry tactics, which was, in a way, notification that they were about to move back into the real war soon. They were moved south again for additional training, and morale was low, given these significant changes in their experiences.[51]

Italy had occupied this French island and part of France as a means of holding the Allies back from ultimately moving into France. Over time, Italy's occupation involved almost 85,000 troops—especially huge considering that the total population of Corsica was only about 220,000. The Italians met very little resistance during their occupation. There was a fairly sizable portion of the population who supported the Fascists and helped control the growth of an anti-Fascist resistance among their fellow Corsicans. However, by early 1943 the resistance to the Fascists had grown to the point that they were receiving arms and ultimately Allied Special Forces personnel to assist.[52]

In early September 1943, after Mussolini was imprisoned in Italy and a year before Dad's unit showed up, 12,000 German troops went to Corsica, taking over the occupation from the Italians, whom they assumed would capitulate to the Allies. Some of the Italians remained loyal to Italy, and after the armistice was signed with the Allies, they fought alongside the Corsican resistance against the Germans until Corsica was liberated on October 4 after severe fighting. The Germans were actively retreating some 30,000 troops from Sardinia through Corsica to the northern port of Bastia. The last of the German units were evacuated the night of October 3, 1943. Corsica was the first French territory to be freed by the Allied forces, and this marked the beginning of the liberation of France.[53]

Corsica was short-lived for the 431st, as they were alerted for movement to southern France on November 1 and were ordered to move to a staging area near Ajaccio, Corsica, on the eastern coast. Here they rejoined the US 7th Army along with other anti-aircraft battalions.[54]

Mainland France

After several cold, rainy days, on November 5 the battalion boarded the *SS Robert M. T. Hunter* and departed for France. It was an exceedingly rough trip on the Mediterranean Sea due to storms and took three days to arrive at the outer harbor of Marseilles, France, then another five rough-water days at anchor before the ship could be berthed and personnel and equipment unloaded. Unloading all the equipment took three days, and several jeeps and trucks had been severely damaged by the salt water and bouncing around in the rough seas.[55]

Finally, the battalion was on land. Over the next three days, they traveled nearly five hundred miles to Brouvelieures, where they set up their command post, and the other batteries were all put into position.[56] At this time, the Allies had launched a major offensive involving all six Allied armies on the western front. The French 1st Army and the US 7th had reached the Rhine River in Alsace. The other sectors were only making small gains against the Germans. The Germans were actively and unexpectedly building up their forces along the front faster than the Allies, despite Germany's great inferiority of ample material resources, including soldiers and fighting equipment.[57] The front was in northern France, near the Belgian border, and Dad's unit was farther west, almost on the German border.

The unit moved north and closer to the front, and as described in the Morning Reports, they began experiencing more enemy activity. On November 20, the battalion experienced its first casualty since leaving Palermo, Sicily, nearly a year earlier, when an engineer stepped on a mine. A medical technician went to his aid with a stretcher. As he stepped off the road, he stepped on another mine, losing a foot and several fingers. They soon found that there were mines and booby traps everywhere that had been cleverly camouflaged, making them difficult to find. As the Axis forces were driven back, they left behind minefields in areas where they thought the Allies would be. As the AAA batteries of the 431st Battalion were moved frequently, battery personnel had to spend a great deal of their time locating and uncovering the mines to get the anti-aircraft guns set up. The training they received in Corsica for these issues was very helpful in assisting them in their abilities to identify and clear the mines and booby traps. Clearly, Dad and the 431st had caught back up to the war.[58]

The day after Thanksgiving, Headquarters and HQ Battery moved southwest to Saint-Dié-des-Vosges.[59] On the day they moved, Dad wrote a letter to Mom. It's important to note that none of Dad's letters ever mentioned things going on as far as the war was concerned. Letters written by servicemen during the war were all read by "examiners" for any content that could potentially be used by the enemy. On the front of every envelope is a stamp that said "Examiner" followed by the signature of the person who approved it and allowed it to be mailed. Dad, of course, very carefully followed these rules.

He began his letter by saying,

There isn't much to write about excepting that I missed church again this Sunday ... There are beaucoup little girls over here, and I agree with you, Darling, they are really about the cutest little devils there are ... The town of Epinal France isn't worth spending any money on either. I was there a few days ago also. I love you, Beaucoup ... I'm going to sign off now, Darling, I'm freezing!

Apparently, Dad had found a French word he liked: *beaucoup!*

On December 1, Dad's section of the 431st was moved again, to Mutzig, France, just twenty miles from Alsace and the German border. All the other batteries were also moved to locations near that area and were providing anti-aircraft protection for several Army battalions. Throughout the month of December, the batteries experienced many raids from German fighter aircraft. Anti-aircraft batteries were experiencing some serious confusion during this time, as they were being attacked by both friendly Allied P-47 aircraft and by captured P-47s flown by the Germans.[60]

On December 10, the problem escalated when American P-47s flew low toward the anti-aircraft batteries—much like German aircraft would do when attacking—and the AA units fired on them, after which the P-47s dove and strafed the gun positions, damaging some of the equipment, but fortunately missing personnel. The batteries continued to have multiple encounters with German aircraft and set up searchlights to help with identification at night.[61]

In a letter to Mom dated December 15, 1944, Dad wrote:

My Darling Wife:
Darling, there is absolutely nothing to write about tonight. I am in the best of health and sitting by a nice warm fire and on that stove is a twelve quart bucket of water heating for your husbands bath, it will be a sponge as I haven't located a tub as yet. It is really cozy here as there are only two of us in the room, they were going to put four in here but two of them decided not to come, so. Just finished a ham and egg sandwich (canned of course) but it sure was good, now the guy in the room with me is making toast and we shall put preserved butter on it; the butter

is mostly cheese. We will also have cup of coffee w/o cream. Someday I shall write you a letter Army style. I love you.

Well right now I'd better get a bath and some sleep 'cause your little man is going to have a busy day.

> *'Tis neither You Nor I*
> *But WE*
> *Jinny Mae and Richard D.*

> *Your Loving Husband,*
> *Dick*
> *I love you, Beaucoup!*

The day after this letter, the Germans launched a big counteroffensive on the front, which surprised the Allied command and their forces and ramped up the action taking place around Dad's location at Mutzig. This became known as the Battle of the Bulge. The Germans made some headway, but by December 26 Allied forces had begun to push them back. The weather had also cleared, allowing some five thousand Allied aircraft to bomb and strafe the German forces and their supply lines.[62]

On 30 December the Advance echelon of Headquarters and Headquarters Battery was bombed and strafed by twelve (12) enemy operated P-47's. The CP, mess hall, kitchen and quarters of officers and enlisted men were badly damaged. The command post was located on the mian road at an intersection and a 1½ ton 6 X 6 truck and a 3/4 ton reconn car, property of 36th Field Artillery Battalion were strafed and burned. The raid lasted approximately 20 minutes. During the raid six (6) Enlisted men were killed. Two (2) officers and thirteen (13) enlisted men received wounds as result. One (1) enlisted man from this organization being among those killed. General Brooks (CG 6th Corps) and General Townsend, Commanding general 35th AAA Brigade, and Lt. Colonel STEVENS, visited the CP shortly after the raid.

US Army Morning Report, dated Dec. 30, 1944

On December 30, Dad's unit was attacked by enemy planes. When he heard the noise of the attack, Dad ran out of the building where he was working and caught a piece of bomb shrapnel in his left forearm. According to the December 30 Morning Report, he was one of thirteen wounded enlisted men. These were the first "in-action" casualties the 431st AAA AA Battalion had experienced since leaving

Sicily. He and the other wounded soldiers were cared for quickly by medics and soon evacuated to England.[63]

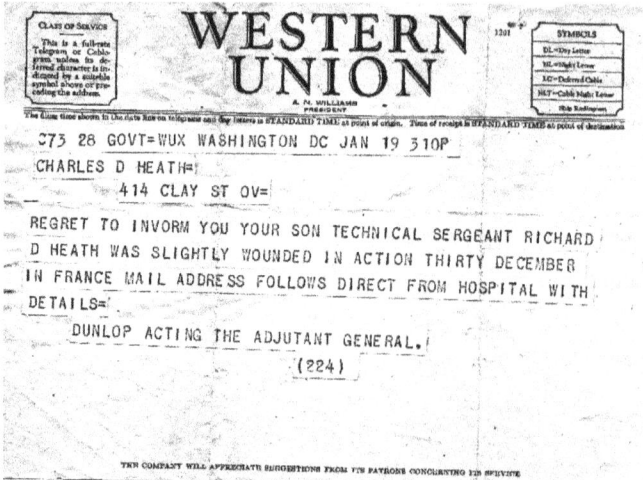

Western Union telegram, dated Jan. 19, 1945

It wasn't until January 19 that word of Dad's injury was received back home. Mom found out two days later when Gramma Peggy came to see her with "teary eyes and a red nose, and I knew something bad had happened to Dick." She didn't wonder why her mother knew about it before she did nor why the telegram went to Dad's parents instead of directly to her. Dad's parents thought it would be easier for Mom if she learned of his wound when her parents were with her. In the end, because the wound was slight, it wasn't terribly bad news. Dad received the Purple Heart in June 1945, shortly after he came back to the United States.

On Dad's birthday, January 26, five days after she received notice of his wound, Mom wrote him a letter but wasn't certain where to send it. Ultimately, the letter was returned to her. Here is an excerpt:

My Darling Husband,
All day, the radios have been booming out about this being General MacArthur's birthday and nary a word did they say about it's also being the birthday of General Ike's right hand man. I missed you so and really had a hard time getting things done. I wouldn't do a darned

thing now, if you were here, but sit close and love you ... There has still been no news from or about you. I am no good for a thing. I stand in the middle of the floor and turn round and round—wondering what to do ... Each day, it becomes more and more difficult to find something to write. We haven't been down to the folks since Tuesday. I'm not going to mail any more letters to you until we get your hospital address. The news seems so good that I wake each morning fearing it has changed. The first thing I do is turn on the radio.

Goodnight, My Darling
With all my Love,
Your Wife and Son

'Tis neither You Nor I
But WE
Jinny Mae and Richard D.

I love you, Darling

On the same day Mom wrote the letter above, Dad wrote the one below while he was still in the hospital in England. It didn't arrive in Manitowoc until a month later, on February 27.

My Darling Wife:
I got so used to talking to Arabs, French, Italians, Sardinians, Corsicans, and Germans that now I'm in England, I asked the nurse the other day when was chow—in Italian, she gave me a very blank look and I realized that you could speak just plain English and she'd understand. Was I surprised. I love you.

Well, Darling, our two years of separation are completed, Our Son will soon be two years old, our marriage will soon be three years old, you will soon be twenty-3 and I sure hope I'll soon be home. If our friends the Russians keep up their drive I know I will be unless they really pull one on us. I love you.

Did I tell you I have a private room, shared with only one other guy? Sink, hot water, stove, and everything. I love you ….
Goodnight, my Beloved.

'Tis neither You Nor I
But WE
Jinny Mae and Richard D.

Your Loving Husband,

Dick
I Love You
But Good

Eventually, Mom and Dad were able to write back and forth to one another. When he was recovered from his wound, Dad was released from the hospital in England in mid-April 1945 and sent back to the United States. Mom and Danny went to Ottawa, Illinois, when they learned Dad would soon be home.

Map of Dad's Movements, March 1943–December 1944

PART II:
RAISING ARMY

CHAPTER 5
BACK HOME IN WISCONSIN
WITH BRAT TWO, 1945–1946

Dad called Mom when he arrived in New York—the first time they had heard each other's voices in two years. He was placed on leave from the Army for thirty days and headed for home. Dad, Mom, and Danny spent a short time with his folks in Ottawa and went around visiting all his aunts, uncles, and cousins. Afterward, they went to Manitowoc and the little apartment Mom and Danny had been living in for just a few weeks. Dad had to report to a hospital in Indiana in early June for a physical and to get discharged from the Army.

Although his wound was slight, and he could have been sent back into action in Europe, the war there was virtually over. All German military forces surrendered to the Allies in May of 1945 after Adolph Hitler committed suicide, and the Allies and Russia had closed off all escape routes.[64]

They bought a car and a small camper to make the trip to the hospital in Indiana, determined not to be separated anymore. On the way, Mom remembered a campsite where she stayed once on a trip to Ohio with her parents. When Dad, Mom, and Danny arrived at the campsite, it was quite late, and there were no other campers. They pulled in, set up the camper, and spent the night. Early the next morning, there was a loud pounding on the camper door. A very irate man was standing there wanting to know who they thought they were to come in there, digging up his yard. Dad and Mom explained to him that they thought it was still a trailer park, that Dick had just come home from the war and was on his way to the hospital in Indiana. By the end of the explanation, the man had seen little Danny, and as he heard that Dad had just come home from the war, wounded, his entire attitude changed. They were invited into his home for breakfast, and he told them they could stay as long as they liked and were welcome to stop there on their way back. Dad did all he could to repair the lawn before they left for Indiana.

On June 10, 1945, while they were still in Indiana, Dad was honorably discharged from the United States Army. While there, Danny (age two) and Dad bonded under the hood of the car. Danny would ask, "What's that, Daddy, huh?" and Dad would tell him it was a carburetor or a dipstick. Later when Dad would point to each thing and ask Danny what it was, Danny could tell him without missing a beat.

Hello, Dave!

Upon returning to Wisconsin, Mom and Dad settled in Waupaca, living in Mom's folks' cabin on the Waupaca River. While he was overseas Dad had written to Mom about the possibility of purchasing the cabin and the property around it from her dad. They sold their car and camper, and the money from that helped Dad buy a milk route, which included a very large truck as part of it. That truck was their sole transportation for the time they stayed there.

Dad's job wasn't one of those milk routes where he would deliver milk to homes in quart bottles. He would go from farm to farm, pick up multiple ten-gallon cans filled with milk—weighing up to about eighty-eight pounds each—then transport them to the creamery. It was a very hard job, which was sometimes quite treacherous on those snowy Wisconsin roads. And, according to Mom, Wisconsin had a terribly cold winter in 1946.

Dad and Mom didn't waste any time creating the next Brat to join the Heath Platoon: Dave was born in February. Two weeks before Dave was due, Mom went back to the doctor she had when she was pregnant with Danny in Manitowoc, and they stayed with her folks. Dad was still at the cabin, continuing his milk route work, but there wasn't a phone there. The cabin was about eighty-five miles away, so they made plans for Mom or Gramma Peggy to call a gas station near there when the baby was on the way. Mom really wanted Dad to be there when his second child was born, and he didn't want to miss it for anything. When he got the news, he took off for the hospital and arrived just in time. Dave had been in a hurry to get born and the roads to get there were really bad with snow and ice.

So Much for Civilian Life ....

Dad sold the route just a few months later in May and they moved to Manitowoc where he got a job in a factory. Even though he grew up with his father working in a factory, Dad disliked the work environment from the first day he got the job. By that time, both he and Mom knew the military was in his blood and that he would most likely not be happy doing anything else. So, on September 26, 1946, one year, three months and sixteen days after his discharge, Dad reenlisted in the United States Army at the rank of staff sergeant, one stripe below his rank when he was discharged at the end of the war. The next day, the family was on their way to Fort Bliss, near El Paso, Texas.

CHAPTER 6
JAPAN AND A FAMILY OF FOUR
BECOMES FIVE, 1946–1949

It was a long road trip to Fort Bliss, which is more than 1,500 miles from Manitowoc. It is on the farthest southwestern corner of Texas, right on the border with Mexico. The trip took several days, and it was still very hot in that part of the world at the end of September.

Arriving in El Paso, Dick and Jinny rented a room in a hotel that didn't allow children—so they "smuggled" Dan (age three) and Dave (eleven months) in and worked hard to keep them very quiet. Fortunately, they were naturally quiet kids, so there weren't any problems, but it was a nasty place, with bugs crawling everywhere. Dad bought bug bombs, and every night they would smuggle the kids out and go for a ride while the bombs fumigated the room. When they came back, they would shake out the bedspreads, sweep the floor, and then do the same thing again the next night. It wasn't a pleasant situation, but there was no need to look for another place to live because Dad was informed right away that he would be going to Japan, and the family was very excited to learn that they were going with him! But, given that the United States had recently conquered Japan, what would the Heath family expect to find regarding the attitudes of the Japanese people toward the occupying American soldiers and their families?

Postwar Japan

Prior to Japan's surrender, more than 250,000 Japanese military personnel and civilians had been killed in intense bombing attacks that had occurred on the Japanese islands, beginning four months after their unprovoked attack on US forces in Pearl Harbor. American planes dropped bombs on Japan from April 1942 through May 1945. Most cities and many urban areas were wiped out with little left but rubble from the destroyed buildings. More than 8.5 million Japanese people were homeless due to the bombings when the Heaths arrived. This intense campaign culminated with the two atom bombs the United States dropped on the cities of Hiroshima and Nagasaki, after which the Japanese immediately surrendered.[65]

According to "Douglas MacArthur's Occupation of Japan: Building the Foundation of US-Japan Relationship" by Mieko Endo, through those years the people of Japan were suffering from serious food shortages, as well as medicine and clothing. One big problem they had was a lack of arable land on which to grow food, so Japan depended on importing food as well as many products from other countries, specifically Korea and Taiwan. Even though Japan's culture had been driven for a long time by a militaristic attitude, hungry soldiers couldn't hold up physically forever, and many died of starvation. Even with these issues, the people were consistently told Japan was winning the war right up until the day Japan surrendered. Through the first three years of Allied occupation—1946–1949, which was our time there—the Japanese people were suffering severe hunger and lacked living materials and housing, and crime rates for theft and robbery were very high. Additionally, they were angry at their leaders for losing the war and were highly fearful of what the occupying forces would do to them. They were told women and girls would be raped, men would be murdered, and what little food they had would be taken from them.[66]

At this time, the American people generally hated Japan for the devastating attack on Hawaii just a few years prior. Americans wanted the Japanese to pay dearly for Pearl Harbor and held very little mercy for them. This prevailing attitude included the cry for war-crimes trials for military leaders and Emperor Hirohito, the divine leader of Japan.[67]

Rebuild or Crush?

General Douglas MacArthur, commander of the occupying armed forces in Japan, recognized the incredible needs and desperation of the Japanese people. His key advisor, Brigadier General Bonner Fellers, specialized in Japanese cultural psychology, and his advice helped in developing a plan to demilitarize the country, feed the masses, rebuild the economy, change the form of government to a democracy, and enable Japanese women to vote. Marriage and divorce statutes were also rewritten, including outlawing contract marriage. Additionally, high schools became coeducational, which was a new concept for the Japanese people. These significant societal and cultural changes were designed to create in the Japanese people a renewed sense of purpose and dignity and to assist them in as many ways possible. These initiatives were made formal in the new Constitution of Japan, which was then passed by the newly reformed Japanese Parliament.[68]

What was likely even more important in convincing the Japanese people that the occupying forces were not hostile to them, was that MacArthur made the decision to enlist Emperor Hirohito in creating a positive thought process among his people. MacArthur elected— not without some serious challenges from US officials—to forego dethroning Hirohito and charging him with war crimes. McArthur recognized that the emperor was highly revered, worshipped, and considered a divine being by the Japanese people, and the response to deposing him could result in riots, bloodshed, and a very difficult transition. MacArthur prevailed. As a result, on the day of Japan's surrender, Emperor Hirohito issued a national radio address to his people in which he ordered them to submit to the occupying forces and obey all the terms of the surrender of their country. Upon Hirohito's address, seven million soldiers laid down their weapons and demobilized the military. The Japanese people had never before heard the voice of the emperor, but they obeyed his instructions, and the occupation and the ability of the people and their conquerors to become friendly occurred easily and quickly. One year after the end of the war, at General MacArthur's request, Emperor Hirohito issued a statement to his people known as the "Declaration of Humanity," in which he renounced his divinity, becoming a human being to his people. After doing so, he toured all over Japan to meet the people. Just as the people had never heard his voice, they had also never seen him in person. This dramatic change in the culture of the country also helped pave the way to embracing a democratic society.[69]

Some of these massive changes didn't last long though, as the advent of the Cold War with Russia and the rise of Communism began in 1947. Because occupying forces felt they may need a more powerful Japan to assist in driving back Russia and Communist China, they began eliminating many of the changes and encouraged the Japanese to remilitarize. Along with this, the United States began in 1950 to push back the Communist movement from Japan, which had been taking root right after the war. However, the democratic constitution enacted in Japan after the war remains in place to this day.[70]

Another Separation, Immunizations

In mid-November 1946, Staff Sergeant Heath was driving the family car to San Francisco so it could be shipped to Japan. Then he was on his way overseas by way of a troop transport ship. He arrived in Yokohama on December 10, 1946, after a ten-day trip, and was assigned to Headquarters Battery, 138th AAA Group.

Meanwhile, the family was headed to Wisconsin by train from El Paso. While the new separation from Dad wasn't pleasing, Mom knew that it wouldn't be a long separation, and she, Danny, and Dave were soon to be in Japan with him! It is likely that Mom was not overly aware of the extent of the trauma the Japanese people had experienced over this time period, as one might expect of most US citizens at that time. Mom, Danny, and Dave spent a couple of months with her folks, waiting for their port call. All three had to get immunizations before going to Japan, and the local doctors didn't have what they needed. Mom learned that they were available at the naval base near Chicago, so they went to Dick's parents' home in Ottawa to be closer when it was time for the vaccinations.

While they were at Grampa Grump and Gramma Nell's home, Grampa Grump volunteered to cut Danny's hair, which was beginning to get a little long. He took him out on the sunporch with Mom, who would distract him during the haircut. Dave was spared the haircut at Mom's request. Dave had his first birthday that February, and if his dad had been home, Dave would have definitely had his hair cut too. All the while, Grampa Grump lived up to his name with his "grump-ing" about his son reenlisting in the Army.

Also during this visit, Gramma Nell introduced Mom and the kids to their first Catholic Lenten experience. Just one Gramma Nell experience with Lent was more than enough for Mom. When it came to anything church-related, Gramma Nell went by the book, and at that time the rules were much stricter than they are now. They were all subjected to some serious fasting until noontime came on Easter Sunday, and then they were really happy to do some serious feasting. As hard as she was about the fast leading up to Easter, Gramma Nell knew how to cook a great feast!

The day came when it was time to get their immunizations, so they caught the early train to Chicago, then took a subway to the naval base. It was quite a long walk from the subway station to the base hospital, and Mom had to carry Dave. Big brother Danny helped out by carrying the diaper bag and held Mom's hand. Danny and Dave weren't used to getting shots and both engaged in much screaming and carrying on, but in spite of that, they all got their first series of shots. Mom was given the serum they would need for the follow-up doses, which would be administered by a local doctor in Ottawa. All three were weary when they took the long walk back to the subway, then the train ride, landing finally back into the arms of loving grandparents. All the Brats of the Heath Platoon were required to get a big batch of immunizations before every trip overseas; this was definitely not a favorite event for any of us!

Reunited

Dave started walking a few days before embarking on their overseas trip in late April of 1947. The trip involved five days on a train, two days in Seattle, and eleven days on a ship crossing the Pacific Ocean to Japan. While on the ship, Dave developed a good pair of sea legs, but once they docked in Yokohama, he struggled when trying to walk on flat, not-moving ground. It didn't take him long to master it though, in true Dave style.

Dave in Yokohama, 1947

Aboard the ship they were fortunate to share a stateroom with two nice ladies who loved children. Mom was very seasick for three days, and those nice ladies took care of Danny and Dave while Mom was under the weather. On the fourth day at sea, she was happily feeling much better. The ship arrived in Japan on the eleventh day, and Danny and Dave were really excited to see their daddy.

The family had a nice two-bedroom Army dependents' apartment in Yokohama and a full-time maid, paid for by Uncle Sam. It was thought by the US military that they would lose face if soldiers' families did their own housework. Mom didn't hear anyone complain about that, and no one heard any complaints from her!

After only a few days in Yokohama, Danny disappeared. This was frightening. The United States was occupying a foreign land after a long and bloody war; there could still be people who hated our guts, and four-year-old Danny had gone missing! He was found after about fifteen frantic minutes that felt more like fifteen hours to Mom—the rascal was hiding behind the china cabinet! Danny had a curious spirit and liked to wander and see what was "out there." Later on, after the family had settled in their apartment, he went exploring outside the apartment area. Somewhere along the way, he got on a honey bucket wagon and got a little tour of that part of Japan. The man on the wagon eventually took Danny back to the American apartment complex, apparently assuming that was where he lived. To this day, Danny can't remember why the man let him on the cart. *Honey bucket wagon* is the term used for the wagons pulled by oxen that carried human waste to a location where it was used for fertilizer; this could explain the unusual smell of the "honey."

Danny in Yokohama, 1947

All the apartment's furniture was government-issued and was very serviceable and nice looking. They even furnished a playpen, which really delighted Dave when he discovered that, since there was no floor in this playpen, he could just pick it up and go. And go he did! A fix for that little problem was found, though, when a padded cloth floor was attached to the bottom of the rails.

The family's maid, Ayako, soon became a good friend to Mom, Dad, and the kids. She was quite young and spoke very little English, but they managed to communicate. She wore western clothing to work but would dress in Japanese attire for special holidays. It was like she was an altogether different person on those special days, assuming her natural Japanese demeanor in reverence to the holiday.

The car arrived in Yokohama about three weeks after Jinny and the kids did, and they were at the port to watch it being off-loaded from the ship. Danny was a very excited young fellow, watching all those cars coming off the ship, and he was really thrilled when he recognized the Heath's Ford! Though they could have managed very well without their own transportation, having their own car made it much more interesting, as they could travel around the country and explore.

The family made several trips to Mt. Fuji, which has an elevation of 12,388 feet.[71] There was a beautiful resort area high on the mountain, and they made day trips there, as it was only a few hours west of Yokohama. The roads were very winding, and one time Dave got carsick all over poor Mom. They were driving through a little village and pulled the car over to deal with it. When the villagers saw what was happening, they came out to the car and helped clean up the mess. In their three years in Japan, Dad and Mom found the Japanese people to be very gracious and always willing to help.

Many small trips were made around the Yokohama area of Japan, just to get the feel of the place. Mom said they saw that the hills were full of caves where the Japanese soldiers might have hidden to fight our soldiers if the United States had occupied the island before the Japanese surrendered. The highway between Yokohama and Tokyo was wiped clean of buildings due to intense bombing during the war; there was nothing left but rubble. One time, while lost way out on a back road, Dad and Mom began to wonder if the people in that area even knew the war was over and what might happen to them if they didn't. They never encountered any problems. In fact, after riding around in the country once, they were heading back toward home and saw Emperor Hirohito's palace. That was pretty exciting! It's also quite interesting that Hirohito's palace was spared, given the intensity of the continuous bombing Japan experienced during the war.

Japanese people came through the housing area every day to check out the garbage cans for any edible food or other items of possible use. These were some of the more than eight million who were homeless following the devastation of the war. There was an area in downtown Yokohama under some railroad tracks where there were dwellings made of cardboard boxes and any other usable materials. The dependents' housing had no air-conditioning, so the family kept windows open at night and could hear the sadness of people crying out in pain.

There was also a busy street fairly close to the apartment area where the Japanese frequently had festivals that always included parades with dragons and music. Mom, Dad, and the boys always loved to go out and watch them as they went by.

There was a Japanese American couple living in the apartment building. The wife was pregnant, and when the time came for the birth of their child, Mom happened to be at the hospital and saw her come in. Her husband was on field duty out of town, and the hospital administration wasn't going to admit her because she appeared Japanese. Mom assured them that she was a United States citizen, so they let her in.

While in Yokohama, Dad and Mom met a young corporal who was in Dad's outfit. Digger was from California and away from home for the first time. He would come to the apartment frequently for dinner and really enjoyed being with the family. He liked Danny and Dave, and they liked him, and he became a close family friend. After leaving Japan, we saw Digger in many places over the years as they moved from one of Dad's duty stations to another.

Mom had her one and only bout of homesickness during their first winter in Yokohama. The two-story apartment had a window at the landing where the stairs turned. On her way downstairs one morning, she looked out the window and saw the ground was covered with snow, and she started to cry. Having grown up in Wisconsin, Mom had experienced a lot of snow in her lifetime, and there aren't many people who dislike snow as much as she did then. Given her dislike for the snow, she couldn't understand why the sight of it suddenly brought about such a reaction of homesickness. As the picture says, though, it was "a long way back home."

a long way back home

Mom and Danny on Hiratsuka Beach, 1947

In April 1947, Staff Sergeant Heath was promoted to technical sergeant, and a few months later was assigned to Headquarters, 8th Army, Special Services Section, also in Yokohama, so no move was required.

Welcome, Bobby!

Around June of 1947 Mom was pregnant with Brat number Three (guess who?). During the pregnancy, the Army hospital provided Mom with a quart of milk daily, which she had to go pick up. Most of the time it wasn't worth bringing home because it was often not drinkable, but she went to get it almost every day just in case it was good. Danny usually went with her. The walk was short and interesting, if not a little concerning, as they had to cross a bridge where beggars were always sitting. They had been told in Army briefings about living in Japan, that they should never give anything to the beggars. Knowing the peril and poverty in which the beggars lived, it was difficult for Mom to not give them anything.

Time—and the pregnancy—went on, and soon Mom had to get to the hospital to deliver the new addition to the Heath Platoon. To get to the Army 106th General Hospital near Yokohama by car, they had to pass the headquarters building where Dad worked. In the wee hours of that morning in March 1948, Dad decided to break all speed regulations as he passed that building. Mom thought he might be disappointed no one stopped him because this was his third child and the first one where he had accompanied the baby's mommy to the hospital for the birth. They arrived at the hospital safely, which was a good thing, as I was apparently very tiny and arrived quickly. About fifteen years after I was born there, the 106th General Hospital became one of the hospitals to which wounded US servicemen were sent for treatment, recovery, and rehabilitation during the Vietnam War.[72]

Two hours after my birth, a nurse came to the room and told Mom it was time to get up. Mom was sure she had made a mistake, but the nurse assured her that she hadn't. Mom didn't think her legs would hold her, and if by some miracle they did, she thought everything in her body would fall out. Keep in mind, that in her two previous experiences with childbirth, Mom was kept in the bed for days. But the thinking in the medical field about these things had changed significantly since Dave came along. Her legs worked, her body held together without any problems, and three days later, Bobby and Mommy went home. However, they went to a different home, which was a big surprise to Mommy.

During those few days, Dad and Ayako had moved everything to a larger apartment. It was brand new with three bedrooms and a bath and a half for the family and a bedroom and bath for Ayako. The place was not completely finished as they learned a few days later when a workman came to the door and wanted to know if they wanted green or red carpet on the stairs. Then he said, "You had better take green because they are all out of red." It took no time at all to make that difficult decision. For several days, Ayako would go to Mom and ask where different things could be found. Mom, of course, should have been asking her, since she had not been in on the move and was having some challenges finding things herself.

A few months later, in July of 1948, Dad was assigned to the 163rd Transportation Car Company, again in Yokohama. Maybe someone noticed him speeding by headquarters that night I was born?

A master sergeant named Bill, who worked with Dad, and his wife, Lena, were my godparents, and on the day of my christening, a bottle of champagne was uncorked, which they all enjoyed. Not long after dinner, Dad, Lena, and Bill disappeared to take a nap while Mom sat feeding me, with a head that was spinning from the champagne. Ayako asked her, "Okasan, you no get drunk?" Mom rarely drank anything with alcohol, so just a little bit had a greater impact on her.

During the day, Mom put me in a bassinet downstairs, usually in the dining room. One morning, it was obvious that mice had been in the bassinet overnight; fortunately, I wasn't there with them. There were large openings around the pipes to make room for them to shake in case of earthquakes, and the bassinet was near a pipe. Dad made sure that some tin was put around all these openings, which took care of the problem.

Later that year, Ayako had some family problems and had to leave. It was sad to see her go, as she had become one of the family in a sense. Shortly before Ayako left, Dad and Mom were starting to be concerned because Dave wasn't talking. Before Ayako left, Mom mentioned it to her. She said, "Okasan, Davy speaks Japanese." Apparently, Ayako and Davy had lots of conversations over the course of the last year and a half. That also explained why he always crawled up and turned the radio from the Armed Forces station to a Japanese station. It alerted them to the fact that they had probably not been talking to Dave enough. Today, there is no problem getting Dave to talk, but he unfortunately didn't hold onto his ability to speak Japanese.

The Army soon provided a replacement for Ayako, a young man whose name was very hard to pronounce, so we called him Boysan. One of the many good things Boysan did for us was keeping the floors really clean. The floors in the living and dining rooms were made of unfinished wood and Boysan polished them regularly. Mom said he really had them looking beautiful, and the shiniest place was right around my playpen, where he would talk to me while he shined the floor. At bedtime, the sheets and blankets were turned down on the beds, and shoes would have a fresh coat of polish on them each morning. Boysan did a great job of pampering the family. Mom and Dad had his name and address when they left to come back to the United States and kept in touch for a while. He became a policeman after we left.

The Army base had a really nice Enlisted Men's Club, and Mom and Dad often took Danny and Dave there for lunch. It was a big brick building and looked identical to several other nearby buildings. The first few times they took the kids, Dave would start crying at the entrance and didn't want to go in. It took a while to realize that he thought they were taking him into the dispensary for more shots. Mom, Danny, and Dave ate their first french fries in that club. After a few french fries and some good lunches, Dave got over the issue of going into the club. Sometimes there would be a band in the afternoon, and Dad always liked to dance. Mom claimed to be a poor dancer and avoided it as much as possible (yet, we remember that Social Dance Club in high school). Dad would ask someone else to dance, and that was fine with her, but it really upset Danny.

When Mom had shopping to do and didn't have the car, she would ride the Army bus, often with Danny. He wasn't shy about speaking out when he wanted to get his mommy's attention. One day, the bus was about to cross the railroad tracks, and Danny said, "Look down there, Mommy. That man has his ass stuck in the tracks, and he can't get it out." The bus passengers really enjoyed that. Mom's not sure just how Danny learned that a donkey could also be called an ass. One other time, a man with a very long beard got on the bus, and they were all informed by Danny that Santa Claus had just gotten onboard. The people were disappointed when Danny wasn't with her; he kept those bus rides very entertaining.

In the fall of 1948, Danny started kindergarten at Yokohama American School, which first opened in 1946.[73] The school was a short distance from the apartment complex, and Mom walked with him. He was not at all happy about staying at the school when Mom left, and she could still hear him crying when she got out to the street, which was about a city block from the school. That first day was the only time he gave any indication that it bothered him. Danny and his siblings had a lot of changes coming beyond just going to school!

Hiratsuka Beach was within easy driving distance, so the family could go and spend several hours before returning home. Mom had never been swimming in the ocean before and found the waves to be more powerful than she was; they knocked her down a number of times. Japanese men would come out to the beach area with huge nets to catch fish fairly close to where they were swimming from time to time. There would be a dozen or more men, and most of them were stark naked. Mom, the quiet Wisconsin girl, saw a lot more than she wanted to see! When the fishermen showed up, it meant swimming time was over.

Apparently, the fishermen weren't the only ones running around naked. One day when Davy was two years old, Mom saw him chasing a naked little Japanese girl down the street! She may have been a very young girl who lived in some of the rubble near the apartments, and it's thought Davy may have been trying to speak to her—in Japanese, of course!

As was mentioned earlier, the United States was providing many opportunities for the Japanese people to earn money to help them rise out of the devastating squalor in which so many of them lived. Many of those opportunities included working for the military as maids and landscapers as well as other jobs. One of those was cutting the grass around our housing complex. The Japanese women who did that cut the grass by hand with shears. Mom often wondered why the military didn't supply them with lawn mowers. Either way, it was helpful to them and the Japanese economy as they recovered from the war.

Sayonara, Japan

In January 1949, Technical Sergeant Heath was promoted to sergeant first class and was awarded the Good Conduct Medal. Along with that came the usual transfer. Dad was assigned to Camp Stoneman in Pittsburg, California, to await reassignment. We all were going home to America together, including Dad, on March 23, 1949, just a couple weeks after my first birthday. We went down to the dock and boarded the ship when Dad suddenly realized he had left his orders on the dining room table back at the apartment! With only a short time left, he ran back to the apartment for them. Our little family was nervous that he would miss the ship, but he managed to make it back with time to spare.

The ship set sail, and the three members of the Heath Platoon and Jinny were in a stateroom with a single lady, while Dad had to bunk with the troops. We got to spend the days with him, and we had meals together. Mom did a little better than she had on the way over, not having much trouble with seasickness. As the ship approached San Francisco eleven days later, it sailed under the Golden Gate Bridge at night, when it was all lit up—I'm told it was a beautiful experience, although being only one year old at the time, I don't personally remember it.

Mom's cousins Mildred and Wayne lived in San Francisco and took us in for the brief time we were on the West Coast. They took us sightseeing all over San Francisco and the surrounding areas. As the time approached to leave, Mom surprised everyone when she told them she would be willing to fly home to Wisconsin. She had never flown in any kind of plane and was very anxious about it. Eight days after our arrival in San Francisco, on April 11, 1949, Dad received his orders for his new post at Fort Eustis, Virginia, and the 76th Transportation Railway Shop, but first he had some leave time. So after flying across country, we went for a visit to Manitowoc, Wisconsin, and Ottawa, Illinois, and I got to meet my grandparents.

CHAPTER 7
VIRGINIA, TURKEY, AND
TWO MORE BRATS, 1949–1952

A few months before leaving Japan, Dad ordered a new Ford and decided it would be a black car. Shortly after arriving back home in Wisconsin, he went to Detroit to pick up the car. It was a surprise when he drove up with their brand-spanking-new 1949 *white* Ford. Well, what could they say; it was a new car! It was also the first new model design Ford Motor Company had created since the beginning of the US entry into World War II due to production having been put on hold by the government so car companies could produce vehicles needed to support the war effort.[74]

Dave and Dan on the family Ford, 1949

Mom's folks were living in a gorgeous new house that Grampa Archie built, as always with the hope and expectation to sell it. Archie showed Dan, age six, how he could hold nails in his mouth and spit them out into the board where he was going to nail them. If he got really good at it, the nail would stick in the wood right where he wanted to nail it. Archie was that good. Knowing by now that her young boys could be a bit mischievous, Mom wasn't too certain that was a good lesson for him. But as far as she knew, Dan never tried it anytime that he wasn't with Grampa Archie.

After enjoying several weeks visiting Grampa Archie, Gramma Peggy, Grampa Grump, and Gramma Nell, Dad's leave was coming to an end. We all jumped into the new white Ford, drove down to Newport News, Virginia, and rented an apartment where we lived for a few months. Unfortunately, the apartment was pretty overrun by cockroaches and mice. "Cockroaches and mice" could almost be a theme song for many of the places we briefly stayed. Since there were many apartments attached in a long row, it seemed impossible to control the cockroaches because they seemed to migrate from one apartment to the other rather quickly. After setting off bug bombs, we were making nightly runs out of the apartment for a couple hours to let them kill the bugs, bringing back unhappy memories of El Paso, Texas! Sure, the bombs killed the bugs and even the mice, but a new batch of them came back the very next day. Yuck! Since it was summer, the windows were opened to air out the apartment, getting rid of the smell of the bug bombs.

Dad and Mom were looking for a house they could buy and finally found a brand new one that was under construction—and they were able to get a thirty-year VA (Veterans Administration) loan for it. The price on the house was $8,200, and they gave the realtor ten dollars down payment. The house had a big back yard and was on a quiet street about midway between Newport News and Fort Eustis. That area was pretty close to the ocean, right at sea level, and there were holes all over the yard dug by crawdads.

Many US military families were buying homes during this time, in large part due to the passage by Congress of the GI Bill just before the end of World War II. This provided those who were in the military, or veterans, to purchase homes with no money down and with lower interest rates, as well as many other benefits. Along with this, the nation's economy since the end of the war was doing exceedingly well, partly due to the fact that the country had dramatically increased the production and manufacture of war supplies and materials, which also increased employment across the United States. With so many employed and earning money, people were able to purchase many other products, which again increased manufacturing and subsequent employment.[75]

Additionally, as the war came to a close in 1945, tensions with Russia —now called the Soviet Union —began to rise, along with the "iron curtain" in Europe. America was suddenly involved in a Cold War with the Soviet Union. With national concerns about a potential conflict with them, the United States continued to manufacture and stockpile weaponry and to develop more advanced and sophisticated weapons of war. All these factors continued to increase the availability of decent-paying jobs.[76] Mom and Dad purchased two of the primary items that were part of the boom in the American economy: a new car and a new house.

While living in our new home in Newport News, Dan (age six) and Dave (age three) wandered the neighborhood, exploring what was around us and making friends with the kids who lived nearby. On one such exploration, they discovered a grape arbor in a neighbor's back yard. The grapes looked ripe and delicious, so they decided they should give them a try. After they snatched a couple mouth- and pockets-full of grapes, the owner of the home spotted them and came out of the house in their direction with a very unhappy look on his face. They took off running toward home with the owner of the arbor on their heels, yelling at them. They ducked into the crawl space under the house, and Dave, with his red cowboy hat, was peeking out, hoping the grape-man wouldn't see them. He did. Mom heard the commotion and came outside to see what was going on. The grape thieves were caught and had to crawl back out, pockets bulging with grapes to face the wrath of the old man, as well as a bit of scolding from Mom.

Fortunately for Dan and Dave, they got off with a warning—and they got to keep the grapes. Some might explain their good luck due to being little and cute. Even at that, if they got caught in a second grape theft, things might not go so well. Be warned, Brats One and Two!

In August of '50, Brat Four came upon the scene. All three of us older Brats—Dan, Dave, and me (age two)—adored baby Mike and did much to keep him entertained. People often remarked that they didn't think they could personally handle a big family, saying that one or two kids are almost too much. Of course, the Heath Brat babies didn't all arrive at once, and the older ones always helped Mom in any way we could or were instructed. With that said, by December Mom and Dad realized there was yet another Brat baby on the way, number five, due in August of '51!

Dad and a friend replacing an engine, 1950

During this time, once again, the family finances had gotten very tight, and Mom and Dad were having difficulty making ends meet. With little other choice, they sold the nice '49 Ford and bought an older model Plymouth. The Plymouth wasn't mechanically in great shape, but Dad put a rebuilt motor in it to ensure we had a dependable mode of transportation.

Then, in April 1951, just a few months before Brat Five was due to arrive, Dad was suddenly on orders to Ankara, Turkey, and was on his way there just one month later in May. He was assigned to the USA Group Joint American Military Mission for Aid to Turkey, 8666th AAU (Administrative Area Unit).

This assignment came about due to the Truman Doctrine, which President Harry Truman introduced to Congress in March of 1947 as a response to geopolitical expansion being undertaken by the Soviet Union following the end of World War II and Communist uprisings in Turkey and Greece. There were many things of significance about the announcement of this doctrine: one being that it moved the United States from its position of isolationism, which it had held prior to involvement in World War II. It is frequently referred to as the beginning of the Cold War with the Soviet Union, and these policies led to the formation of NATO (North Atlantic Treaty Organization) in 1949.[77]

Our Growing Family
This was a one-year assignment for Sgt. Heath, and families couldn't go, which meant another unhappy separation for Mom, who was six months pregnant. I had just turned two in March, and this would be my first separation from my daddy—and I didn't like it!

Dan had been in first grade when we left Japan and completed that grade after the move to Virginia. He was then going to second grade at a Catholic school in downtown Newport News about five miles from the house when Dad left for Turkey. A military school bus from Fort Eustis took him to and from school. They were only supposed to pick up kids from Fort Eustis, but Dad had managed to get them to pick up Dan on their way. This may well have had something to do with his duty station being at the 76th Transportation Railway Shop, which was where the bus came from.

Dave started kindergarten in this same school that year. One of the things Dave learned at the Catholic school was that students must obey what the nuns/teachers told them to do ... immediately. When his teacher said, "Dave, stop talking!" and he didn't, Dave learned how long he could stand in one spot with his nose in the chalk circle his teacher drew on the blackboard. Although Dave didn't enjoy the nose-in-the-blackboard thing, it took a few more incidents for the lesson to finally be learned. Unfortunately, that is one of many lessons Dave would periodically forget during his years in school. He was certainly not the only Heath Brat who struggled in the lesson-learning department.

Speaking of lessons, Dan had a BB gun while in Newport News, and several of the neighborhood kids who had BB guns would shoot birds with them, thinking that was a very fun thing to do. Even though he wasn't a good shot and rarely hit anything he aimed at, there was one exception to Dan's poor marksmanship. One morning while out running around with the neighbor kids and his BB gun, he saw a bird sitting on a limb in a tree. So he aimed, pulled the trigger, and shot that bird right in the eye, and it fell to the ground, dead. Dan looked at that dead bird, realized that he had just killed it and killed it for nothing. In spite of the neighbor kids giving him a lot of loud "Hurrahs!" Dan felt really terrible about that poor bird. He never shot another animal again.

Apparently, Dan was pretty well armed with kid weapons because he also had a bow with blunt-tipped arrows, which were homemade out of some kind of reed that grew in the area. This was another toy many of the neighbor kids had, and they would run around shooting arrows at one another. Among the factors common among the kids was that most of them removed the blunt tips from their arrows. I mean, how are you going to stick an arrow into anything with that kind of tip? So one day they're running around the neighborhood yelling and screaming at each other and occasionally shooting off an arrow, sometimes randomly at a tree and sometimes at another kid. Dan stopped, took aim at one of his buddies, and let the arrow fly. And fly it did, right into the middle of the kid's forehead—and it stuck! Thank goodness, it stuck just under the skin, but that had to hurt! It's not certain whether Dan gave up shooting arrows or just got a little more careful about where he shot them.

In addition to his adventures around the neighborhood, Dan had continued spending time with Dad under the hood and around our family cars. While doing that, he learned a lot about cars, how they worked, and how to fix things. When Dan was seven years old, one day the old Plymouth had a flat tire in the driveway of the house. Dad had already shipped off to Turkey, and Mom had no idea how to change a flat. Dan said, "Mom, I can change the tire." Outside he went, and soon the tire was changed! How many seven-year-old kids can do that?

Dan came home from school one day through the back door, which was the door we all were required to use, to change into his play clothes so that he could join his friends outside. There was an oil furnace heating grate in the middle of the floor in the hall, and he was standing on it warming his feet when he heard Kate Smith singing "When the Moon Comes Over the Mountain" at the end of her TV show, *The Kate Smith Hour*. That was the song she sang at the end of all her shows. Dan knew when he heard it that we had gotten a television, and he very excitedly ran into the living room to look at that beautiful, new black-and-white TV. All Dan's friends had televisions, so it's likely he had heard Kate's closing song at one of their houses before. Needless to say, he didn't go out to play that afternoon.

Unbeknownst to Mom, as part of their many outdoor activities, Dan and Dave would go to a store at a nearby street corner store and café. Among other things, they sold cigarettes and had packs of matches in a box on the counter for people to use to light their cigarettes. Dan would sneak in and help himself to a pack of matches from time to time. Dan, Dave, maybe me, and some of the neighborhood kids went into the woods across the street from the house, which is where we engaged in lots of different games. The woods, of course, had lots of dry leaves and limbs, and one of the games was to start fires. It was something they did pretty frequently because, you know, it was fun! One time, they started a fire that got big, fast. Really fast. Realizing it was getting out of control, they got really scared, thinking they were going to burn down the whole woods. They all stomped on it frantically and finally got it out. That was their last fire adventure—Dan and Dave learned their lesson. If I was along, I must not have learned that lesson; Mike and I would learn ours later in Lake City, Washington.

When Dave was five years old, he liked to collect rocks and other paraphernalia that he found. One day he came home from playing, and Mom was out on the porch. His pants were dragging, and he was struggling to hold them up. It was obvious his pockets were as full as pockets could be. He had been collecting lots of rocks on this particular day. He looked at Mom and said, "Mommy, I can't hold up my pants!" One of the things Mom noted was that her son was picking up a bit of a Southern accent; "can't" sounded like "cain't" and "pants" sounded like "paints." This was Dave's shift from Japanese to Southern English, although the Southern drawl didn't last very long. Maybe his rock gathering would have worked better if he put his rock collection in my wagon. I always pulled my little red wagon around wherever I went. This made it easy for Mom to find me; all she had to do was look up and down the street, and wherever she spotted the wagon, I was nearby.

Our Newport News house, 1951

Helping Hands

When it was nearly time for Brat Five to arrive, Dad being far away in Turkey, and Dan, Dave, me, and little Mike already in the nest, Mom was in need of some help. She called her mom to ask if she and Archie could come, but Gramma Peggy didn't see any way that they could right then. Mom then contacted Gramma Nell, and she was going to come to help, but then Gramma Peggy and Grampa Archie changed their minds and were able to come. Nell was likely a bit disappointed. While there, Grampa Archie screened in the front porch and scythed down all the high weeds that had grown in the back yard. We were all highly impressed with Grampa Archie's big, strong arms—arms we all enjoyed swinging on frequently.

Archie and Peggy were there about a week before Brat Five—Girl Brat One—Rachel, was delivered. Peggy drove Mom to the Fort Eustis hospital faster than she had ever driven. When Gramma Peggy found out that she would have to check in at the gate to the post, she was really unhappy about being delayed—but people don't just drive into a military post without permission. Fortunately, once the guard recognized Jinny was in labor, it didn't really take any time at all to check in, and they quickly drove on to the hospital. It turned out to be a good thing she hurried because Rachel didn't waste any time in making her arrival to the Heath Platoon!

After Rachel's birth, the doctor went to the waiting room and told Peggy that she had her first granddaughter. She was so excited that she was almost breathless. A funny sidenote: Mom and Dad had decided that if they ever had a girl, her name would be Diane. When Mom sent a telegram to Dad announcing his daughter's birth, she neglected to tell him her name was Rachel. He later told her he'd celebrated *Diane's* arrival with all his buddies in Turkey.

Mom's folks stayed with us for a week after Rachel's birth. After they left, Mom felt very blessed to have Dan, Dave, and even three-year-old me with her to help out with things. It couldn't have been an easy task that soon after giving birth to have to take care of the baby, a one-year-old, *and* three active young children without any help!

One other important reason why Mom was very thankful to have help from Gramma Peggy and Grampa Archie was that before Rachel's arrival, and shortly after Dad left for Turkey, I quickly earned the nickname "Teeny the Meanie." I was into my "terrible twos" at the time Dad left and apparently didn't understand why my daddy had to go away. Obviously, I must have wanted to make my position on that very clear. I started coloring my bedroom door with crayons and hiding things—for example, Mom's watch—in my dresser drawer. I started saying things like, "When Daddy gets home, I'm going to beat up his leg." Fortunately, Mom fairly quickly discovered my hiding place and was able to retrieve the missing items as soon as she realized they were missing.

I was still actively engaged in my Teeny Meanie-ness during Gramma Peggy and Grampa Archie's visit. While Gramma Peggy was there, she baked cookies and put them on the table to cool, which we all loved. Much to her surprise on one occasion, when she got ready to put the cookies away, there was a "Teeny" bite out of every cookie next to the edge. Needless to say, Teeny the Meanie accurately got the blame! I further accelerated my Teeny Meanie reputation the day I threw a peanut butter jar lid in the toilet and flushed it—that didn't work out well!

I reputedly continued my Teeny Meanie antics until immediately after Dad returned from Turkey. It's a good thing I quit my shenanigans too; the Sarge wasn't known for leniency with bad brat behavior! Any member of the Heath Platoon will confirm that Sergeant Heath was a very strict disciplinarian. When he said, "No," he meant it and didn't have to repeat it. We knew it. In our family, a child didn't go running to Mommy to try to get a different answer to a question posed to Daddy. There was no different answer.

Together Again

In May 1952, I was very happy to see my daddy again—and I didn't even "beat up his leg." Dad had been in Turkey for nearly a year, and he returned home having earned the promotion to master sergeant (E-7). Rachel was eight months old, and it was love at first sight for both of them. He already had orders for his next duty station, and the Heath Platoon would be heading for Pittsburgh, Pennsylvania, where Dad would be teaching ROTC at Duquesne University. The house was put up for sale, and it sold in just one week.

When looking at the many good things about being a military family, one of them was the length of leave time Dad always had between duty stations. This provided time to travel to our next destination and usually time for visiting parents/grandparents and a few cousins. Dad's sister Pat was very excited when she learned that her brother would be stationed only an hour away from her home in

New Castle, Pennsylvania. She invited our family to stay with her and her husband and kids until we could find a place in Pittsburgh. Mom and Dad took her up on that offer without a second thought.

CHAPTER 8
PITTSBURGH AND BRAT
SIX IS BORN, 1952–1955

We stayed in New Castle with Aunt Pat, Uncle Phil, and their two girls, Patty (age six) and Melissa (two), for three weeks in June of 1952—and we had a great time. The weather was perfect the entire time, and the Heath Platoon—Dan (nine), Dave (six), Bob (four), Mike (two), and Rachel (one)—played with and got to know our cousins. Each day, as soon as breakfast was over, we were sent outdoors and couldn't come back inside unless we had to use the bathroom. Either we developed very weak bladders during that time or possibly the plethora of Brats was the problem because "AUNT PAT, I GOTTA GO POTTY!" almost became a litany. With each and every visit after that one, upon arrival at their house, the Heath Platoon would unload from the Ford wagon, line up oldest to youngest, and yell in unison and as loudly as possible, "AUNT PAT, I GOTTA GO POTTY!" She would always run out of the house laughing and with a huge grin on her face to welcome us.

Bringing that many extra people into their home should have been a burden, but Aunt Pat and Uncle Phil always made all of us feel welcome—even as there were always more of us with nearly every visit! And we did visit with every return from a faraway duty assignment, as well as frequently while Dad was stationed at Duquesne.

Uncle Phil was a very quiet man, and Dad was just the opposite, yet they became very good friends. It was good having family nearby, but that was the only time Dad's duty station was close enough to family to make regular visits. Those three weeks remain in the Brats' happiest memories of growing up Army.

By the end of the three weeks, Dad found an apartment and we moved in with the few things we brought on a small trailer from Virginia. The Army had shipped the rest of our household goods, but they somehow had gotten misplaced. Dad's boss at Duquesne, Colonel Schmeltz, went to work on it, and before long the rest of our belongings arrived. Colonel Schmeltz and his wife were older and never had children. They took our family under their wings during those three years in Pittsburgh.

At this post, the commanding officer had an annual New Year's Eve party, and it was a tradition that enlisted men made appearances with their wives. Colonel Schmeltz told Dad to be sure to bring his children along as well. Dad coached us on what we could and could not do while at this party. As a result of that very serious coaching, Dad and Mom were both very proud of the way all five of us conducted ourselves.

While in Pittsburgh, our family became best friends with another couple, Les and Naomi. Les and Dad both taught in the ROTC program. They remained good friends, and over the years we visited them in many places around the United States. Les and Naomi didn't have any children when we first met, but they fell in love with all of us. When visiting at our apartment, they would often ask Mike if he wanted to spend the night with them. Mike always responded, "Only if Rachel can come!" Of course, they were more than happy to have Rachel come along too.

One time when Dad and Les were in the field on training maneuvers with their ROTC students, Naomi was close to having their first child. Because Les had taken their car to work and left it there while out in the field, Naomi had no transportation. One morning, Mom couldn't get Naomi out of her thoughts. They lived only a few miles away but didn't have a phone, so Mom piled us into the old Plymouth and went to see her—and none too soon! She had gone into labor and even though she didn't seem too concerned about it, Mom soon had her loaded in the car and on the way to the hospital. Good thing because it didn't take long for little Cindy to make her appearance. It's also a good thing that Mom had "been there and done that," or Naomi could have been birthing her first baby at home on her own!

Welcome, Jim!

Soon after Les and Naomi welcomed their firstborn, the next addition to the Heath Platoon was on his way. Our family's budget demanded Mom go to a military hospital facility, and the closest one was at Carlisle Barracks, about two hundred miles due east, near Harrisburg, Pennsylvania. They went there a few days early, and the doctor induced labor on August 12, 1953, since he learned that Mom couldn't be away from her ever-growing family for long. Dad took a leave of absence from work so he could stay home with us while she was at the hospital, but we weren't too fond of Dad's culinary skills. He only had three dishes, two of which were not overly appealing to us Brats. Breakfast was scrambled eggs and toast, which was actually a happy change from the usual oatmeal or cream of wheat. Lunch was peanut butter and jelly, which involved the mixing of the two before applying them to the bread, which NONE of us liked! In our minds, it was required that the bread be buttered on one side, jelly applied, then peanut butter on the other piece of bread. Right, Mom? Then, the third dish was some kind of not-so-tasty spaghetti. HURRY HOME, MOM! We survived, just as we did during the birth of the rest of the Heath Platoon—and the same exact menu every time.

Mom and Dad were starting to have difficulty naming the new boys coming into the family, but after being nagged by the hospital to let them know a name for the birth certificate, they finally picked James John. Not Johnathan, but, John. Gramma Nell liked to call him Jamie, and he didn't like that moniker much as he grew older; he preferred Jimmy.

We spent six weeks of the following summer in Manitowoc with Grampa Archie and Glamich in a tiny house while Dad was at a summer training camp for ROTC personnel at Fort Sill, Oklahoma. Who's this Glamich? Gramma Peggy decided she didn't like being called "Gramma" because she thought it made her seem old. So someone came up with "Glamich," which was a testimony to our glamorous Gramma. She liked that and was our Glamich from then on.

Very sadly, about six weeks after Peggy and Archie went home from Newport News following Rachel's birth, Grampa Archie suffered a severe stroke. He was paralyzed on his right side and could only say a few words. He was only fifty-seven, and he lived until he was sixty-eight. He always needed a wheelchair, but he managed to relearn a few words over time. This came as a bit of a shock to us kids that summer, which was the first time we had seen him since his stroke, but we all still loved our Grampa Archie.

My brothers, sister, and I all slept in Glamich and Grampa's attic and the only toilet was a bucket that Dan had to empty every morning. Well, there was an outhouse, but no one was going to run out there in the middle of the night.

The local high school offered a swimming program for Dan and Dave's age group, and they were quite excited to go. As they stood in line to get in the day it started, some of the boys asked them why they were carrying towels and swimsuits, since none of the other kids would be wearing them. Dan and Dave did an immediate "about face" and headed for the house. Swim naked? In front of all these other kids? No. Apparently, this was a gene they picked up from Dad, who was always very modest.

Back to Pittsburgh

When Dad's ROTC summer camp was over, he came to Manitowoc and drove the family back home. Our Pittsburgh apartment had been sublet while we were away, and when we got home, the renters were gone and left everything nice and clean. Mike, being the caring little gentleman that he was, took little Rachel by the hand and said, "I'll show you around, honey."

After returning to Pittsburgh, Mom and Dad discovered that little Jim, who was only about a year old, had a hernia, so they had to make the two hundred–mile trek back to the hospital at Carlisle Barracks.

He had to have surgery and was there for ten days. After he got home, Jim was kind of grumpy for a while, which was understandable under the circumstances.

Mom and Dad stayed in touch with friends they made in various duty stations around the world and would occasionally have an opportunity to see them. Digger, the friend from Japan, was passing through Pittsburgh and came to visit. He was studying Chinese in preparation for a job over there and was no longer in the Army. When Digger or Les and Naomi visited, the grown-ups would play cards, laugh, drink a little beer, and have a good time.

Meanwhile, the Brats would be here and there, but we wouldn't be disruptive to the fun. Dad would permit each Brat to have one sip of his beer. We were all happy to get our sips, and the absolute rule was *one* sip. One night, one of the Brats griped about only getting one sip. He kept griping, so suddenly one sip turned into no sips—for any of us! Griping and whining didn't work on Dad. That's part of growing up Army.

Pittsburgh is where Dan learned about Big Business and the value of hard work. A swimming pool was being constructed down the hill in an open space behind the apartment complex. We would go out there and watch while it was being built and get excited about going swimming. That excitement waned once we learned we would have to pay a membership fee to swim there for the summer. The Heath family didn't have any money for trivialities like that. So Dan (age ten) and his friend Benji came up with the idea of selling pot holders to raise enough money for the membership fee. The two of them made those tiny pot holders on a little handheld loom and sold them as fast as they could make them. Pretty soon, they earned almost enough money to pay for their memberships for the pool. Mom made up the difference, and they had a great time down at the pool that summer!

Apparently, the pool wasn't quite enough fun to fill the day, so Dan and Dave (age seven) found a place near the apartments where they could camp out. There was a cool little creek that ran by it. A little way down the creek, it washed over the edge of a hill over a concrete spillway, down to where there were some railroad cars. This was kind of a waterfall made out of concrete, probably to keep the water from eroding the ground. Dan, Dave, and some friends would jump into the creek and slide down the spillway. It was really slick. The reason it was so slick? It seems this "creek" carried sewage, and of course, that created a smelly, slimy, slippery, greenish-colored surface on the cement. The kids knew about the source of the water and slippery surface, but they were unabashed because it was too much fun—even though it stunk! It was also a bit of a suicidal leap over the edge of the spillway, and that, combined with the sewage, provided them with the name for their camp: "Camp Sewercide." One might wonder if the parents of Camp Sewercide's participants didn't detect a certain odor when they came home after playing there ....

Dan, being the oldest of the Brats, was assigned the job of taking Dave to school in Pittsburgh to get registered to attend second grade. The elementary school wasn't very far, so they walked there. This was the first Brat encounter with having two parents with the same last name prior to their marriage. Mom had always dealt with registering the kids for school up to this time. (If you recall, Mom was a Heath and Dad was a Heath prior to their marriage.) On every school registration form, there is some reason for needing your mom's maiden name. It's uncertain that anyone can explain the reasoning behind that need, but it's always there. Dan filled out the form. The secretary at the school couldn't accept that Mom's maiden name was Heath. She kept re-explaining to Dan what exactly a maiden name was. Of course, he kept explaining to her that his mother was a Heath both prior to and after marriage and that, yes, he did understand what a maiden name was. It's uncertain how that ever got resolved, unless the secretary called Mom. Dan knew that lady never believed him. Each member of the Heath Platoon can offer at least one similar story as we grew up having to fill out those forms. I started writing, "This *is* my mother's maiden name!" above the space where that had to be filled in and still got questioned about it every time! In our second year in Pittsburgh, I went to kindergarten in the same school, and to avoid confusion, Mom went to the school and filled out the paperwork herself.

Also in that second year we moved from our first-floor apartment to a bigger one on the second floor. The room the four oldest kids—Dan,

Dave, me, and Mike—shared overlooked the playground. I remember that room because it is where I learned my times tables one bright and sunny Saturday while everyone else played on the playground right outside the window. I longed to be out there with my friends, but that wasn't happening until I could multiply. I was in the first grade then, and Mom had gotten a note saying I was lagging a bit behind in my grasp of the multiplication tables. Once assigned to my room and told, "You will stay in your room until you memorize your times tables," it didn't take me long. Apparently, Mom was quite certain the view of the playground would provide all the incentive necessary to motivate me to get it done—and I did, in less than an hour! It's amazing what a little incentive can do. As I look back, it's also pretty amazing I was expected to learn the times tables in first grade!

A lot of our family free time was spent with Les and Naomi, going on picnics. Dad had sold the old Plymouth and bought another Ford sedan, but it was getting quite cramped with two adults and six Brats. So they traded it in for a Ford station wagon, but didn't let us know about it. Les and Naomi came over to follow us to the park for a picnic, and some of us wanted to ride with them, still thinking our family car was going to be crowded. As we were loading up in the other car, we saw the rest of the family getting into the nice big Ford wagon, and we were sorry about the decision to abandon them. Every family car after that one was a Ford wagon.

Summer of '54

The next summer, Dad was back in Fort Sill, Oklahoma, for ROTC training camp, and Aunt Pat wanted Mom and the Brats to spend some time with them in New Castle, Pennsylvania. Getting to New Castle from our apartment in Pittsburgh required Mom to drive through downtown Pittsburgh. Since she had not done much driving in cities, she was a bit nervous about it, so she got the Brats up before dawn to make sure she missed the morning rush-hour traffic. Leaving that early for a one-hour trip to New Castle meant an early arrival at Aunt Pat's. That had our relatives all scrambling to get up at the sound of a very loud "AUNT PAT, I GOTTA GO POTTY" ringing out from the Heath Platoon. Once they got their eyes open and a little breakfast in their tummies, everyone was happy and, of course, had lots of fun.

At the time Dad first reported to Fort Sill that summer, an alert was sent, saying he was to be shipped to the United States Army Forces in the Far East (USAFFE), and he was to report to Fort Lewis, Washington, on August 5–6 for transport to his assignment. Colonel Schmeltz immediately sent a request to the commanding general at the Pennsylvania Military District "to eliminate MSgt Richard D. Heath … from this shipment on the basis that no suitable replacement is available and the fact that this will result in an 80% turnover of enlisted men at this Detachment." Even though Colonel Schmeltz went on vacation for a couple weeks right afterward, he contacted the command by phone several times to try to get Dad removed from the list. A few days later, Dad received a note from the assistant adjutant.

Dear Sgt. Heath: We have received another telegram from District telling us to disregard their previous telegram which alerted you for shipment to USAFFE. It looks like the Colonel got you off the hook again. I know this will make you feel a lot better. Maybe now the District will lay off you for awhile.

So Dad didn't have to go to the Orient … for now. Strangely, he returned from Fort Sill determined that we needed to learn how to behave in restaurants—not that any of us thought we would be allowed any shenanigans at any meals, at home or away. Financially, we couldn't afford to eat out very often but, for some reason, Dad felt it was important. No one knows what brought about that need suddenly, but we began going out once a month. In the beginning, the waitress assigned to our table would not look very happy about it. Think about it: you just got assigned the table with *six* kids! But we Brats knew what was expected of us, and it was a real treat getting to go out to eat in a restaurant! As a result of our excellent behavior, when we went back to the same restaurant, we never had any trouble getting the same waitress. We were all really cute kids after all, and when you combine cute with good manners, we were irresistible!

CHAPTER 9
WISCONSIN FUN BEFORE
THE NEXT BASE, 1955

Maximum Army tours of duty were typically three years, so Dad knew he was soon to be on orders again, and this time, he was given a list of choices of where to go next. In January 1955, he made a formal request to be stationed either in Europe (first choice) or Latin America. He specifically requested Norway, Denmark, Sweden, or Spain. Since we would be following him, the whole family had to pass tests to determine if we could endure the extreme climates in Norway, Denmark, or Sweden. No one can remember just what these tests were, or whether everyone "passed" or not. Dad's orders came on May 17, 1955, and he was going to the semitropical island off the coast of China, Taiwan. He was to report to Oakland Army Base, California, on June 15, 1955, to ship out.

It isn't clear, and there was never any explanation offered by the Army about this extreme difference in location, far, far away from the ones requested. Extreme climate tests, maybe? Consider that Dad was born in Illinois, and Mom was born and raised in Wisconsin. Probably a better explanation is that, since he got out of going to the Far East the previous summer, the Army was not so subtly letting him know who was really in charge here. So it was time to pack, kids! We're off to Taiwan!

But First, Farmhouse Fun

After Dad left for Taiwan, Mom was several months pregnant again, and she and the Brats went back to Wisconsin to be with her folks until she received our port call for Taiwan. Glamich rented a big farmhouse and we all stayed there. We had never lived in a house with that many bedrooms! We were there for the whole summer and had the time of our lives. We had all kinds of wide-open spaces to run and explore; cows, horses; no hot water, no indoor plumbing, lots of poison ivy— well, all good things have a price.

Rachel, Mike, Jim, Bob, Dan, Dave posing on the family Ford at the farm, 1955

Since there was no running water in the house, there was an electric pump in a shed several feet from the house. When we needed a lot of water, we formed a bucket brigade to bring the water into the house. Mom had to wash clothes in one of those really, really old wash tub, wringer-type washing machines. She put a big tub for the rinse water on a chair next to the washer. One day the chair collapsed, and the tub of rinse water splashed out all over the floor. That wasn't fun.

Then, when it was bath night, another bucket brigade from the well to the kitchen was formed. The water was poured into kettles so Mom could heat it up on the old cast-iron stove and then pour it into a big metal wash tub, which was set out on the floor in the middle of the kitchen. Then the Brats would be called in one at a time to take a not-so-private bath. All six of the Brats were bathed in the same water, but didn't think anything of it. After all, these were the same kids who played at Camp Sewercide!

Another fine attribute of the old farmhouse was that the only facility for going to the bathroom was the outhouse. There was a path behind the farmhouse that went to the outhouse. To the Brats, it was a smelly, scary place inside. Dave described his attitude about going in the outhouse: "One slip of your little tush, and the rest of you could be down in that smelly hole! And what lives down there in that smelly place, anyway?" None of us really wanted the answer to that question. Another important factor was that there was a bee hive in the outhouse, so it was really important to do one's business without making the bees unhappy.

Something interesting about living out in the country is that there were no city lights to light the sky. If someone had to go to the bathroom at night, they couldn't see their way to the outhouse because in the country, nighttime is very, very dark, except when there's a nice bright moon up above. Bladders were largely held in control during the night at the farmhouse. What fun that outhouse would have been in the middle of a good ol' Wisconsin winter!

There were lots of apple trees all around, including near the barn and pasture where the farmer who owned the house kept his cows. He milked the cows and worked the farm, but must have had a better house somewhere nearby. He almost kicked us out because we fed the apples to his cows—which they loved. The farmer didn't love it though. Apparently, apples aren't good for cows to eat. So he made the Brats quit feeding the apples to the cows and let us stay for the rest of the summer. Fortunately, we got the message and did as we were told. Other than that, we had the run of the farm and would spend time in the barn jumping from hay bale to hay bale, playing tag or hide and seek. It's probably a good thing Mr. Farmer didn't see us doing that, or there could have been another eviction notice.

Mike had his fifth birthday that summer, so Mom made his favorite birthday dessert from Jell-O in the form of a boat. It was loaded with fruit cocktail and remained his favorite dessert for many years. That same summer Rachel turned four, but she was happier with a good old birthday cake with lots of frosting on top! The rest of us were happy with whatever dessert showed up!

The Brats would also go to a small lake to do some fishing from time to time. The lake had a small dock, and we would go out there with makeshift fishing poles and throw a line in the water. One day, Jim (two years old) was playing close to the end of the dock, lost his balance, and fell in. The water was pretty deep, and he soon disappeared. Dan saw him go into the water, jumped in immediately, and hauled him back up sputtering and spitting, but no worse off for the cold bath. There isn't anything much better than an older brother who looks out for you!

Swinging

This farm had a huge, wonderful oak tree with long, thick limbs protruding from the trunk, just begging us to climb it. The lowest, really large limb had a single strand of a stout rope tied to it. That limb looked like it was a hundred feet high to us. It was decided that it would be good if someone stood where the rope reached the ground and held it at about chest height, and then the rest of us would grab the end of the rope and run with it until it reached full extension, snapping the slack out of the line and launching the "rider" into the air. Dan, being the oldest and biggest, was convinced he should be the first to try, especially since he came up with the idea. He grabbed the rope and stood in front of us, while we—Dave, Bob, Mike, and Rachel— grabbed the long end and took off running. Well, Dan outweighed the smallest three of us who were pulling the end of the rope with Dave, and even though we were able to get him off the ground, he didn't go high enough to feel any thrill. So Dan joined the "run-and-snap-the-rope" team, and Dave took his turn hanging on to it. Again, not much of a snap. So then it was my turn, followed by Mike. Still no great results.

Then there was little, tiny, barely four-year-old Rachel. She was really excited and eager to get her turn to do what her big brothers just did. Well, she grabbed hold of that rope, and all four boys took off running with the other end; that rope went taut and snapped! It was like Rachel flew to the top of the tree, squealing in delight the whole way! Wow! She went so high on the end of that rope that she looked like a little rag doll when she reached the top of her flight. All the boys thought it was great! Rachel kept yelling, "Do it again!" And again! And again! We were having a whole lot of fun snapping the rope and watching our little sister fly way up in the air, squealing and screaming in delight! It was like we had engineered the perfect Disney World ride and had the happiest customer in the whole world!

This was all really great, right up until Glamich heard the squealing and laughing and came out to see what was going on—and nearly had a heart attack from fright when she saw the only daughter in the family flying through the air toward the limbs above her while all the boy Brats were totally engrossed in the delirious abandonment of the moment. Needless to say, Glamich very loudly, quickly, and firmly put an end to that fun! To this day, every member of the Heath Platoon who was involved remembers how much fun that was at the time—and shakes his or her head at how crazy it was, and expresses their thanks that Rachel survived!

Off to Taiwan, More Shots

All fun things must come to an end, and the port call came to drive across country to the West Coast and our flight to Taiwan. First, we had to go to an Army facility several miles away from the farm to get the required vaccinations, of course. Mike told everyone that he would be last to get his because he wasn't afraid of shots. When his turn came, he passed out. He said he never felt a thing. In the meantime, while Mom and the rest of us boys were getting our shots, little Rachel had moved off into another room and was hiding under a table. When they found her, she grabbed hold of a table leg and held on for dear life. It took a lot of work from Mom, Dan, and Dave to get her loose. She had practice getting a really tight hold on something from her flying adventures in the tree!

Glamich was left with the job of getting the household goods packed and shipped, then moving herself and Grampa Archie back to their home. Mom drove to Ottawa, Illinois, to pick up Dad's youngest brother, Paul, who was eighteen years old at the time. Paul and Mom took turns driving to the West Coast. Apparently, it was a nail-biting trip for Mom when Paul was behind the wheel. Gramma Nell always said Paul was accident prone, but Mom would say he was an accident looking for somewhere to happen. Fortunately, Paul never found that "somewhere" on this trip. He was a bad tailgater and liked to talk with his hands, so sometimes both of his talking hands were off the steering wheel at the same time. When it got toward evening one day, we were in downtown Salt Lake City, and Mom said, "Paul, I will look for a motel on my side, and Dan will look on his side. You drive." Of course, two people looking weren't enough for Uncle Paul because he had to look too! Fortunately, we found a motel without any driving mishaps.

After several days, the drive was finally over, and we reached our destination, Hayward, California, none the worse except for Mom's nerves. We stayed again with Mom's cousins Mildred and Wayne and got another tour of San Francisco while Paul went back home on a train. Wayne went with Mom to get the car ready for shipping to Taiwan and then took us the 550 miles to Edwards Air Force Base to catch our plane. Mom was seven months pregnant and was not supposed to fly after the sixth month. She was really surprised when she learned that the Army had asked four soldiers to help her with the Brats on the flight. The soldiers enjoyed our comic books, and Mom was very grateful for the Army's consideration of her pregnant condition.

The flight to Taiwan took us to an air base on one of the Aleutian Islands in Alaska where we had a brief layover. We got off the plane at night in a frozen wonderland. We saw wolves running across the runway, and Mom was concerned that the plane would hit one on takeoff. It didn't, and we continued our long trip, stopping in

Hawaii for refueling. Again, it was nighttime, and we didn't leave the terminal. Mom learned that there was good reason why a pregnant woman shouldn't travel after six months when she looked at her ankles and saw they were badly swollen. Soon, however, we would arrive in Taiwan and be reunited with Master Sergeant Heath at our new country to call home.

CHAPTER 10
TAIWAN AND THE ARRIVAL
OF BRAT SEVEN, 1955–1956

Taiwan was the Chinese name for the island we would call home for the next three years, but it was named *Formosa*, "beautiful island," by the Portuguese in 1544.[78] The Japanese gained control of the island in 1895 and maintained control until the end of World War II.[79] As we lived on and explored the island, we found it to, indeed, be beautiful.

This photo may look like it was taken for The Addams Family, but it is the passport photo for our trip to Taiwan in 1955. Back then, passports were provided for parents and children together. As you can see, we all complied with the instruction to not smile!

The island is oval in shape, approximately two hundred forty miles long and ninety miles wide. It is separated from the southwest coast of China by the hundred-mile-wide Taiwan Strait. The Chinese Nationalist, also known as the Republic of China (ROC), government reinstated the island's original name, Taiwan. The ROC, along with two million Chinese people, escaped from Communist China in 1949 after years of civil war, so the natives of Taiwan didn't get much respite between the occupation of the Japanese and that of the Chinese ROC.[80]

Dad was a motor pool sergeant—one of about 10,000 US military personnel living in Taiwan. The US Army was there to support the Chinese Nationalists in their independence from mainland Communist China; the United States had hoped we could support the ROC's elimination of the Communists from China.[81] The reasons behind why our family was there was lost on the Heath Platoon, and we had absolutely no idea of the politics of it all. It's not even certain we were aware there had been a world war eleven years earlier, or if Dad had fought in it.

We landed in Taipei midmorning on a suffocating, hot, and humid September day—and there was Dad, with a big smile on his face and as happy to see us as we were to see him. We went home to a gorgeous, big, stucco house on the outskirts of Taipei. After settling in as much as possible rather quickly, we had to make a quick trip to the military medical dispensary to get Mom's swollen ankles checked out. The doctor who was on duty was the one who finally delivered Steve, and he told her to just put her feet up and relax. He had a snippy nurse who told him Mom shouldn't have made the trip as far along with her pregnancy as she was. He asked her, "Do you think we should send her back?" He was unmarried, but he said he wanted to have ten children, and he admired a woman who was willing to have a large family. Interestingly, the same nurse assisted him at Steve's birth, and she was still harping on the fact that Mom had "broken the rules."

Living "on the Economy"

Our house was really nice, had plenty of room, and was in a good location not far from Dad's motor pool post. It had concrete pillars out front supporting a second-story balcony that overlooked a small courtyard. There was no air-conditioning in the house, and it was really hot, but almost every afternoon, there was a nice, cooling rain. Mom usually went out on the porch and let the breeze from the rain cool her. Dad bought a large fan, which helped make things feel even cooler. A stucco stone wall separated our house from the small Taiwanese village that stretched down below.

There were only three houses with American occupants in our small area during the time that we lived "on the economy." That phrase means that we lived in a privately owned house, rather than in military dependents' housing. The house behind us was a little higher and about the same size as ours, and the one next door was quite small. Carl, an Air Force sergeant, and his wife, Jo, lived there. They had two German shepherds and a guard, and they still got robbed regularly. We were told that robbers would never come to a house with lots of children because the kids were up and down all night. Thankfully, we never did get robbed during our time there. The wall around the three properties had broken glass embedded in cement at the top to discourage thieves. It obviously didn't have much of a deterrent effect though. In front of and below the houses was a Taiwanese village with a concrete ditch between the wall and the road. The ditch was used for outdoor laundry and other not-so-sanitary purposes by the villagers. We were encouraged to stay out of the ditch.

Our house had very fragile windows all along the porch that bordered the living room, and they nearly reached the floor. Actually, all the windows were very fragile. Someone was always breaking a window! One afternoon we were upstairs in one of the bedrooms that had a chest of drawers located at the end of one of the twin beds. Someone decided that we could do flips off the chest of drawers onto the bed, and of course, we all jumped in to do it. Nobody took notice of the one most serious logistical concern with this acrobatic entertainment. At the end of the bed, on the end opposite our launching pad, was a window. Rachel discovered this problem when, after a beautifully performed flip, she put her foot through that window. After much bleeding, Rachel's foot was bandaged up, and we all were sent to bed for a long afternoon's nap. Dad did his share of grumbling about the cost of repairs any time a window was broken. One day, he broke one, and we all gave him a standing ovation. He said, "It was my turn."

Another interesting feature of the house was that all the big windows had canvas awnings over them. These were the kind of awnings we could roll up so that they did not shade the window. As little kids, we thought it would be fun to roll them down and roll them up, and roll them down, and roll them up ... Much to our delight, there were critters that lived in those awnings that we had never seen before. We had no idea what they were, but they were really cool-looking little mousey things with wings. We discovered that if we would roll the awnings down early in the day, they would be asleep and wouldn't wake up right away when they hit the ground. So we decided to open the awnings and drop the critters to the ground, then catch them in glass jars. We punched holes in the lids so they could breathe. Well, we did do that, and Mom freaked out when we showed her our new little friends. To us they were really cute, but she *really* didn't like our little bats! We weren't allowed to play with them anymore. I have no recollection as to how we disposed of them!

Shortly after arriving, Dad had hired a local lady, Ah Sing, to be the family's maid and who very shortly started answering to "Seeny." Seeny was a big help to Mom during our time in Taiwan, especially after our new little brother Steve arrived on November 5.

Dan, Dave, and I were enrolled in the Taipei American School, the only school available and where all the military dependents in the area went as well as some Chinese children. The school was founded in 1949, and with the influx of US military personnel and their families in 1953, a larger facility was built to accommodate the children. This was a private school, and tuition for military Brats was paid by the US government.[82]

There wasn't a kindergarten, so Mike had to wait a year, not that he seemed to mind. And of course, Rachel, at just over four, happily stayed home with Mom and Seeny as well. In fact, Rachel thought new baby Steve was her little doll baby. Mom left them with Seeny one day, and when she got home, Rachel met her at the door with Steve in her arms and a huge smile on her face. Seeny had no problem with that because Taiwanese children, at a very young age, carried their baby siblings around. Rachel didn't have any problem with that either! Mom wasn't a big fan, though, but didn't make a fuss about it.

As part of our education, we learned about the cultures of our countries. One day, a Chinese lady came to our class and taught us to sing the Chinese National Anthem. This song is often called "San Min Chu I," from the first line of the anthem. The song was actually the national anthem for mainland China when it was controlled by the Kuomintang government, which was the ROC ousted by the Communists in October 1949 after several years of civil war. The ROC used the same state symbols and anthem they had on mainland China. "San Min Chu I" is banned on mainland China today.[83]

In the second grade, my classmates and I performed the song for a group of visitors, but I can't recall what the occasion may have been. Under the right conditions, I can still remember this song. This may be due to my strong connection with the leader of the ROC, Chiang Kai-shek.

Chinese National Anthem (English Translation)

San min chu I, our aim shall be,
To found a free land, world peace be our stand.
Lead on comrades, vanguards ye are,
Hold fast your aim, by sun and star,
Be earnest and brave, your country to save,
One heart, one soul, one mind, one goal!

SECOND GRADE P. M.

Third row: Bruce L____, Timothy M___, Van A___., Dennis T___, Linda F.
Deborah W____, Elaine O____, Tom K.
Second row: Paula F____, Gordon R.___, Peter W___, Mary F___, Brian W___, Roger
B___, Rebecca V___, Joey O___.
First row: Robert Heath, Arthur S.___, Patty G.___, Craig L.___, Ken F___, Stephen
C___, Alan A___, Jeffrey G___, Pam M___, Bonnie M___.
Teacher: Mrs. J. M

Bob in second grade at the Taipei American School, 1955

Because all school-age military dependents in the area went to the same school, we were transported there on military buses. Dad was in charge of the motor pool, so he knew all the soldiers who drove our buses to and from school. Sometimes we thought that Dad had eyes in the back of his head when he would come home from work and confront us about something we had been up to on the bus—which would not be a pleasant turnout for our behinds! GIs took turns riding the school bus as monitors to ensure the kids all behaved. For some reason—probably because he did the scheduling—Dad was almost always the monitor on report card day. We did a great deal of groaning about that, but as we know, groaning, griping, whining, and that sort of behavior never got us anything we wanted.

One bus incident involved Brat Dan. We would wait along with the kids who lived behind us for the bus, and it infuriated Dan that the bus driver would pass us, pick up other kids somewhere down the road, and then pick us up on the way back. So one day, Dan apparently had about all he was going to put up with, and he attacked the problem directly. As the bus came by, Dan ran after it, leaped on the narrow ledge at the door, and pounded on the door. The driver stopped and made Dan get off and go back to the bus stop. It might go without saying that Dad and Dan had a little "prayer meeting" that evening. After that, we waited patiently for the bus to come back to get us ... well, maybe not "patiently."

Another bus incident involved me. When I was in second grade, I was sent to the principal's office for misbehaving in class. The principal sent a note home with me for whatever my behavior problem was—I can't (or choose not to) remember what it was—but it mysteriously flew out of the bus window on the way home. Apparently, someone was supposed to sign it or something because after a couple of days, I got my butt smacked since that note never got home. Who could help what the wind did to a note? Anyway, whatever I did to create the need for the note, I probably didn't do anymore.

Adjusting to the Culture

In the village below our house, the native children who were not potty trained wore "shimdy pants." The crotch section was not sewn together, so all they had to do was spread their legs and go. The children were always curious around us but never bashful about going potty when we were around.

The Taiwan village below our house, 1955

Another thing we saw and found very strange in the village and around Taiwan was how some of the Taiwanese women had very, very tiny feet; this was something very unusual to us. We learned it was customary to bind the feet of girls when they were very young in order to prevent their feet from growing any bigger. The intent was to preserve the "dainty-ness" of their feet to make them more attractive to men and to create the thought that they were more genteel. Foot binding was incredibly painful for the young girls, and fortunately was ultimately banned, even though many Taiwanese and Chinese people continued to practice it well after that.[84]

Of course, there were many things about Taiwan, the people, and their customs that were very different from things most of us had experienced before—with the exception of Dan, who had more memories of his experiences in Japan than Dave or I did. Mike once mentioned to Mom that he was really tired of all the foreigners around where we were living. He had a very dumbstruck look on his face when she informed him that *we* were the foreigners.

For the most part, Mom and Dad didn't get too worked up about things; they just dealt with them. For example, our driveway in Taiwan began at the top of a short hill, and there were bright red gates at the top. Mom was backing the car in through the gates one day and scraped the side against the gate; it did some damage to the car door. Seeny said, "When Mastah come home, you better hide." Dad was very calm in dealing with it. One thing about Dad that we came to recognize more and more as we grew older: the bigger a problem was, the calmer he became in taking care of it. It's a trait that we've all seen in ourselves as we grew older.

After scraping up the door, Mom drove across the capital city of Taipei, which was close to where we lived, to get to the Army base and the commissary to get groceries. The entire time we were near Taipei, road work was being done on some section of the road we had to drive through to get to the commissary. The workers carried gravel and dirt in two baskets, held across their shoulders connected to a pole made of bamboo. Most of the workers were women. There was always the smell of tar in that area, and it often took lots of time to navigate through the construction.

On Mom's way back through Taipei one day, she passed a man on a bicycle—there were lots of bicycles and pedicabs on the streets of Taipei. The man had extremely long fingernails, and he swerved in so that he tore his fingernail on the side of the car. He made a big fuss about it, but that was a common practice to try to get money from Americans. He got nothing from Mom. Actions like this one from some of the Taiwanese were fairly common during our time there.

Another instance of this occurred one day when Dan and Dave were out roaming around some of the many footpaths near our house, and they started throwing rocks over a ridge on the hill. They could hear the rocks hit, and kept hurling them. Well, they were unknowingly throwing those rocks onto the clay roofing tiles on a Taiwanese house down below! They discovered this when a very annoyed man came up to the top of the ridge and took them to a local police office down below. He was demanding lots of money to fix his roof, only it was probably enough to build a whole new house. After a while, Dad came to the rescue and convinced the man to take enough money to replace a few roof tiles. How Dad knew where they were is a mystery, and perhaps even more mysterious is how Dan and Dave avoided getting their butts whipped after that little event! Perhaps their argument that they weren't aware of the houses down below could explain that part.

It is important to note that Taiwan in 1955 had a great deal of poverty, even though the island was in the midst of a fairly major economic improvement cycle. The streets were dirty and narrow, especially the side streets, with the aroma of Chinese cooking filling the air, merging with the exhaust fumes of buses and trucks and the smell of tar from roadwork. The streets were always busy with people, cluttered with bicycles, buses, pedicabs, scooters, cars and trucks, and all the bells, horns, engine, and transmission noises that they make.

The streets were lined with shops and "shotgun" houses. A shotgun house has an opening—not necessarily a door—at both ends. Usually it was just one large open room, and the children would toddle around wearing nothing but their birthday clothes, accompanied by dogs, cats, pigeons, chickens, and an occasional pig. There was little if any furniture. Beds were often just a pallet on the floor. Cooking was done outside, or with a pot over a small flame inside. Bathrooms were either outhouses or just the ditches that ran along both sides of the road. There were shops mingled among the houses where the people sold all manner of anything you can imagine. One shop had a sign stating that the owner was an "Ox Hopn Makef," which meant that he carved artifacts like ships and vases out of ox horns. Another might sell pots, baskets, or furniture, all of which were handmade. Dan liked to go to one of the shops and get a drink called *chi suey*, which the Taiwanese referred to as "air water." It tasted like soda water but lots sweeter and with lots more fizz. We liked to shake them up and spray each other and anything else nearby.

There were little roadside stands everywhere that sold vegetables and fruit. We bought all our fresh vegetables, fruits, and meats in those local markets. Any fruits or vegetables that were grown touching the ground had to be cleaned in chlorine water before we could eat them raw, according to information provided by the military. This was probably because of the prolific use of human waste as fertilizer. Bananas, apples, oranges, and tangerines just had to be washed and dried. We bought bananas by the huge bunch for about a dime, and had a hook on the wall in the kitchen for them. We could help ourselves to bananas whenever we wanted.

A man came around the house selling fresh eggs every week. We got beef from the locals too, but the beef that Mom and Dad bought was very tough. It had to be simmered all day to tenderize it enough to eat. Unfortunately, steak meat could never be tenderized enough. The beef was from water buffalo, which were beasts of burden, and they were only butchered after they were no longer able to work, which explains why the meat was so tough. We could also get pork, and it was excellent. Apparently the pigs never had to do any work, so they were nice and tender. Even though we had eggs, we never did have chicken while there, but we could see them running around all over the place.

There was also a man who would come by the house once or twice a month calling out in his own little song, announcing his trade. He would sing out, "U ka na way wo, way wo U ka naaaa!" as he pushed his bicycle through the alley, wearing black pajama-like clothes and a coolie hat, ringing the bell on his bike. He had a manually operated grinding wheel mounted on the back fender of the bike, and his song translated to something like, "I will sharpen your knives and your scissors too!"

For a short while, we bought bread in the local bakery, but that changed when Mom found a course black hair in one of the loaves. From that day on, Mom baked all our bread, which we all loved. Mom always made the *best* homemade bread! There wasn't an oven on the stove in our house, but we had a separate electric roaster oven, which was big and had a lid on the top. Two loaves would fit in it, so bread baking was pretty much an ongoing job considering there were seven, then eight Brats to feed! That may seem like a lot of work—and it was—but Mom didn't have to clean the house, wash or iron clothes, or wash any dishes. She considered it a good thing that she had something to do, as if the care and feeding of eight Brats wasn't enough!

For about the first year we were there, we kept our food cool in an old-fashioned ice box. It was a wooden cabinet with a section on top for a block of ice and another section for the food. There was a drip pan underneath that had to be emptied often. Mom and Dad's dear friend Tommy, always affectionately known as Godman, went to Hong Kong one time and brought us back a refrigerator. We called him Godman because he was godfather to Steve and Rick. On another trip to Hong Kong, he bought Mom an Elna sewing machine, and he had even taken enough lessons so he could show her how to operate it. This was her first sewing machine with zigzag and embroidery stitches. Mom loved to sew and was really good at it! Tommy was a bachelor in Dad's outfit, and he enjoyed being around our family. He wound up marrying a Taiwanese lady, and they eventually had two children.

Adventurous Brat-foolery

It is difficult to share the essence of how we felt while exploring such a busy downtown area by ourselves as children from a foreign land. There were no restraints, and we had no fear. For a few cents we could buy interesting looking and smelling food to eat, or resupply our fireworks cache for the next coffee-can bomb we might build. One of the most interesting things to do was just observe the people.

Of course, we never sat still watching people or anything else for very long.

There were many things that seemed common to the people who were both natives of the island and those who had fled Communist China to form the ROC. Some observations were shocking, almost painful to us kids. Many of the people were missing parts. Often it was an eye, or an arm, or maybe a leg. We remember seeing one woman whose nose and tongue were gone. At the same time, these people seemed to have a kind of innate peace, almost a built-in sense of humor that made most of them congenial. It was like, after what they had been through, life was good.

One day, we were playing on the balcony when an old woman came into the yard to beg at our front door. The old woman didn't have a nose, making her face unusual at best, if not scary looking. When we spotted her, we began to shout down from the balcony, generally making a racket in an effort to get her to go away. Naturally, all that noise got Mom's attention, and when she saw what was going on, she went outside and gave the old woman some money. Obviously, we shut up when we saw Mom go out there. She then rounded us up, chewed us out for being insensitive and mean, and put us in our beds—the ultimate punishment before the belt. We all would have preferred to get the belt; once you got the belt, your punishment was over. That is, unless you did something really bad and got both the belt and sequestered to your room for the rest of the day. Mom never used the belt on us though; that was always Dad's job. Regardless of all that, being kinder people to those in need was a very good lesson to all of us.

If Dad had known about this next escapade involving Dan and Dave, there very well could have been a belt event ....

In a great example of our lack of fear in freely roaming about Taiwan, one bright sunny day, Dan, Dave, and a couple other kids went into Taipei with an idea in mind to have a pedicab race. A pedicab is a three-wheeled bicycle that has one wheel in front and two in the back, with a seat that can hold two or three people. They're called *pedicabs* because they have a driver who pedals people around wherever their passengers want to go. There were hundreds of these in Taipei, and they served the populace much as taxicabs do in the United States. The Brats had ridden around in them before, but were thinking it might be more fun if they were doing the driving with the drivers sitting back in the seat while they had a race down one of the side alleys of the city! Amazingly, Dan and Dave were able to talk two pedicab drivers into accepting their plan, though it's pretty certain they told them that they would take the work of pedaling off of them and just let them rest in the cab as they pedaled around. No one mentioned there would be a race involved.

Quickly, they mounted up, feet on the pedals and hands firmly on the handlebars; Dan yelled, "Ready! Set! Go!" and the race was on! Almost immediately, the two pedicab drivers in the back seats were getting really ticked off, but Dan and Dave were going too fast for the drivers to be able to reach up and stop them! Dan and Dave were not to be denied: they were racing neck and neck, ringing the bells on the handlebars as loud as they could, with each jockeying for the lead while careening down the alley at breakneck speed. Just as they approached the end of the race, a chicken ran out in front of Dave. He lost control of his pedicab and found himself driving right through the front then back doors of somebody's house! As if that wasn't bad enough, while plowing through the house, the pedicab took down the family's laundry that was strung up across the room to dry! When he finally got the vehicle stopped, he quickly and apologetically returned the laundry, but the previously congenial pedicab driver was red in the face and very, very unhappy! It's quite likely the Pedicab Drivers' Union took a vote, and Dave and Dan were blackballed from the pedicab driver ranks forever. Also, due to Dave's catastrophic finish, Dan was declared the winner of the 1955 First and Forever Final Taipei Brat Pedicab Race!

A related incident did actually result in Mike's first spanking—that he could remember! A bunch of us were riding around in a pedicab one day; no one hijacked it, but at the end of the ride, one kid tried to jump off the side before the pedicab stopped and fell on his arm. When he got up, he was holding his arm and was clearly in pain as he ran to his house. It turned out that he had broken his arm and showed up the next day with a cast on. The kid was about Dan's age, was well liked, and just part of the gang. In every way he was just like the rest of us and was the only African American kid in our immediate group of friends. One of the other kids used the "N" word in reference to him when he saw him wearing the cast on his arm, and for some reason, Mike repeated that word at our house. Dad overheard it, and that resulted in Mike's first whipping. He said later the spanking wasn't especially painful, but he knew Dad was making a point. He did, and Mike never forgot it. I never heard that word used by any of the Brats since that day. Actually, I never heard any Heath Brat use that word *before* that day either!

Tamsui River, 1955

Another incident involving Dan and Dave that could have ended very badly included overt curiosity coupled with temporary theft of equipment. Our house overlooked the Tamsui River, which frequently had large ships out in the middle. The road below our house ran alongside the river, but was high up from it, with a stone wall at the edge of the road that dropped straight down to the river. Dan and Dave noticed there were several large ships moored in the river that never moved, and that seemed odd to them. There was a rowboat tied at the base of the wall that they could get to by climbing down a ladder built into the wall. So, of course, they went for the rowboat.

After they got there, they decided to "borrow" the rowboat and row over to one of the large vessels in the river that never moved to explore it. Apparently there was no thought about just what they might find on that ship.

They rowed to the closest ship and found a place where they could tie the rowboat to it next to a rope ladder. When they climbed up the ladder, they found a Chinese gentleman, perhaps thirty years old, up on the deck. The man was quite friendly to Dan and Dave and offered them some green tea. They learned through his broken English that the ship was owned by the Communists and had been impounded by the Republic of China. Somehow he was able to live aboard the ship, and the Brats thought that was pretty cool. They weren't too sure what "impounded" meant or who these Communists were though. After finishing their tea and conversation with the gentleman, they climbed back down the ladder, rowed back to shore, tied the boat back where they found it, and never breathed a word of this little adventure—until Mom's eightieth birthday.

We Brats weren't thoughtlessly causing mischief only with vehicles though. You may or may not know that the Chinese invented gunpowder and firecrackers.[85] Just about any caliber of firecracker you can imagine can be found in Taiwan! We had never really been around fireworks that much, but we could suddenly buy *tons* of fireworks for what amounted to about thirty cents. Some of them were those long strings of small firecrackers, and all you had to do was light one fuse, and they would pop and bang and leave a big smoke cloud. We would buy big rolls of those firecrackers, light them, and listen to them pop. After a while we must have decided that was a little boring, so Dan and Dave figured out that we could take the paper wrapping off of the little ones and combine the gunpowder to create our own, bigger, louder explosive devices. That sounds logical, right? Dan and Dave took each firecracker, unrolled them, and dumped the powder into a big, forty-eight-ounce coffee can. Then they tied all the fuses from the little firecrackers together and put the new long fuse down in the powder. Next, the can was packed with paper, then rocks were put on top, and Dan lit the fuse. We all backed away, and it blew up, making a monster noise! It blew the rocks into the air, and they showered down, but no Brats got hit by any—or if we did, no injuries occurred. Lucky, lucky, lucky!

We also had what were called M-60s and M-80s, which were the mother of loud firecracker technology. They were probably the inspiration for us to attempt to create our own little bombs. Dave began to wonder what would happen if he put an M-60 in our neighbor's mailbox—the one right across the alley. Well, he did; then he found out what an M-60 would do to our neighbor's mailbox—it destroyed it. Dad was really mad, and then Dave was really sad and didn't feel much like sitting down for a while.

How none of us got hurt and how we were even allowed to do this right in front of the house makes us all shake our heads today. We were very inventively, mindlessly creative, and exceedingly lucky to have survived our crazy creativity! This was yet another one of our many fortunate survival situations in Taiwan.

Mike still remembers his first near-death experience. We drove into the countryside surrounding the city often on the weekends and saw some very beautiful places. One day we were swimming in a spot that was far from civilization; that is, as far as we could get on this tiny island. It was hilly and green, and there was a rushing stream and boulders. Little Steve had stayed home with Seeny, and we were all really having a great time. Mom and Dad were sitting in front of Mike (age six) on the bank of the stream, and he was backing up and pushing off toward the water. Each time he pushed back, he took another step back to see if he could push all the way in. That worked pretty well for him until he stepped off a ledge under the water and sunk in well over his head. He didn't seem to panic because he could see Mom right in front of him when his head bobbed back up, and he thought she would grab him and pull him back out of the water. But the current took hold of him and started to wash him quickly downstream! Dad moved really quickly, leaping into the water, and had little Mike in his arms almost before most of us realized he was being swept away. All the Brats were quickly whisked out of the water and herded into the car. We left in a hurry and never went back to that spot!

Not everything that happened was caused by us little Brats though. One of the scariest events—scarier now in retrospect than it was to Dave then—was when he came down with jungle rot in his feet. We learned the hard way what people meant when they told us not to run around in bare feet. He didn't know how serious it was at the time, but he could have lost use of his feet from it. You have possibly never seen (or smelled) anything as nasty as his feet were then, and in case you have a weak stomach, I won't describe them here except to say the word *rot* is an understatement. It happens mostly in hot, tropical areas to children or young adults, and it is a bacterial infection that attaches to a wound and begins to rot the flesh, emitting a nasty smelling pus. His feet really hurt. He had to soak them every day in a purple-colored solution. After quite a while, they got better. I think they were healed by the time we moved up to Green Mountain, and they never bothered him again, not even when he went to Vietnam in 1969.

Revenge on the Neighbors

There were some kids who lived in the house behind us, the house at the end of the alley. It was a little to the right and a bit higher than our house. I remember that there were two girls, probably about ten and twelve years old. Somehow, those kids managed to tick off Dan and Dave, who decided they were going to get even with them. They spent some time kicking around ideas about how to get back at the girls and finally came up with a plan. On the second floor we had an open porch on the right-hand end of the house. Dan and Dave made a couple dozen containers out of sheets of paper, filled them with dirt, and threw them from our upstairs porch at the other house. Boy, I guess Dan and Dave taught them a lesson! Yessir! And Dad taught Dan and Dave one! And neither of them wanted to sit down for a while. Many, many lessons were learned in those early years!

By now, it probably sounds like there were a lot of spankings going on in our house. I want to be clear that none of us ever felt that we were being abused in any way by these spankings. It's also important to note that these were all isolated incidents. In talking with my sibling Brats, every one of us agrees that when we got a spanking, we were very much deserving of it. They weren't terrifically painful, but did sting enough to get our attention. I would have to say that when you're the parent of this many very creative, active Brats, it's very important to establish boundaries. We all knew and accepted this, and it is probably why the frequency of the spankings seemed to have diminished through our growing-up years. Dad had eight siblings, too, and was raised with this form of discipline, so for him it was a pretty normal way to make a point to kids. It's also important to know that we all never doubted the love we were provided by Dad and Mom.

CHAPTER 11
UP THE MOUNTAIN AND
THE PENULTIMATE BRAT, 1956–1958

When military dependents' housing became available, we moved a short distance from Taipei to a housing area on Green Mountain. There were a dozen homes, all very nice and in a beautiful location. Both noncoms and officers lived there. Our four-bedroom home was close to Chiang Kai-shek's compound, and Mom said she would often see him and his entourage out walking in the beautiful park across the street. It's not hard to imagine how much we appreciated having all four of those bedrooms once the eighth Brat, Rick, was born in September 1956!

Our Green Mountain house, 1956

Mom and Dad had not told anyone back in the States that she was pregnant with Rick. They were concerned that their parents would worry, since Steve and Rick would be born only ten months apart. Once Rick was born, they couldn't keep it from them though. They weren't concerned at all; quite the opposite in their joy to have another healthy grandson and to know that he and Mom had come through the birth with no problems.

Shortly after Rick was born, Dad took a second job as a bartender at the Officers' Club on base to earn a little extra money. One night after he got off work, Dad drove the car into a rice paddy. He sustained a minor injury and spent a night in the hospital. The car needed a good cleaning after being pulled out of the paddy but fortunately didn't sustain any other damage. Following that incident, we had rice growing in our car for a while, which seemed a little weird.

The rice paddy event happened as a result of Dad apparently imbibing in a toddy or two himself while making the officers' drinks. This was the absolute only period of time when I can recall Mom and Dad arguing. The arguing began not long after the rice paddy incident, and Mom was not happy with how things were going. Dad came home from working at the club one Saturday afternoon and had been drinking. They began to argue, and after a few minutes, Dad stormed out of the house and was headed across the front yard, very angry. I was seven years old—and keep in mind what a brat I had become as Teeny the Meanie when my dad left us to go to Turkey! Well, here was my dad leaving again! So even though I was five years older, I was afraid and ran out of the house after him yelling, "Daddy, please don't go!" He stopped in his tracks, walked back, picked me up, and said, "Son, I'm not going anywhere." We went back to the house, he quit the part-time job at the club, and I never heard another argument from them. Ever.

Mom always appreciated having Seeny around to do the housework and sometimes the cooking. It gave her lots of time to spend with all of us and especially for taking care of the babies, not to mention giving her a rest period from birthing two babies a mere ten months apart! All of us older Brats loved our new little brothers and fussed over them a lot. That was especially true of Rachel, the fifth child and only girl, who was not only the Little Princess of the family, but was now also the younger kids' self-appointed Little Momma. She engaged in both roles happily and extremely well!

All the dependents' houses had maids' quarters, and Seeny, her husband, King Shun, and their baby, who was born shortly after Rick, lived with us. The two babies shared a playpen and were really cute together. King Shun and Seeny had two other young children who were cared for mostly by their grandparents. I went with her to their home in Taipei once and got to play with her kids.

King Shun did yard work for us and some of the other neighboring families, and there were other yard men who worked in the area. One afternoon Mom found five-year-old Rachel sitting on the ground at the side of the house with some of the yard men, trying to smoke a cigarette. The men may not have understood what Mom said to them, but they must have gotten the gist of what she meant because she was yelling pretty unhappily at them. Needless to say, they never sat near our house again. It probably goes without saying that Rachel understood perfectly what Mom said to her! Rachel will tell you that she never tried to smoke again.

Mom and Dad kept busy as much as we kids did. A new NCO Club opened shortly after we moved up the mountain. It was a large facility with a swimming pool, which we all frequented often. They served meals and had bingo once a week. Mom and Dad would take one or two of us with them to play bingo. I remember winning fifty dollars! Whatever became of that money, I wonder …?

Downtown Taipei had bowling lanes, and Mom and Dad played in bowling leagues. Dad was a pretty good bowler. There was a movie theater nearby, and the movies were free for military families.

Mom and Dad's friends Jo and Carl, whose mailbox Dave blew up when we were in our economy house, had also moved up the mountain, directly across from us. And the adults made good friends with other couples in the neighborhood, including Ann and Norman, with whom they played cards and maintained friendships over the years.

Mom and the ladies frequently got together for lunch. One day, Ann, who was born and raised in Germany, was having a bad time with homesickness, so Mom and her friend Alice did their best to make her feel better, although they, too, were likely feeling a bit of homesickness.

Curious Adventures in the Mountain 'Hood
We had a dog named Prancer—it was pretty unusual when we didn't have a dog. Prancer and the Brats would all be off running the countryside during the day when we weren't in school. When it was dinnertime, Dad would let out a very loud whistle, and Prancer and all the Brats would come running back to the house. Unfortunately, Prancer apparently had an affinity for the local chickens, a fact we didn't know about until he came home with a dead chicken tied to his neck. That wasn't acceptable to Dad, so Prancer had to go bye-bye. Dad gave him to some GIs who lived downtown and wanted a watchdog. I hope they didn't have any chickens ….

One Saturday morning, we were outside playing and noticed something strange. Inside our housing area, a group of ROC soldiers had moved into the very first house inside the entrance to the compound and were standing around the entrance. When we asked Mom and Dad about it, they said it was nothing to worry about, but there was some rioting going on down in Taipei, and the ROCs were just there to be like police for us.

This was late May 1957. Just prior to this, a US soldier shot and killed a Taiwanese prowler who had been looking through his bathroom window at his wife who was taking a shower. There were no witnesses to the incident, but the soldier claimed that when he confronted the prowler, he was attacked by him with a stick. The soldier then shot him twice, killing him in self-defense. Following this, the soldier was tried in a US military court on May 23, found not guilty, and sent back to the United States. His release created a great deal of anger among the Taiwanese people and resulted in a mob storming the US Embassy in Taipei.[86] Hence, the ROC soldiers at the gate to our housing compound to protect us. As I've grown older and have considered these things, it's a little surprising to me that these were ROC rather than US troops protecting us, or at least some combination of the two.

Ignorant of it all, we started hanging out with the soldiers because, well, they were there. As you may have noted by now, we required very little incentive to have some fun. The soldiers would make jokes and play tricks on us, and we would do the best we could to do the same back to them. One day we convinced the soldiers to play "war" with us. We had some slingshots, and so did they, so we got to firing cherry bombs at each other with our slingshots. Cherry bombs are round wads of very thin paper that have gunpowder and little pieces of gravel in them. If you threw one of them down hard on the pavement, the compression of the little rocks on the gunpowder would cause them to blow up with a loud POW! If you got hit hard enough with one of them, sort of like in paintball wars today, they would go off too. It would sting a bit sometimes, depending on where it hit, but it seemed like it was great fun at the time. It should be noted that Dave was the lead Brat in this little adventure, although there were plenty of neighbor Brats involved too.

On a warm afternoon, we were warring with the ROCs, but nobody was winning. Typically, the ROCs weren't very good shots and would miss us. Thinking back on that now, if they really were lousy shots, what good would they have been to us if that riot had come up the mountain? Of course, they probably wouldn't have been using slingshots to defend us. I don't know if they missed on purpose or not, but we were having fun, and they were all laughing, probably at us silly kids. Suddenly, everything changed: Dave was able to get a good angle on one of the soldiers. He pulled back his slingshot as far as it would go and let his cherry bomb fly. It smacked the soldier on the forehead and POW! It went off right between his eyes! Nobody was laughing. All the neighborhood kids quickly retreated, and that was the last day we played "war" with the ROCs. Those guys should have known better than that, don't you think?

Not long after our "war," Dave decided he needed a homing pigeon. He had always been fascinated by flight and enjoyed watching birds fly. When he watches a bird fly even today, he will tell you that he is still amazed at the combination of ease, grace, and beauty as they soar through the air. In fact, he would often dream that when he grew up, he would be an airplane! He told us that he dreamed that he could run through a field, flap his arms, and sail through the air. One time, when we were visiting Glamich and Grampa Archie in Wisconsin, Dave was sleeping on the top bunk dreaming about flying as he fell off the bed onto the vacuum cleaner! Even though his crash landing broke the vacuum, he didn't get hurt at all. Maybe the rest of his dreams that night involved crash landings?

Dave made a small cage for his bird-to-be with boards and chicken wire that he found. Then he went downtown on the bus to Taipei and searched around the streets and alleys of the city until he found a man who had homing pigeons to sell. He paid the man the equivalent of thirty cents for the bird, which was probably too much by about twenty-seven cents. The man kept saying in broken English, "You no ret bird go, he fry away, no come back you!" In other words, if the bird got away from him, Dave wouldn't see it again. Dave assured him he would be careful not to let the bird go and very happily went home with his new pigeon friend.

Dave and the pigeon got home at about 3:00 that afternoon, and he put it in his homemade cage, closed the door, and sat there admiring it. It was slate gray with blue bars on its wings. They call them "blue bar" pigeons for that reason. Dave proudly showed the pigeon to everyone who would look. Somewhere between 4:30 and 5:00 p.m. he opened the cage door to put in some water for Mr. Pigeon. It got spooked, jumped out, and flew away. *He no come back to Dave!* Being a homing pigeon, it's probable that it flew back to the fellow in Taipei where Dave bought it. It turned out to be a very short-lived experience, but Dave didn't give up his love affair with pigeons, as we'll see in the next chapter.

Mountain Memories

As can be noted in the pictures of us growing up, we always had short, military-style haircuts. Dad was our barber. When it was the babies' turn for their haircuts, Mom would hold Steve or Rick across her lap, and Dad would cut their hair while they screamed their little hearts out. One time, our next-door neighbor, a colonel, came running over to see if Mom and Dad were abusing their children—a trip he only made once. It should be mentioned that our haircuts were done in true Army style: very short on the sides—we called them "whitewalls"—and not very long on top. It was the way it was, so we didn't whine about it, but as we all grew into our teens, we appreciated the haircuts less and less. This was particularly true for those of us hitting our teens in the mid- to late-sixties, as hair was being worn longer by many of our friends. Unfortunately, the Beatles were not permitted to influence our hairstyles. At all.

Dave, Dan, Rachel, Mike, Bob, Steve, and Jim, 1957

In several of the pictures of us when we lived on the mountain, the area between the houses shows a large grassy lawn where we played as well as on the swings right behind our house. Jim had a little friend named Susie, and they would play together for hours, but a day never went by that they didn't have a big argument. When Mom called Jim in for lunch one day, he said, "I'll be there as soon as I have my fight with Susie." No matter how much they fussed, Jim and Susie were fast friends during our time there. Susie was one of the younger members of the family of six girls living right behind us.

Their big family of girls and our big family of mostly boys were in constant battles over daily ownership of the swings behind our house. Ah, the swings. Remember Mike's first spanking experience for using inappropriate language? Well, one bright Saturday morning, we were finishing breakfast and could hear some noise coming from the area behind the house at the swings. That meant the swings were being claimed by some of those neighbor girls. Mike heard the noise, quickly consumed the remaining food on his plate—we weren't allowed to leave food on the plate—excused himself from the table, and took off out back. Soon we all heard someone yell, "G#d d#mmit!" Dad leaped up from the table, grabbed his belt, and ran out back. He picked up Mike, brought him back in the house to our bedroom, and guess what? That's right, Mike got his second whipping! That kind of language wasn't permitted around the Heath house. Another important lesson learned, and not only by Mike. *All* the Brats were paying close attention!

We had a water tower right behind our house, and King Shun would climb the metal ladder up the tower in his bare feet. He was also our walking rat trap. Mike got up early one morning and watched King Shun scurry around the house barefoot trying to corner a rat that was running around. He finally got a toe on the rat's tail then snatched it up by the tail and carried it outside where he whopped it a couple of times on the walkway and threw it in the trash. Mission accomplished!

King Shun also did the honors of preparing a live turkey we had acquired to cook and have for supper. It's important to understand that we were a lot more used to the frozen turkeys we got at the commissary. So the process of getting this live turkey ready to cook was a bit different and very new to us. Mike was right there when King Shun grabbed it by its head, cut it off, then dropped the turkey on the ground. Almost as amazing as watching it get beheaded was watching the turkey fly over the dog house with no head and blood spurting all over the place! Mike was very quiet for a while. He can't remember if he ate any of the turkey or not. Probably not.

Our house up on Green Mountain had a telephone, which was something we weren't used to. Because of that, some of the older

Brats liked answering it when it rang. We were given very clear instructions on the proper way to do this. We were to say, "Sergeant Heath's quarters, […] speaking." Every one of us continued to answer the phone in that manner as long as Dad was in the Army.

Dave's Boy Scout Days

Dave was in the Boy Scouts while we were there, even though he wasn't all that excited about it. He saw it as very much like being in the Army, with uniforms and such, and he felt he was already getting quite enough of that. Nonetheless, during our second summer in Taiwan, he was a Tenderfoot and the troop went to camp on the southern coast of the island. There had just been a typhoon somewhere in the Pacific, and the waves on the beach were really pounding.

A typhoon is the same thing as a hurricane, but it occurs in the Pacific Ocean not the Atlantic. Historically, Taiwan gets four or five of them a year; we were fortunate to only experience two through our three years there. During the two we experienced, the wind howled, and there was torrential rain. There were no large trees in our neighborhood, so we didn't have to worry about one being blown over on our houses. Fortunately, no roofs were blown off, and none of the houses experienced any significant damage during our tour of duty.

Anyway, the battering waves at the beach that day put excitement in the hearts of all the scouts and fear in the hearts of the leaders because they could just see their scouts getting swept out to sea. They set up a "buddy system" where each scout had to know where the other guy was all the time.

Tenderfoot Dave learned two things at summer camp that year: one sad and one full of mystery, adventure, and wonder. The sad event was about one of the scouts in the troop, Billy Miller, who was also Dave's assigned buddy. He was about ten years old and just a little kid like Dave, away from his parents trying to do what the adults told him to do and still have fun in spite of that. Billy had a little problem. He wet the bed one night and his fellow campers in the tent found out about it. On the last night, he wet the bed again. This time, his fellow campers had a surprise waiting for him when he woke up that morning. He couldn't find his uniform trousers anywhere, so he put on whatever he could find to go out and see what everyone was having such a good time laughing about. When he came out of the tent, he discovered that they were laughing at him: there were his pants for everyone to see, run up the flagpole with a great big sign pinned to them reading, "LEAKY MILLER!" Billy may have never gone camping again. One thing that incident burned into Dave's mind and heart that year is just how mean kids can be to one another when they think they're being funny. To this day, Dave is not interested in camping, and the remembrance of this event is why. He's also not interested in being mean to other people.

The second and most interesting thing Dave experienced came while he was exploring the sand dunes early one morning. There was some patchy ground cover that grew out of the dunes, just as it does on most beaches, and he was making his way through and around it. He reached the top of one of the dunes and turned around to look out over the ocean. As he turned around, he saw the strangest thing coming straight at him very fast. It was a flaming yellow ball of fire, and it was both beautiful and scary at the same time. Suddenly it was shooting across closely above him, and he whirled around to watch it flame and smoke away as it sped past over the dunes. It was the first meteorite he had ever seen, and he couldn't believe how close it was! He ran in the direction it had gone, but couldn't find where it landed. It had been wonderful and exciting and here and gone in seconds! No one else had seen it, and no one believed that he had seen it. But he definitely saw it, and it didn't matter to him if anyone believed him or not. From that little incident, though, he learned that it didn't matter in life if other people see things the way you see them, as long as you don't allow that which they don't see to make you blind too. A very good lesson!

The Incident in the Grove

It was the summer of 1956; I was eight years old, and Mike was six. We had heard the name Chiang Kai-shek a number of times, as the leader of the people of this island. Even though Mom said she saw him walking nearby our compound, I don't remember ever seeing him. Our compound was surrounded by one of those thick, six-foot-high concrete walls, similar to the one at our house on the economy. Really, the wall could have been shorter than that, but so was I back then. Embedded in the concrete on top of the wall were shards of glass, which stuck up like quills on a porcupine's back. Again, as with the wall around our economy house, it was probably there to keep out intruders. It wasn't very effective: the Heath Platoon along with neighbor Brats used to love to walk on top of that wall and break off the shards by kicking them with our shoes. It's difficult to say what was so fun about it, but we spent hours doing it. Besides, it made it easier to scramble over the wall! For us and likely for intruders trying to get in! On the other side of the wall on one side of the compound was a grove of trees where we occasionally would wander around and play.

Just as we did everywhere, we all ran pretty loosely and freely around the countryside surrounding the compound, and the Chinese and native Taiwanese people there mostly ignored us. No one ever bothered us, or behaved as though we shouldn't be around—well, unless someone broke something and got caught. At least, most of the time. It never occurred to us it should be any different than that. Little did any of us know there were significant tensions between the US government and the ROC government during part of our time there.[87] Beyond those tensions, there were tensions between the native people of Taiwan and the ROC for taking over their island. It would be decades later before we would begin to understand more about the history of the countries in which we grew up.

All that aside, Mike and I strapped on our cap pistols one day, loaded them up with fresh rolls of caps, and fired off a few rounds to make sure they worked. We holstered our pistols, climbed over the shard-topped wall, and dropped down into the tree grove on the other side. Then we started running through the woods, in a completely unscripted, shrieking, ruleless game of blasting away with our cap pistols, playing cowboys and Indians, cops and robbers, soldiers in a great battle, or anything the game evolved into from moment to moment. Our cap pistols were *kapowing* all over the place, with little puffs of smoke curling up with each pop. We occasionally stopped and argued whether one of us had been fatally shot by the other. Nobody ever won those arguments. Even at that, we may have "killed" each other a few times, but we always managed to resurrect ourselves so that we could continue the mock bloodshed.

I really don't know how long we ran around in that grove of fruit trees, but it doesn't seem that it was very long. Suddenly we both stopped running. It wasn't just me and Mike in the thickly shaded tree grove. It was Mike, me, and a bunch of Chinese soldiers—and these guys had *real* guns. We stood there for what seemed like a very long time looking at the soldiers. They stood there looking at us and talking to one another. Two of the soldiers walked over to us and took our cap pistols, then herded us toward what seemed to be the center of the tree grove, prattling back and forth in their fast-paced language the whole way. There, on a porch in front of a thatched hut, on a big chair—maybe it was a throne—sat a bald man in a Chinese Army uniform. I mean, the "throne" wasn't gold-gilded or anything; it was just a big, wooden, ornately carved chair. Mike and I stood there, looking at the bald soldier in the chair. He was clearly the lead soldier.

The men talked to the bald soldier, occasionally pointing at us and the cap pistols; then the soldier who took our cap pistols handed them over to the throne soldier. He looked them over carefully, pointed one in the air, and pulled the trigger a couple times, letting loose two puffs of smoke. He laughed, and all the other soldiers laughed too. Mike and I didn't laugh. I looked over at Mike. I was about to pee my pants, clueless but highly fearful as to our future here with the Chinese soldiers. Mike didn't look worried; Mike never worried about anything. Suddenly the chief soldier said something to two of the others and handed them our pistols, gesturing for them to go. These two soldiers took us through the tree grove and back to our wall. They gave us back our pistols, then disappeared back through the trees. We scampered over the wall and ran back to the house. Nobody said anything about not going back there or anything else to us. I don't really remember what I did the rest of that day. I know neither

Mike nor I mentioned it or talked about it; we certainly never told Mom or Dad about our little adventure with the Chinese soldiers. I mean, Dad might have really been ticked if he knew we had been captured by some Chinese soldiers. Today, such a thing would be an "incident." Back then, I guess it was just some soldiers wondering why two little American kids were running around their grove of trees with guns. I have always wondered if the soldier who got smacked between the eyes from Dave's slingshot popper was one of the soldiers who detained us …?

Well, at this point it may not be very surprising that this little adventure never came up again until Mom's eightieth birthday party in 2002—some forty-seven years later. We had all conspired to tell a tale of growing up, and this is the story I told. We really heard some great stories that day. Mike didn't remember a thing about the Chinese soldiers. I guess when you're five or six, you don't remember some adventures in your life. When I finished telling the story, I said, "I don't have any idea who those soldiers were, who the man in the big chair was, or why they detained us." Mom said, "That was probably Chiang Kai-shek; his compound was right next to us!"

Mike and I were briefly captives of Chiang Kai-shek, leader of the Republic of China in 1956. Mom just kept shaking her head and repeating, "I should have been paying more attention!" as we all told our stories.

★★★

When Dave thinks about "growing up Army," particularly our childhood experiences when we lived in Taiwan, it almost seems like a dream. The freedom we had as kids and the things we wandered off and did amaze his concept of childhood today. I don't think he's alone in that thinking as we all look back in wonderment at those times. Without a doubt, reading about these adventures may well explain some of the reasons parents pay more attention to what their kids are up to in today's world.

During one of our adventures around our housing area, we discovered a small cascading stream just a short distance up the mountain. It was a sulfur spring and smelled bad, but the area was beautiful. Springs like this were fairly common around there; they fed some of the sulfur baths in the area, as Dan and Dave discovered.

One day, Dan and Dave and another boy decided to visit the hostels where unmarried soldiers lived up on Monroe Mountain. That probably wasn't the real name of the mountain, but its shape gave the distinct image of Marilyn Monroe, a very popular, well-endowed movie star back then. We're not sure who came up with that name, but it's the name we all were told.

Dan, Dave, and their friend caught the bus up to the hostels and decided the most impressive thing about them was that they had sulfur baths. Sulfur baths are very hot and smell like rotten eggs—just like that stream near where we lived. They explored the hostel for a while, then decided to get into the sulfur bath. They hadn't brought bathing suits, so they just stripped down to the buff and went on in. Man, it was hot! *Really* hot! Soon, just being in the sulfur bath became hot and boring, so they decided it would be more fun to turn the cold water on in the showers on the other side of the room and have a race to see who could get from the far side of the steaming hot sulfur bath and into the ice-cold showers first. It sounded like fun at the time, but they only did it once. The heat of the sulfur bath just seemed to be magnified by the cold of the showers. When Dave got in the cold shower straight out of the bath, his legs got really weak, and he thought he was going to pass out! Somehow, winning that race did not seem like a victory.

Thinking about it now, Dave has no idea why he and Dan or anyone would want to subject themselves to a really hot, smelly sulfur bath rather than just taking a regular hot bath. But let's face it, there was much more adventure in a sulfur bath. The oddest and most amazing thing of all was that no adult came around to interfere with their fun. It was like they had the run of the place. The soldiers who lived there were most likely off at their jobs in the Army, which could explain the absence of adults to keep them straight.

I Wonder What's in Those Big Jars?

On another typical day, Dan and I, Dave, and a few other kids from our housing area headed out to explore the mountain. First, we found some bamboo sticks and had some sword-fighting battles in the banana orchards. Then we climbed to the top of the water tower next to our house so we could spy on other enemy combatants and catch them by surprise when they came. After a while, the mock battles waned, and we went on about our conquest of the island in the best Indiana Jones-style we could muster. Of course, we didn't know anything about Jones way back then.

We were wandering through the woods and came upon a mysterious field of potentially undiscovered treasure right out in the open at the top of a high grassy mound. We had to walk through a field of strange monuments to get to them. Once we got through that field, we came upon the "treasure jars." The clay jars—or urns—of treasure were about chest-high on Dave. We inspected them on the outside quite carefully. They had domed metal lids and the openings at the top were ten inches or more in diameter. It was quite exciting to us that these would be left out in the open for us to plunder. We got into a conversation to determine who should be the first to look inside the jars to see what we had discovered; Dave was assigned the duty of opening the first one. He stepped up to the large jar in the middle of all the others and gingerly opened the lid and lifted it off. Then he craned his neck over the opening and looked down into it— his legs went weak because looking right back at him was the skull of another human being that had passed on long before us! Under the skull were the rest of the bones belonging to that person. *Yikes!* Dave's face turned green, and he backed away from the urn very quickly, nearly falling down, after which we all *had* to take turns looking in, especially after seeing Dave's reaction! Dave was the only one who turned green, but it's safe to say that the rest of us were ready to vacate the premises, posthaste! We picked up the lid to the urn that Dave had dropped and replaced it before we ran back to our compound.

We had stumbled onto a Chinese burial ground. It turns out that the Chinese buried their dead for seven years to let the bodies decompose, then they dig them back up, pick off all the remaining flesh, and place the bones into urns in the exact order that they were in the body, with the skull on top. They were then stored in a place above ground having good "feng shui," an ancient Chinese practice that harmonizes something with the spiritual forces surrounding it.[88] I'm not sure how they figure that out, but I do know that instead of discovering treasure, we had discovered sacred, scary culture. It did not take us very long to leave the treasure behind and get home! I suspect we didn't add any additional positive vibes to the feng shui of the area either. Mom said Dave was still quite green even later that day! Dave said all of us probably learned from that experience that many things in life that look good on the outside aren't quite so good upon closer inspection.

Looking back, I think one of the reasons we were so actively running about the countryside was because we only went to school for a half day each day, even though the standards were tough.

Beyond the half-day school days, Dave had developed his own curriculum for seventh grade. He did this without consulting anyone, including Mom or his teacher. He's not really sure how it came about, or how it went unnoticed until the end of the year. Maybe most of the work was easy enough for him that he could ignore his homework or do it on the way to school and get away with it—right up until the end of the school year. That year, Dave fell in love with reading. Looking back, he thinks it started with an assignment to read *The Call of the Wild* by Jack London. That book took Dave on an interesting adventure into a frozen wonderland, and he was in awe! He felt like he was there, in the story. Then he checked a book out of the library entitled *The Black Stallion* by Walter Farley and fell totally into the experiences and life adventures that reading can bring. Next it was *The Island Stallion*, and soon it was everything Walter Farley had written that had a horse and adventure in it. Every day Dave would check a new book out of the library, read it that night, and take it back and get another one the next day. Dave was very likely the best-read student in the entire school. Best-read kid or not, the end result was that he failed the seventh grade and had to repeat it when we were transferred to Fort Lewis, Washington, the next school year. In spite of that, Dave still loves to read.

Dave had another somewhat memorable experience in seventh grade: a girl named Jane. Dave was beginning to take notice that there were definite differences between boys and girls, and Jane was physically very mature and a very good example of those differences. According to him, sometimes she would wear somewhat revealing blouses to school, which got Dave's attention as well as that of the other guys in the class. Dave would come up with various excuses to walk by her desk so that he could get a good peek at her, and one day he came up with a surefire method. He concluded that if his schoolwork was going to be crisp and sharp, he needed to keep his pencil very sharp. As fate would have it, the pencil sharpener was on the back wall of the classroom, requiring him to walk by Jane's desk. He also discovered that the lead on the pencil would break quite frequently if he would just press it a little harder on the paper. Needless to say, Dave went through a lot of pencils that school year! And now we know the whole reason why Dave had to repeat seventh grade: excessive reading *plus* excessive gawking at Jane!

Another Transfer Is Upon Us

Early in the summer of 1958, Dad got orders to go to Fort Lewis, Washington, near Tacoma. He took leave since it was summertime, and we went to the NCO Club every day, swam in the pool, and drank iced tea.

Rachel fell in love with ice-cold tea there during that summer. She would get a great big glass of ice tea and put as much sugar in it as she wanted, and did she ever load her glass up with the sugar! She would stir and stir and still about a half inch of sugar would remain on the bottom of the glass, and she loved that last sip! Rachel still loves ice-cold tea, but has backed way off the half inch of sugar.

We all learned to swim and do front and back flips off the diving board, and Rachel was no exception to any of that. She always did everything her big brothers could do. We had a lot of fun splashing and playing around in that pool.

On the summer morning we flew out of Taipei, it was 95 degrees—much like the day we arrived three years earlier. That night we landed in Sitka, Alaska, in the snow. We were each given a wool blanket and waited inside a heated building while the plane was fueled, then boarded the plane again and flew to Seattle. It has always puzzled me why a trip such as this would fly 860 miles north of its destination, refuel, then fly the 860 miles back down to where it was going in the first place!? It would seem so much more efficient just to go straight to Seattle, wouldn't it?

Anyway, Dad still had some leave time since he didn't have to report to Fort Lewis until late September, so we had time to visit family in Wisconsin and Illinois, then come back to the Tacoma area to find someplace to live and get all of us registered for school. Since we didn't have a car—Dad sold it before we left Taiwan—we took a train from Seattle to Manitowoc, but we had to wait a couple days for our train. We stayed in one room in a hotel while we waited. The room had two beds, so Mom and Dad put the mattresses on the floor; some of us slept there and others on the box springs. We finally got on the train, and because food was pretty expensive, we just ate sandwiches that we brought with us. When we changed trains in Chicago, we had time to go to a restaurant for a real meal that didn't cost too much.

While in the Midwest, we made our usual rounds visiting family and friends. We often spent some time on the farm with Mom's old friend Dorothy, her husband, Johnny, and their ever-growing family. Dorothy was expecting their seventh child, which would have made them just one kid less than us, except that time they had twins. The visit to their farm was always one of the highlights of our trips home. Our two big families got together with another of Mom's old friends, Doris, and her husband, Cliff, and their family of eight kids, for a picnic. Just our three families amounted to twenty-three children. Of course, we also visited Dad's and Mom's folks while in the area. This is where Grampa Grump began calling Mike and me "Mikey named Bobby" or "Bobby named Mikey" because he couldn't keep our names straight.

CHAPTER 12
BACK TO AMERICA—FORT LEWIS, WASHINGTON, 1958–1961

We Brats were good travelers, but some of us always had a problem with leaving for another posting. It was an everlasting complaint—one that Mom could have recorded and played every three years. "Oh, do we have to move again? All of our friends are here." It usually took us a week or less to make new friends. I don't ever remember having those emotions. For me, it was, "Oh, time to go? Where are we going? When?" And off we would go to whatever and wherever was next. Besides, we always had all of us to play with. We were very fortunate to always move during the summer because it's much easier to start over someplace when it's the first day of school. Once we were in our new schools, we were never the only new kids in class because the schools we attended were near Army bases, and there were always other Brats there too. Fort Lewis was no exception; what was difficult, though, was finding suitable housing for a family with eight kids.

There was no available dependents' housing in Fort Lewis, and it wasn't easy to find a place to rent for such a large family. We stayed in a motel for three weeks and finally Dad found us a very small house. It was in a beautiful place right across from a large park. The house had only one bedroom and one closet and a large unfinished attic that was used as a bedroom for all the Brats except the babies, who shared Mom and Dad's room. The house was a step up from the motel, so we were grateful to have it, but it wouldn't be suitable long term to have all of us sleeping in the attic.

Mom was having an unexpected problem. After three years in Taiwan of not having to do any work she didn't want to do— remember, we had a maid—there were no calluses on her hands. Now, the household chores she was doing caused painful blisters. On top of that, the day our household goods arrived, Mom sat on the front porch and cried because she had no idea where we would put everything in this tiny little house. That said, military families move and travel lightly; there aren't lots of household goods like furniture. Maybe some pots, pans, dishes, and pictures along with clothes. Even at that, it was a small house. Then came the day she had to enroll six of us in three different schools and had to go through the "what was your maiden name" discussion each time—even though she had written a note in advance that Heath was her maiden name, and yes, she was fully aware of what the term *maiden name* meant. Sigh.

The rather desperate search for a suitable house soon paid off when they found a five-bedroom house located in Lakewood, which is a small town near Tacoma. It was a great big castle to us. I only shared my room with Mike while we lived there, which was very rare; normally, there were four of us in a bedroom. This was nice.

The house was quite old but in very good condition, and we all fell in love with it. To this day, many houses later for all of us, that one is the "castle." The front of the house had stucco with German-style exposed timbers. We all thought that was very cool and definitely a sign of a big house. It didn't have a separate dining room but had a good-sized, U-shaped, cafe-style breakfast nook in the kitchen area that most of us could squeeze into. We had to slide in and around to get seated, and it took some maneuvering if someone in the back had to get out during a meal.

We had a beautiful, nice-sized yard with lots of trees, shrubs, and flowers. There was a large tree in our front yard with one of those big, far-reaching limbs that cry out to you, "Come, sit, and relax on me." Mike kept answering that call, and he could spend hours stretched out on that limb, with his legs hanging over. Mike was one of those "tagalong" kids. He was always ten steps behind everyone else, just kind of moseying along in his own world. He never seemed too worried about much, even his shirttail. One thing I never could personally abide was a hanging-out shirttail, but Mike always seemed to have at least one part of his hanging out. That limb was a perfect place for Mike.

Lakewood, WA house, 1959

The house also had a garage, which became Dad's barber shop for us, a little shed out back, and a huge basement for storage and laundry. There was also a root cellar in the back yard that had a glass-paned door on the top, kind of in the shape of a small roof. Dan (age fifteen), Dave (twelve), Mike (eight), and I (ten) helped Dad take down the part that was above ground, then fill it all in with dirt. Our picture window in the front of the house perfectly framed Mt. Rainier off in the distance on a clear day. We had a fireplace, which we used a lot, and it had a beautiful fresco of Mt. Rainier built into the hearth.

When I visited the house forty-four years later, it seemed kind of small compared to my memory of our "castle." Interestingly, the people who bought the house from us were just moving out that day. They raised six children there. Apparently, it is a good house for having lots of kids running around. They let me go in the house and take some pictures and told me I could go anywhere I wanted.

The diner booth in the kitchen was gone, as was the old wooden garage and the pigeon coop. The garage had burned down twenty or so years prior to my visit. I looked for Mike's tree limb so I could get a picture of it. Sadly, the whole tree was gone. Most disappointingly, a two-story recreation building had been built right across the street twenty years earlier and blocked the beautiful view of Mt. Rainier, both from the picture window and from the yard. The people there had even forgotten that view had been there. It was a weird, unusual experience going back to that house, but I'm glad I did it. I went to my old room on the second floor, and it was really small. There was a bookcase where my bed used to be. I went into every room, including the basement and took lots of pictures.

I haven't had the opportunity to visit any of the other places where I lived growing up, and I don't think any of my siblings have either. It's not like they're down the block or across town. When I say it was pretty weird going back there, I guess I really mean it was just very unusual for me to have that glimpse into a place of my past. Every member of the Heath Platoon who has had an opportunity to go to Washington state has made a point of going by to look at the house. I think I was the only one fortunate enough to go inside.

Diversions

We had our first color TV there, and Dave remembers, still with some awe, the NBC peacock along with the phrase, "In living color." Mom let us watch the *Howdy Doody* show every morning before we went to school, and we would spend every Saturday morning watching cartoons. These were new, very enjoyable entertainments for us! Because of our numbers and limited available seating in the living room, all the Brats sat on the floor in front of the TV. Dad always watched the Friday night fights, and Mom and Dad watched *The Lawrence Welk Show* and the *Ed Sullivan Show;* we all enjoyed *Leave It to Beaver* and lots more.

One Saturday morning, Dad was engaging in Brat Barber Shop duties in front of the garage. Apparently, I was first to get my haircut and went outside; Dad sent me back in to get the stool we would all sit on while he cut our hair. Being the good little soldier, I went in and got the stool, then as I was passing the living room, there was Woody Woodpecker up to something on the TV, and my good little soldier persona departed. A very short time later I got smacked on the side of my head, and when I looked up, there was Dad the Barber staring at me, sitting on the stool watching Woody Woodpecker, with a very unhappy look on his face. I leaped up, said, "Sorry, Dad!" grabbed the stool, and ran outside to the garage. The haircuts commenced without further ado. I would have liked to blame it on Woody, but that wouldn't have worked out. He would have just said something silly like, "Heh-heh-heh-HEHHHH-heh!"

Odd Jobs and Dart 1.0
Because of our family circumstances financially, we kids didn't get anything like a weekly allowance, and running to Mom or Dad with a request for money for something wasn't productive. This meant that if we wanted money, we needed to go find a way to earn it.

That first fall in Lakewood, leaves were falling from trees, so Mike and I were exercising an entrepreneurial spirit in looking for profitable work for kids aged nine and eleven. We canvassed our neighborhood looking for someone who would let us rake some leaves for a few dollars, until we finally had a taker. He gave us a couple of leaf rakes, two big boxes, and showed us the leaf-covered back of his yard, where we got to work.

For a short while, we worked pretty hard on those leaves. We filled the boxes and dumped the leaves in a big pile in the corner of the yard. Somewhere along the way, one of us found a dart. It was a pretty average dart as darts go, with plastic blue feathers. I remember the blue feathers because I would soon get a close-up view of them.

I threw the dart in Mike's direction, after which it came arcing back. Making a game out of anything was an art form for kids back then, and we were a couple of kids who were serious about the art of playing a new game. In any case, Mike and I were engaged in our newest game with this blue-feathered dart.

Before long, the dart was being launched high into the air and would slide perpendicularly into the ground with a "chunk." Leaves ceased to be raked by this time. We were now a couple of dart-throwing fools! But there had to be some way to enhance this game, we thought—and we had no fear. Maybe there should have been some fear ....

After Mike launched a particularly high dart, I ran under it with my box, throwing it up to catch the dart inside the box. It landed right in the bottom. This game became more and more fun, as the dart continued to be launched higher and higher into the air. I discovered there was an open slot in the bottom of the box, through which I could sight the dart. So as it dropped from the sky, I zeroed in on it through the slot, and at the last split second, threw the box up to catch it. "Ka-thunk."

Back and forth went the dart, *ka-thunking* with each trip into the bottom of the box. Mike really launched a beauty, and I sighted the dart gliding gracefully up, up, up, then down, down, down toward my box. At just the right moment, I threw my box up to catch it. Something brushed the side of my face, right next to my left eye with a *ssshhhhhtttt* sound, and I realized I never heard the *ka-thunk* in the bottom of my box. I dropped the box, and I could see something that looked like blue dart tail feathers out of the corner of my left eye. I heard Mike yelling, "Bob! Bob! *Bob!*"

I reached up and grabbed the dart and yanked it out of my head, still hearing my brother yelling my name. Mike was running over to me, his box abandoned on the ground across the yard.

"Bob! Are you all right?" I could hear fear in Mike's voice, and I began to panic as well. I mean, nothing really bothered Mike, remember? I held the dart out toward Mike with my right hand and reached up to my eye with my left, checking for eyeball placement, blood, or any other abnormality. Nothing. No blood. Eyeball in place. Sight good.

Mike was staring at me with wonder, disbelief, and shock in his eyes. It seemed the dart flew right through that slot in the bottom of the box and lodged itself just under the skin next to my left eye. I mean, *right next* to my left eye.

I said, "Do you see any blood?"

"No, nothing."

"Nothing?"

"No blood, nothing, except a little hole in the skin by your eye," Mike said.

"What time is it?" We were due to have a family picture at 1:00 that Saturday afternoon.

"I don't know. What time do you think it is?"

"It's probably pretty close to 1:00; we'd better get home, or we'll miss the picture, and Dad will be really mad."

We ran home, leaving the dart, boxes, leaves, and any pittance of money the man might have paid us for halfway raking his yard. In less than an hour, we were in front of the camera with our sister, brothers, and Mom and Dad. It turned out to be a good picture too. I think my smile is quite handsome; Mike's too. You might note in looking at the picture that my head is turned slightly to one side. That pose was intended to leave any mark left on my face by the dart out of the photo. Even now, it makes me tremble a little, thinking about how close to my eye that dart landed. Lucky, lucky, lucky—again!

Family photo, post-dart, 1959

Dan took a slightly different approach to earning money. He would ride his bike over to the Tacoma Country and Golf Club to caddy. It was just under two miles from the house. Three things about caddying he remembers: caddying wasn't any fun, he didn't like it, and there were really nice people at the golf club. Caddying meant spending hour upon hour sitting in the caddy shack waiting for someone to pick you. It had to get down to pretty much Dan being the last caddy available for him to get picked, mostly because he didn't really know much about caddying or golf.

He went early one morning and managed to get a caddy job. It was very cold out that day, with lots of dew on the ground. By the time they got to the ninth hole by the clubhouse, his feet were soaking wet, and he was freezing. His feet were so cold! The man for whom he was caddying told him to go home, get some dry shoes and socks on, and come back. By the time Dan got back, the man was getting close to the eighteenth hole, but he still let Dan finish caddying for him and gave him five dollars, which was pretty good pay then. Even though he found there to be generous golfers, Dan's career as a caddy was very short.

School, Scraps, and Squabbles

Our house was only fifteen minutes from Fort Lewis, and all the schools we attended were close by. Lake City Elementary, which was across the street from the house, is where I took up the violin in fifth grade, although I can't recall what it was about the violin that appealed to me. I was second chair in our orchestra, which really burned me. A kid named Nils got first chair. We had to perform for the teacher, and the teacher would assign us to our "chair" based on who was best, etc. I didn't like that Nils got first chair, even though he was the better violinist. Actually, he played the viola and must have been pretty good at it.

I had my only childhood fight after a school dance one night with a kid named Kenny. What we were fighting about is a mystery to me at this time in my life, but lots of fights between two guys are generated over a girl, and this was happening just after a dance—where there was a plethora of girls. I remember running home to change into my play clothes because I didn't want to get in trouble for getting my good clothes dirty. Mom sent me right back to defend my honor, in my good clothes! I got whooped in the fight, more or less. I mean it wasn't really much of a fight. There was a lot of yelling by the fans, and Kenny and I did a lot of dancing around poking our fists at each other—much more of that than hitting by either of us. He got me pretty good on one eye with one poke, which didn't hurt much, but did turn it a little black and blue. I got to stay home the next day, which was unheard of at our house. One thing we always did was go to school. I saw two sides of Mom I never saw before that night: go defend your honor in your good clothes, and stay home from school with a black eye.

The elementary school had an old two-story schoolhouse in addition to the more modern (for 1958) single-story school wings. That building had an old-timey bell tower, which certainly inspired some interest. Mike claims this adventure was due to my instigation, of course, and it may well have been. One of us came up with the big plan that we would "break" into the schoolhouse one night. After some study, we determined that we could climb a fir tree that grew above the edge of the roof and make our way onto the roof. We then crawled up the tiled roof to the old bell tower, into the bell tower, through the hatch, and then down the ladder into the school. I can't fathom how we had any idea whatsoever that we could actually get into the school through the bell tower, but we did. The empty school smelled of children, the sawdust that they used to use to sweep the floor with, and chalk. The smell is Mike's most lasting impression of that adventure because, once we got inside, we didn't have any other mischief planned. We weren't into stealing stuff or tearing anything up; just exploring what a school looked like when no one else was there. Any misstep going up or down that tower that night would have resulted in at least a broken bone or two, all to accomplish something that we could do any day of the school week by walking through the front door. But would that have been any fun? I'm glad we didn't get caught!

Dave started his second seventh grade year at Mann Junior High and fortunately was able to successfully finish it that year. Early in seventh grade, Dave had an issue with this kid constantly bullying him—something he really couldn't understand. The kid started intentionally bumping him in the hall, and Dave was getting highly annoyed, so he decided to do something about it. The next day as the kid approached him, Dave slugged him in the chest as hard as he could, then walked on down the hall. The kid never bothered him again.

As I think about this incident, I recall many times when other kids would say or do things that weren't nice or kind to me. I was never bothered by that; I just brushed it off and went about my business like it never happened. I think it was like that for most of us Brats, possibly because we had such broad life's experiences that little things didn't matter much.

Dan went into tenth grade at Clover Park High School and was in the drama class there, acting in minor roles in several plays. He had one class he really hated, Family Life Relations, which was kind of an early sex-education kind of class. He remembers it as being "a really stupid class with a stupid teacher who asked lots of stupid questions requiring very stupid answers." So he wouldn't participate in anything and failed that stupid class. In his words, "I guess I showed 'em!"

Dan was riding home on the bus one day, and a kid was trying to pick a fight with him. Why, Dan had no idea, but the kid kept nagging at him, even after they got off the bus. The kid was bigger than Dan, so my brother didn't want to fight him. But the kid kept messing with him, so Dan beat the crap out of him. As far as Dan remembers, that was his first fight. Later in high school he signed up for the Boys Club smoker, which was the boxing club, and boxed for two years. He won his weight division in the eleventh grade, so he signed up again in the twelfth grade. In the twelfth grade, everyone kept telling him about this other guy with a boxing reputation, who was going to pound Dan and that he should withdraw. They said he would hit you so fast that you wouldn't see it coming. Even though Dan was a little worried about that, it raised his adrenaline levels so high that he went into the ring and just pounded the guy for the entire three rounds.

Dan said, "I hit him as hard and as fast as I could. I guess he just never got a chance to hit me 'so fast that I couldn't see it coming.' Everyone was pretty shocked by my big win; some even thought it was a fluke, especially since I was kind of a nobody. But I won my weight division for the second year in a row."

I think Dan was channeling Muhammad Ali, who said, "I'll beat him so bad he'll need a shoehorn to put his hat on." This time, Dan really did show 'em!

It seems a little odd to me that Dan, Dave, and I each had our first-ever physical confrontations with other kids in our first year in Lakewood. It makes me wonder if the local kids had some issue with Army Brats, which would be a little surprising, considering that Fort Lewis had been around since World War I. Then again, Fort Lewis was also responsible for a never-ending influx of new kids. It's just a thing to ponder. Those three incidents aside, the kids in the area were mostly friendly and lots of fun to play with.

Beyond the possible issue of negative attitudes toward military kids, a contributing factor to Dan's skirmish with the kid on the bus could be that he would go to the community center down the street from our house every Friday with his friend Raleigh to look for girls to dance with. Mom taught Dan how to dance at some point along the way before a school dance. Dan loved dancing from then on, just like Dad. He would come home absolutely soaked in sweat from head to foot after dancing. We don't know how the girls stood all the sweat, unless Dan was that good at dancing. So if Dan had been dancing with a girl of interest to the guy who pushed him into fighting, that could explain the other kid's desire to fight.

Teen Esteem

On top of being a good dancer, Dan became very cool, man, during our time in Lakewood. He had a ducktail haircut … well, he had ducktails to the highest degree a short Army haircut would allow. I'm pretty sure he used Brylcreem in his hair back then, which was all the rage for guys to keep those ducktails slicked back and looking good.

Dan wore his pants down low on his waist with his shirt collar turned up in the back, which was the thing to do, and he had these cool beatnik-ish friends who looked and dressed like the guys on *Dobie Gillis* on TV. I tried to wear my pants like Dan a few times, but I kept finding myself pulling them up, afraid they were going to drop to my ankles. I abandoned that style pretty quickly. My pants had to be snugly around my navel; cool was apparently not for me at that time in my young life.

One day Mom saw that boys' clothing in the stores was coming out in many colors, and she really loved it. She bought Dan a pair of orange slacks, which he really liked because they looked totally cool—like him!

"One day, a teacher talked to me about wearing those pants, and she told me that I shouldn't wear them to school. I did anyway. I got called to the office by the principal," Dan said. "He told me that those pants belonged on a golf course, not at school, and that I was not to wear them back to school. I told Mom about it, and she said, 'If you want to wear those pants to school, you wear them to school.' And I did. I don't remember anyone bringing it up again. Go figure Mom letting me defy the school authorities. And us in the Army."

Also at this time, Dan had an LP record album by the name of *Green Door*, by Jim Lowe. We heard Dan playing that record all the time. I still remember the lyrics and tune to the signature song. It was a group of guys singing the song in this soft, quiet voice. It's odd that I still remember that. Dan played it a lot. He said it was the only album he owned at the time. I guess it helped him get all that Brylcreem smoothed onto his ducktails just right.

Dan had gotten a great big speaker, called a *woofer*. It was the first woofer he had ever heard of, much less owned. He would open up the window in his upstairs bedroom and turn that woofer up as loud as he could. Then he would phone Raleigh and ask him if he could hear it from his house. He could. So could Mom, who would very quickly tell him to turn it down.

Raleigh lived in the attic of his parent's house, about a block from us. It was a tiny mill-type house, and Dan would climb up on the roof and go into Raleigh's room through a window. He rarely went in through the front door.

Raleigh was an amateur electrician and knew about ohms and stuff. One of the things he and Dan liked to do was become human resistors and test their electrical resistance with an ohm meter. Raleigh would grab one of the wires of an electrical circuit with one hand and one lead of the ohm meter with the other. Dan would grab the other lead of the ohm meter with one hand and then grab the water faucet with the other hand, which served as the electrical ground. Then, while they were being shocked by the electrical current, they would read the ohm meter to get their resistance. They did this more than once. There isn't any scientific proof of this, but I have a suspicion that these little electrical "zap" sessions may have been a factor in Dan's ability to pound those guys into submission—both the fight with the kid who was pushing him around and the ones in the boxing ring.

Summertime

That first summer, Mom broke her ankle. Mike said she stepped on one of his petrified-wood rocks that had somehow made its way to the bottom of the back steps. As a result, she needed help from the older Brats to keep the house clean. Rachel, Jim, Steve, and Rick were deemed too young to participate in what I refer to as Enslavement Summer. That left it up to Dan, Dave, me, and Mike to take care of the chores for Mom while she recouped. We had a rotating schedule. Each of us was assigned to be at Mom's beck and call throughout our assigned days each week and to clean whatever she decided needed cleaning.

That summer, a lot of stuff needed a lot of cleaning. I seemed to always get kitchen floor scrubbing duty. I hated that. It didn't occur to me that Dan, Dave, and Mike had equally irritating chores. I just hated scrubbing that darned floor! Even more, I hated giving up those summer days each week! I mean, a guy has really important things to do, like playing with darts and cardboard boxes. I do know this: each and every one of us was mighty happy when Mom got that darned cast off and we were released from duty! After our release, I wondered if Mom was wishing for a Seeny reincarnation …?

We all played hard in the summer, except when we had our help-Mom duties. We ran hard and stayed outside all day, just like everywhere else we had lived. Mom just wasn't about to let us camp out in the house driving her crazy, and who can blame her? Of course, there wasn't much to do in the house anyway, other than Saturday morning cartoons, so it just made sense that we would run around outside and play. We were pretty bad about arguing and fussing over just about everything we did while we played, but it must have passed the time. Whether it passed the time really didn't matter; no way was Mom going to let us hang out in the house anyway.

Fire II

A consequence of sending us outside was that it required that we inspire our imaginations to come up with fun things to do, as was our custom, growing up Army. Not boring things, but fun ones. Remember back in Newport News when Dan, Dave, and some friends started a fire in the woods and had a really hard time putting it out? Well, Mike and I were eight and ten years old and had been messing around, ending up in a vacant lot next to our house that we often used for whatever it is that young boys use vacant lots for. It had some trees and deep weeds, and the usual stuff growing on it. On this day we happened to have a book of matches and idle hands. Sound familiar? I thought it would be interesting to light one of the matches and throw it into the tall, dead, very dry grass in the empty lot. When I did, the grass immediately caught fire, and then we promptly stomped it out. That being pretty cool, we continued lighting matches, setting the grass on fire, and then stomping it out. This was true juvenile bliss. We finally came to our last match. I lit it, tossed it into the grass, and let it blaze up. Mike went to stomp it out, but I, not wanting to let a good thing die, or in this case, a small blaze die, said, "Wait!"

"What about now?"

"No."

"How about now?"

"Not yet."

"Bob, we better put this thing out!"

"Just another minute."

"BOB!"

"Oh, okay."

Whoops, too late!

We couldn't stomp fast enough to get that fire out. We finally realized we'd messed up big time and went for help. The fire department got called, and in the confusion, we got separated before we had a chance to put our story together. We both had to go check out how things were going with getting our fire put out. So Mike went over toward the fire truck to watch what was happening. Someone near a fireman pointed Mike out to him, and he went over to ask Mike what happened. He told him, "Bob and I were playing in one of the trees, and we saw smoke. We went to see what was smoking and found the fire, but we couldn't put it out, so we went to get help." He then asked Mike which tree they were playing in, so he pointed to a big one near where the fire was.

Later that night when everything had calmed down, Mike and I compared notes. I had also been collared by one of the firemen who asked me the same questions. Strangely, I told the fireman the identical story except that I pointed to a different tree. I never knew if we just got lucky or if the fireman figured out what had happened and decided to let it go. My bet is that he let us walk because who would ever believe such a lame story? Let's face it, it takes pretty unusual circumstances for something in the woods to just arbitrarily catch on fire.

Feeding the Family

Since we were required to be outside any time we weren't in school, the Heath Platoon knew that lunch was served at noon and supper at 5:00 p.m. As a result, we paid attention to the time and were there for meals. Every day. No exceptions. If you missed, you didn't eat. I can't ever remember missing a meal until I was in high school and playing sports. Even then when I missed dinner, it was up to me to find something to eat when I got home from track (or whatever) practice.

In Lakewood during the summer and weekends, we all converged on the house at noon. Mom would be seated at a small, foldout card table at the back door of the house. She had several loaves of bread, a couple jars of peanut butter, a pound or two of butter, and a couple jars of grape jelly. We would line up and give her our order for how many PB&Js we wanted for lunch. Mine was four. In the fifth grade, I would eat four peanut butter and jelly sandwiches. Four. I think maybe I weighed all of eighty pounds—but probably only *after* eating four sandwiches. We loved PB&J. Considering our numbers, it's not hard to imagine how many loaves of bread, etc., Mom went through every day for our lunches. Each school day morning, Mom would pack a bunch of PB&Js in brown paper bags and write our names on the outside for us to take to school.

Of course, the cost of feeding eight Brats isn't cheap, and Mom and Dad didn't have a lot of money. In an effort to save money, Mom and Dad bought our first freezer and filled it with a side of beef, which they purchased from the commissary on Fort Lewis. They were written up in the newspaper because of the size of that order. It was a little over $100—and $100 worth of anything was a lot—but buying that much beef at once saved a lot of money over time. We all pitched in and wrapped all that beef, which we enjoyed for quite a while.

Year Two in Fort Lewis

My sixth-grade year was in the Navy School, which was a converted old naval yard building; it was where all the district's sixth graders went for just that one year. My *most* significant achievement was that I became the all-world—nay, *all-universe*—tetherball champion. Being short and skinny, I think I snuck up on people. There were times when my right forearm was some color between black and purple from the bruises of pounding the ball or catching the rope wrong. I could wrap that rope like no one's business. The trick to wrapping the rope is to hit the ball at a down angle just right so that it flies over the head and out of reach of the person on the other side. Once you get that going, you can't be stopped. After I worked my way through one of the tetherball lines, I rarely got unseated. I owned it for the rest of recess. You can tell my academic pursuits there left a deep impression on me ....

In fact, I did have a rather unique educational experience at the Navy School, one of two that I had in the Lakewood school system. I would labor like crazy over every math problem. I would retrace repeatedly each addition, subtraction, multiplication, and division of every number—to make absolutely certain I got it right. The result was that I rarely finished a test and therefore got low grades, even though almost every problem that I completed was correct. One day the teacher said, "Bob, do each problem one time, then move on to the next one. I guarantee you at least a B if you do that." So I did, and got my B. I'm pretty sure I earned it, rather than was given the grade. Good advice.

During this time, Dave had created a pigeon loft in the shed behind the house. I don't think we ever knew how many he had but he took good care of them and always protected them from any of us. He became quite the avid pigeon boy, and had several homing pigeons, which actually "homed" as I recall. One thing I learned the hard way was not to mess with Dave's precious pigeons. He'd kick your butt! Mom liked them because she found their cooing to be very soothing. I found Dave's attitude annoying. I wonder what happened to all those pigeons when we left Lakewood ...?

Jim was in first grade at Lake City Elementary at this point. He decided one Wednesday that it was "Backward Day" for him. So he put all his clothes on backward and did everything he could, like walking, backward. I'm not sure he could quite grasp talking backward, but even so, Mom got a call from the principal. Mom's response was, "I'm not worried about it; if he's not hurting anyone, let him do it!" And he did continue every Wednesday with his backward days. I don't think he started a trend or anything like that.

Jim had another significant memory from that year, but this time it involved Rachel. Their "head over heels" memory of Lakewood involves Rachel's bicycle and Mom having told the two of them,

"No," to doing this. They went on a bike trip on a sunny Saturday; Rachel was eight years old and Jim was six—just right for riding on the rear fender of her bike. They rode around for a long time that day and were on the way home when they came to a long hill that they had to push the bike up on the outward leg of their trip. Jim had been looking forward to the fast, smooth glide back down that hill, but Rachel was less excited—and a bit nervous. She warned Jim, "If traffic forces me into the gravel and the handlebars start shaking real bad, we might fall." Jim often wonders if she can still prophesy with that same, great, understated accuracy.

Jim thought they must have been hurling down the hill at a speed of at least fifty miles per hour. They were forced into the gravel along the side of the road, and the handlebars didn't shake—they vibrated—and somehow that caused the front wheel of the bike to get turned to the side, causing the bike to skid and launching Jim head over heels, right over Rachel and skipping along the gravel on his head until coming to rest right in front of the bike; very fortunately for Jim, she didn't run over him! Even at that, there was blood running down his forehead. Kudos to Rachel, who responded immediately with all her emergency training. She got him up and walking—never let a person with a concussion fall asleep—and took him to the nearest house and knocked on the door. They frightened the lady who lived there, but she got them in her car and drove them home. Jim's head was hurting for a while, and in school the next week, he told his class that they should obey their parents because he had been told not to ride double. Jim still has the scar of that bike ride on his forehead at the hair line.

Another neighbor who helped get Jim to the hospital after that spill played the role of Santa Claus at a local store during the Christmas season. When we came home after sitting on Santa's lap around our first Christmas there, Jim said, "Santa sure did sound like Mr. Gleason." Jim had a scrape on his head and cut on his elbow from that bike wreck. Mom called Mr. Gleason to see if he could drive them to the hospital, which he did. While Mr. Gleason was driving Mom and Jim to the hospital that time, Jim kept saying, "Hurry up, Mr. Gleason, before it's too late." The poor man was a nervous wreck by the time he got them back home. As Jim recalled it, all this intensity could have been avoided if Mr. Gleason would have just hooked up Rudolph, Dancer, Prancer, Dasher, Donner, Blitzen, Vixen, Comet, and Cupid to the sleigh; Rudolph would have gotten us there quickly, no problem!

Boating on Puget Sound

There were lakes nearby, and Puget Sound was close. Just about everyone in the area had a boat, so Dad bought our first boat. It was a Chris Craft wooden hulled boat, probably fourteen or sixteen feet in length. People around the Sound today revere their wooden-hulled boats; they even have a festival in their honor.

Us at Puget Sound Beach, 1961

We went waterskiing on Mother's Day that first year we had the boat, and it was so cold that we were all shivering and covered with goose bumps, but it didn't faze us. Our first waterskiing adventure on Puget Sound was a whole lot of fun! Other than our trips to and from Japan on a great big troop ship, none of us had ever been on a boat before this—well, except for Dan and Dave's little adventure in Taiwan.

Dad loved to fish, and having so much water—both fresh water and salt water—so close was really the best. One time Dad and a buddy were out on Puget Sound fishing, and a huge whale surfaced suddenly alongside them. Then it gave them a shower with its blowhole. You don't have that experience every day! The Chris Craft headed for shore instantaneously! Apparently, it was an experience Dad didn't need to repeat: that Chris Craft never saw the Sound again, well, at least not in Dad's possession. He sold it right away!

It rained a lot in the area where we lived. It rained often in Taiwan, too, but not like this. Even in June, it would be so foggy and misty that the temperature wouldn't get above fifty degrees until noon. But fog, mist, and rain make everything grow lush and beautiful, according to Mom. There weren't any flies or mosquitoes and no electrical storms. In winter, of course, we had a good bit of snow. Weather, among many things, was quite a change for us, having just come from a tropical island. But like many things growing up Army, it was just one of many differences to which we all adjusted quickly and without a thought.

CHAPTER 13
LEAVING FORT LEWIS AND LAKEWOOD, 1961

Dad began to be called "old man" by the soldiers at the motor pool at Fort Lewis. He was the head sergeant there. He didn't like the old man thing and didn't like the soldiers dealing with him like he was too over the hill to do things for himself. Dad was a good soldier and took his work very seriously. Toward the end of the old man's second year at Fort Lewis, in April 1960, he was promoted to master sergeant (E-8) and then got orders to be in Bamberg, Germany, at the end of September. It didn't look very promising that we would follow him due to concerns of rising issues between the United States and the Soviet Union. These concerns had escalated after the failed Bay of Pigs invasion and the subsequent US placement of ballistic missiles in Italy and Turkey. Our placement of those missiles resulted in a buildup of ballistic missile capabilities by the Soviets in Cuba.[89]

Rachel (age nine) was very upset about Dad being away from us and that we were not permitted to go with him, so she wrote a letter to President Kennedy, to which she actually got an answer. The response wasn't very encouraging, but we were able to go the following summer, in July of '61.

Sometime after Dad left for Bamberg, Dan (seventeen) and Dave (fourteen) made a game of throwing the little red berries from our holly trees at each other. Mom told them to stop but they ignored her so she went out to spank them. Dan and Dave were bigger than Mom by then, and Dad had always been the designated administrator of spankings. People driving by laughed at Mom for trying to spank them, and when Dan and Dave noticed this, they quit their game. No way were they going to have anyone laughing at Mom!

Dan was a senior when Dad headed for Germany, and he realized he wasn't going to have enough credits to graduate—by a whopping half a credit. He was taking a class in radio and TV broadcasting at the technical center, which he really liked. It took half of the school day, but he only got half a course credit for it. To graduate that year, Dan would have had to drop that class and take some other full-credit course. Even though he knew it, he wouldn't change classes and therefore didn't graduate. Dan said: "I guess I showed 'em. Again!" This is somewhat reminiscent of a seventh grader we know deciding that reading novels was much more educational than doing his homework!

I was in seventh grade, at Mann Junior High, when Dad left for Germany. I was still in the orchestra, but now playing the cello. As the only cello player in the orchestra, I knew I would be first chair in that section. Take that, Nils!

I borrowed Dan's old blue bike that he used to deliver newspapers, which had a great big wire basket on the front. I'm guessing he didn't know I used it too. That's how I carried my cello home and back to school any day that I needed to practice when Mom didn't have the car to transport me. That must have been some sight: me and my eighty pounds on that big bike with a great big cello in the basket.

We had our orchestra concert near the end of the year. Mom came to see it, and I was really excited about that. It was difficult for Mom and Dad to attend many of our school functions, simply because there were so many of us, and thereby just as many school functions to attempt to attend as well as the need for someone to take care of the rest of the kids at home. The cello is, of course, just one of many instruments in an orchestra, so after the concert I asked Mom if she could hear me playing. She said, "Of course I could hear you. You were wonderful!" Truthfully, I had a few doubts regarding both of her responses, but it was nice to hear her say it.

My English class had only three boys in it along with a bunch of girls. That was a new and somewhat exhilarating experience for a seventh-grade boy: three boys and all those girls! I think the teacher had an idea just how exhilarating the three of us might have found that situation. The students' desks were lined up in a U shape around the room, and the three boys all had to sit together at the end closest to the teacher's desk. Oh, well. We would have to interact with the girls at lunch, I guessed. Besides, the pencil sharpener was up near the teacher's desk, so I couldn't have used any of Dave's tricks to check out the girls.

In that same class, we had to diagram sentences, and it was a task I really didn't like, which must have shown in my work. One day the teacher told me, "Bob, you don't have to diagram any more sentences. You have excellent writing abilities, and I don't think you need the 'help' that diagramming would offer." He ranks as one of my all-time favorite teachers! Can you imagine telling a kid he doesn't have to diagram sentences anymore? That would rank pretty close to not having to do fractions, although I never had a teacher offer that option. Two happy, memorable teacher experiences in Lakewood.

Interestingly, I majored in English in college, and we did big-time sentence diagramming in one of those classes. I disliked it even more, but learned to do it because good grades had become much more important. As a student and later a teacher, I never saw any purpose in diagramming sentences, so when I taught English in high school and middle school, I never made my students diagram. I have no doubt there are English teachers who would love to argue with me over that issue.

Sorting Out Overseas Schooling, 1961

When we found out that we were going to be able to join Dad in Germany, Dad checked into the schools that would be available. The dependents' school in Bamberg was only for kindergarten through eighth grade, so high schoolers had to board away from home at the

Nürnberg American High School, which was about forty miles away, during the week and could come home on weekends. Mom, Dad, and Dan decided Dan would stay with Mom's folks in Manitowoc and retake his senior year there. This suited him and was good for Glamich since Grampa Archie was in a wheelchair.

When it was nearly time for us to leave, Mom put our house on the market and had no trouble selling it. A retired pastor with a large family bought it, and we were soon on our two thousand-mile trip to Wisconsin. We had most of the summer and were going to spend a lot of that time with Glamich and Grandpa Archie.

As we were preparing to leave Lakewood, Dave was experiencing a change in his previous ease and comfort with moving. He was twelve years old when we got there and fifteen when we left the shadow of Mt. Rainier and headed for Bamberg, Germany. This time, he was feeling the loss of leaving behind people he had built relationships with. He was growing up, maturing, liking girls—not that liking girls was new for him. He's not sure the girls were overly concerned about his departure though.

I have to admit, for me, it was just what it was (again). We were moving.

Dan shared the driving, and we made good time, even though we stopped often to rest and see the sights. Some of the states didn't have speed limits, which bothered Mom when Dan was driving because he didn't seem to believe in speed limits either. Mom would make Dan stop driving from time to time, and she would drive. That said, it's one reason we made good time!

We hadn't planned it, but one afternoon we happened to be on Highway 16, which went right past Mt. Rushmore and its famous residents. After we got out and enjoyed that awesome sight, our car had mechanical problems. We were close to a small town with a car repair garage, so we got a day's reprieve from traveling; that never hurts! To us, the western towns looked like you would see in a cowboy movie. We didn't have air-conditioning in the car, mostly because pretty much nobody had it at that time. Rachel wondered how Dave could wear his hot-looking letter jacket all the way across the country.

After several days' travel, we arrived in Manitowoc. This time, Mom's folks were living in a one-bedroom house with an unfinished attic. We all bedded down in the attic, which was accessed by a ladder that came down into the kitchen. Our nighttime bathroom facilities consisted of, literally, a pot to pee in. This was our second outhouse experience. Personally, I wasn't all that thrilled about the outhouse thing. Indoor plumbing has its benefits. Smell, temperature, smell, smell … that sort of stuff. The whole idea of all that "stuff" down there … well, we'll leave it at that. One interesting thing is that it was a two-seater. I really don't think any of us went in there at the same time.

Grampa Archie was not at all well. One day a prayer group came to the house, and we all assembled in the bedroom while they prayed and prayed for "Archie." After we said our "amens" and as they were leaving, eight-year-old Jim said, "I hope this Archie, whoever he is, gets better." We didn't call him Grampa Archie; we just called him Grampa.

The summer of '61 was the last time any of us German-bound Brats or Mom got to spend time with Grampa Archie. Rachel was summoned by him many times to come in the house and do something for him because he wanted "Rachie." She's glad he wanted her and glad we all had that summer and that memory.

I think the stress of watching Grampa deteriorate got to us, though I don't think we recognized it then. An elderly woman was walking down the street in front of Glamich and Grampa Archie's house one morning. A bunch of us were out there messing around in the street, mostly just being us, playing, arguing with each other over some stupid point of order of the game we were playing, just being noisy Brats. The old lady was walking by and said something like, "Hmph! All of you children living in that little house! Hmph!"

Well, that really ticked us off! This old bag had just totally shown disrespect to *our* Glamich! We came right back at her and let her know beyond a shadow of a doubt that this was *our* Glamich and *nobody* disrespected her. I mean, we were a bunch of sassy-mouthed Brats!

This was very much not how we were taught to talk to adults by Sgt. and Jinny Mae Heath. Somehow, it seemed okay this time. It seemed like it was exactly what we should have done. We even bragged to Mom about telling off that old bag. As far as I can remember, Mom approved. The old lady hustled her old bustle on down the street. We never saw her again. I guess she wasn't going to put up with all of us ill-mannered children. Hmph!

Before we left Glamich and Grampa Archie for Germany, we had an opportunity to visit Aunt Max and Uncle Punk, which for most of the Brats was a new family experience. Aunt Max was the youngest of the eight girls and three boys in Glamich's family, and it was very rare that we ever visited any of them. As far as I can remember, this may have been the only time we ever were with them.

Dart 2.0

In Manitowoc, we would frequently walk down to Lake Michigan. Dan, Dave, Mike, and I were walking along, and one of us found a dart. This is a little bit of scary déjà vu, thinking back to Dart 1.0. This dart had white plastic feathers.

There we were, walking along, on our way to the lake, and we had a dart. What could go wrong? We were walking behind a school building that had a loading dock right off the road in the back of the school. The driveway to the dock had a sloped, grassy bank on each side. We decided to stop there for a rest. Two of us sat on one bank, and the other two sat on the other. Mike was opposite me. I had the dart. I threw it over at Mike, sticking it into the grassy bank between his legs. He threw it back, sticking it in the bank between mine. Cool game! So back and forth it went a few times. A very few times. About the fourth time back at Mike, I stuck it directly into his thigh. His eyes got big, and he grabbed the dart and yanked it out. After he removed the dart, we went on down to the lake, dart hole in the thigh and all. It was, thankfully, our last dart episode. The place where the dart stuck in Mike's leg never got washed or otherwise sanitized, except maybe while we splashed around in Lake Michigan. He never complained. I'm pretty sure the dart was left on that grassy bank for some other bright, young kids to play with.

Glamich, Dave, Bob and Smokey, 1961

One of our favorite pastimes was to go fishing in Lake Michigan, but prior to going fishing we had to come up with some bait. Nothing was better for bait than crawdads, and the best place to get crawdads was in the streams around Glamich's house. We would set out in the morning with an old sheet, hiking through fields of corn that was way over our heads. Once we got to the stream we would wade in, stretch the sheet out between us, and drop it to the bottom of the stream. We'd hold it there for a while and then pull it up, let the water drain out, and take it to the bank and dump the crawdads into a bucket. We would then pull the bloodsuckers off our legs and wade back in to get another haul. Once we had a load of crawdads, it would be back to Glamich's to fetch our lunch and bamboo fishing poles, and off we would go to catch some fish. I have no recollection as to who knew of this way of catching bait for fishing. Furthermore, who knew there was anything called a crawdad, or where we would find some? It was a great summer of playing in the fields, streams, and lakes of Wisconsin.

Our port call came, and we had to say goodbye to Glamich, Grampa Archie, and Dan. We would never see Grampa Archie again. It was good for them to have Dan there to help though.

This time, Mom was the lone driver, and our first stop was New Castle, Pennsylvania, close to six hundred miles away, where we spent a few days with Aunt Pat and Uncle Phil and our cousins. There should be no doubt Aunt Pat got our loud, "AUNT PAT, I GOTTA GO POTTY!" when we arrived.

Mom and Dad's friends from our Taiwan days, the Johnstons, were stationed in New Jersey, another four hundred miles east, where we would get the car on its way and catch our flight to Germany. Along the way to New Jersey, a long trip in our old Ford wagon loaded with Brats, we rarely missed an A&W Root Beer stand. The first night on the road, after checking into a motel on the highway, we went out to supper at a local diner. In addition to a café, they had a bowling alley and trampoline bouncing place. I don't think any of us had ever seen a trampoline before, so we stood and watched other kids jump on them for a while. Then back to the diner where we all got our fill of hot dogs and hamburgers, along with a promise of ice cream before we left. Most of the Brats went back to look at the trampolines.

To eight-year-old Jim, however, the trampolines were a bit too one-dimensional to hold his interest. Instead, he went into the bowling alley and apparently got engrossed in that, losing all track of time. That is, until he recalled the promise of ice cream! He jumped up and ran out to the trampolines, looking for the rest of the Heath Platoon. Nowhere to be seen. He then ran out to the parking lot; no car. Then into the diner where there was no one but the cook.

"Do you know where my mom is?" he asked, tearing up.

"That bunch in the Ford station wagon left about ten minutes ago. Were you with them?"

Jim, now crying, responded, "But I didn't get any ice cream!" Even rising third graders must keep their priorities straight.

Mom rarely missed a head count, and we don't know what happened that night for sure, but riding down the road to the motel she saw Mike in the back seat with two ice cream cones. When she asked him why he had two cones, he said, "Jim didn't want his." At that moment Mom invented the technique of power sliding a Ford station wagon into a 180-degree turn because she knew Jim was not in the car.

That cook was pretty smart too. He figured out the best way to quiet a lost and left-behind kid was to give him enough ice cream to cause a permanent brain freeze. It gave Jim something else to think about until the Brat wagon came back for him before much time had passed. Jim was safe, back in the car, happily eating his ice cream, and we headed back to the hotel once again. Wait a minute … did Mike get to keep *both* ice cream cones?

The next day we arrived in New Jersey, and Johnny Johnston went with Mom to take our car to the port for shipment, and the next day, he took the family to the airport for our flight. That was not the last time we saw the Johnstons; they remained good friends to our family.

Our previous overseas adventures had been in Asia. This time it would be Europe. Dad finally got his request for his duty assignment to Europe. Our plane landed in Gander, Newfoundland, because of engine problems. We left there after dark, and there were large areas of forests on fire, which we could see from the airplane.

We made another stop in Ireland for fueling, and when we finally got to Frankfurt, we were completely socked in with fog: frightening for Mom; exciting for the Brats. We landed safely, but when we got to the waiting room, we didn't see Dad at first.

Rachel recalled, "I could hardly wait to see Dad—there he was, not even looking for us. He was reading the newspaper. But then I saw his smile, and I knew the truth!" He jumped up, and we barely had time to say hello before rushing to the train station. We just managed to catch our train, and later we had to rush to change trains. The sergeant had it all planned down to which Brat would carry which bag.

Hallo, Deutschland!

CHAPTER 14
BAMBERG, GERMANY, 1961–1962

We arrived in Bamberg mid-July 1961. It was a pretty town on the Regnitz River with a population of about 85,000 when we lived there. We were billeted in a large apartment complex and were lucky to have a sparkling clean first-floor apartment. When moving out, people moaned and groaned about the strict cleaning policy the military had, but it really was great to move into an apartment that was spotless.

Our arrival was ten months after Dad got there; the delay was due to the tensions between the United States and the Soviet Union over East/West Germany. The United States, British, and French occupation forces were in West Germany, and the Soviet Union occupied East Germany following the end of World War II. Bamberg was only about forty miles south from the East German border and about 250 miles from the center of the tension, Berlin. Many of the people living in East Germany did not want to live under Communist Soviet rule, and tens of thousands of them were leaving to live in West Germany. The Soviets didn't like that all those people were fleeing to the West, and one month after we arrived in Bamberg, the infamous Berlin Wall was being built to stop the exodus. Needless to say, the building of the wall didn't ease tensions at all.[90]

It took two months for our household goods to arrive, and we never knew why it took so long. Dave made up his own song about it, which mentioned the bottom of the deep blue sea, and he teasingly sang it to Mom often. Our "belongings" mostly consisted of our clothing and Mom's sewing machine. Fortunately, the apartment was fully furnished, which was the norm for dependents' housing. Being out of the United States meant that we were once again without a TV, but I doubt any of us missed it. After all, we had a whole new country with a different language, customs, food, and countryside to explore! Who needs TV?

Dan was enrolled in school back in Manitowoc, living in the attic of Glamich's house. As he said, "Because I only needed one half of one stinking little credit to graduate from high school, this was a unique experience—I could take anything I wanted to! So I took algebra because I liked it, but hadn't done well before. This time, I got an A in it. I took Spanish again and did well. I really enjoyed being in school for the first time in my life, maybe because there was no pressure at all. I only needed that one little stinking half credit. Now, I guess I showed 'em for real." Dan was the only Brat to graduate from high school in the same town in which he was born, which is something very unique for our family.

Every day after school that fall, Dan worked in potato fields on a local farm while he finished high school. Dan rode on the harvesting machine, pulling clogs out of the machine and picking up good potatoes that fell on the ground, then throwing them back in the truck. He helped unload the big bags of potatoes off the truck, and after the unloading was over each day, the guy who was in charge had cases of beer for everyone to drink until they couldn't drink any more. Dan would usually drink a beer or two, then go home.

After all the potatoes were harvested, he worked at the Mirro Aluminum Factory, where they made the handles and knobs for pots. Dan ran the plastic machine and was the second-best plastic machine runner they had. The foreman begged him not to go in the Army after he graduated so he could stay there making plastic knobs for the rest of his life. Dan was pretty sure there was something better out there for him. Every Friday night, Glamich and Dan would have what they called their end of the week "fix" once she got home from work. They would split a beer to chase a shot of brandy.

Dan did a funny but kind of mean thing to Grampa Archie that year: "I had a stereo with a big speaker. I figured out that I could use a speaker as a microphone, a trick I learned from my friend Raleigh in Washington. Anyway, I rigged my speaker to the speaker in Grampa's TV down in the living room. I would talk to him during his TV shows, and it drove him crazy! He couldn't figure out where that was coming from. This little trick didn't make Glamich too happy though." The "microphone" was quickly disassembled.

Dan and a friend on horses in Ethiopia, 1961

After graduation, Dan determined that he wasn't interested in being drafted into the Army and being assigned to an infantry unit. Instead, he volunteered to enlist and got trained to be a Morse code intercept operator. He wound up at Kagnew Army installation near Asmara, Ethiopia, attached to the United States Army's 4th Detachment of the Second Signal Service Battalion. He recalls that this was known as a listening station and was on a mountain at 7,300 feet above sea level close to the equator. The altitude in addition to the huge 2,500-acre antenna farm made this location ideal for listening to and typing the Morse code signals his radio was able to pick up from nearby African and Arabian countries. These were translated and used to determine activities that might be going on in those areas. This was all part of the Cold War buildup between the United States and Soviet Union.[91]

You might notice in the picture of Dan on the horse that his blue jeans look scuffed up at the knee. Not long before this picture was taken, he and the horse had been riding merrily along in a ditch, when suddenly they came upon a culvert. For some reason, this spooked the horse, and it came to an abrupt halt, throwing Dan over the horse's head. Undaunted, Dan jumped back up on the horse and continued riding into downtown Asmara, where the picture was taken.

School Away from Home

When we arrived in Bamberg, Dave was going into the tenth grade. As Dad learned, Bamberg had no American high school for him to attend. So every Sunday night around 6:00 p.m., Dave and the other high school Army Brats would gather at a bus stop and be transported to Nürnberg, Germany, to dormitories where they would spend the week while attending Nürnberg American High School. The trip to Nürnberg wasn't bad, Dave said. He remembers that a guy named Herb and his girlfriend, Mary, really liked the bus ride. Herb was a high school letterman on the football team, and he and Mary would put his letter jacket over their heads and make out all the way to and from Nürnberg. At that time, Dave thought such public displays of affection were pretty gross, but he later changed his mind. Dave's memories of Nürnberg revolve mostly around the dormitory, rather than academics.

"Not a lot of kids my age got to live in a dorm away from their parents," Dave said. "One of the guys in the room across the hall from me, Willy, had a nice radio, and he kept it tuned to the BBC for all the latest hits. I will never forget that very British radio voice crackling through the air announcing, 'You're listening to the BBC, and now, here are the Beat-els singing, "It's Been a Hard Day's Night!"' and Willy would crank up the volume so we could all enjoy the music."

In the fall of that year at Nürnberg, the guys played tackle football out in the yard of the dorm, without pads, of course. Toward the end of the season Dave had to stop playing because he hurt his shoulder trying to tackle the ball carrier when someone else behind him tried to help with the tackle.

"The collision caught my upper arm and shoulder with the runner going in one direction and the tackler behind me going in the other direction. It hurt pretty bad, but I must have recovered because that spring, I went out for wrestling and could climb a fifty-foot rope, arm over arm, while holding my legs out horizontally in front of me."

Just before Christmas break that year, Dave picked up a bout of hepatitis, possibly in the school cafeteria; they called it yellow jaundice. His skin and eyes turned yellow, symptomatic of the disease. Unfortunately, hepatitis is very contagious, and while at home, he passed it on to Mike and me before he returned to school, where it was quickly recognized by school staff, and he was promptly admitted to the Army hospital. According to Dave:

> This was a low and somewhat scary time for me. I was all alone in the hospital with grown-ups all around, but no one that I knew. Kids from school couldn't come and see me, and my parents were tied up with the plague I had left at home and couldn't come and see me. I don't remember them even calling me during that time. Up until then, it did not bother me to have my blood drawn, but one day that all changed and took me years to get over. One afternoon, a very large medic, wearing the white jacket that medical people wear, sort of backed into the room through the doorway. He was carrying a tray of other test-tube samples of blood he had drawn from other patients that afternoon, and they were rattling in the holder as he came in the room. When he turned around facing me to prepare my forearm to draw my blood, his jacket was crimson with blood spilled down the front of it! All the blood drained out of my face, and I felt weak. I'm not sure why that affected me that way. After that, all I wanted to do was get out of that hospital and get home.

The rest of the family had to have shots, as did all my and Mike's classmates at school, none of whom were happy about it. Jim said there was no way they were giving him a shot. He was so belligerent and did so much squirming and squalling that the medics put him in a strait jacket—and he did get the shot! After several weeks at home, we were cleared to go back to school, and life became more normal again.

Neighborhood Doings

Not only was Dad one of the lead enlisted men at his motor pool in Germany, he was also assigned to be building coordinator in our apartment buildings in both Bamberg and, later, Heidelberg. His job was to try to keep peace and see that folks behaved.

On the second floor in the apartment directly above us, there was a dad who was a "Bible disciplinarian." He would beat his little kids while holding and quoting the Bible, loudly. When it came to Dad's attention, he told the man that there would be no more of that. I know, it does seem a little contradictory considering Dad's disciplinary methods, but I think it had more to do with the loud Bible-yelling than the spankings.

Mike recalled that the family was nearly as large as ours. But, he said, "The size of that family was where any similarities ended. While all of us were skinny, those kids were emaciated. We wore hand-me-downs; they wore *our* hand-me-downs. The mother was scraggly and worn out. There was a sadness to that little family that was hard to miss. I don't ever recall seeing the father of that household …."

Rachel became good friends with another fourth-grade girl who lived on the third floor of our building. Jane really liked french fries, and Mom sometimes made them for lunch. We all walked home from school for lunch every day, and one day Jane stopped in to wait for Rachel and enjoy a few fries. When they stepped out of the door, Jane's mom was standing at the entrance to the building, looking out toward the street. Jane acted terrified, jumped back inside the door, and said, "Mom doesn't want me stopping at anyone's home!" So our mom opened the large dining room window at the back of the apartment, and Rachel and Jane jumped out and ran merrily off to school. Jane reported that she didn't get a spanking or anything, so apparently no harm was done. Our mom was an aider and abettor to her escape. Isn't that what moms are for sometimes? Had Mom finished one-room school teacher training and gone on to teach, I think she would have been a very fun teacher.

We started school in the fall, and Rick (age five) was very happy because he finally got to go to kindergarten. It had been lonely for him when his best friend, Steve, was away in kindergarten the year before in Lakewood. Steve (now age six) went to first through third grades in Germany. In first grade, he had a weak bladder, which is still kind of a sore spot to him: "I would raise my hand to go to the bathroom, and the teacher would ignore me, thinking I was just trying to get out of class. I would occasionally go home with wet pants. Dad told me to tell them I had to go. I said, 'Dad, I tried! They just wouldn't listen!' You'd think the teacher would figure out that I wasn't bluffing after the first wet experience or two, but she didn't." I mean, the kid's in first grade, Ms. Teacher, and you're gonna make him sit there and wet his pants every day? I'm surprised Mom didn't jump in on this one.

Steve remembers the huge "capture the flag" games we played with lots of the neighbor Brats. We didn't have television or any kind of electronic devices, so it was easy to find lots of kids who wanted to do anything fun. Steve said:

> Capture the flag was a game where each team had a flag that they put in a particular spot and protected it from the other team. We had a dividing line between our two territories. If anyone was caught across the line, they could be captured by any member of the other team and taken to prison, where they were kept until the game was over or someone snuck in and tagged them without being captured. Then they would all be free to go back to their side. The goal of the game was to capture the other team's flag and get it back to your side without getting caught and to protect your flag in the process. One time, I saw Dave dressed up like a woman sneaking through the line, and he got away with it and got their flag. Looking back, it was a fitting game for a bunch of military Brats in Germany during the Cold War.

Due to this Cold War, Dad was often gone for as much as a month when his unit went out on maneuvers. *Maneuvers* were times when the US Army units would go out into the field and practice defeating Russians. At that time, it was presumed the Russians were poised on the eastern side of Germany waiting to pounce on the NATO soldiers. The Russians pretty much presumed NATO soldiers were poised to do the same to them.[92] Fortunately, it never happened.

Bamberg, located roughly in the center of Bavarian Germany, was built on seven hills, and the residents sometimes like to compare it to Rome. Bamberg is one of Germany's most picturesque medieval towns with narrow winding streets and quaint, ancient architecture. The city is divided into two boroughs by the Regnitz River. Bishop's Town is located on the west bank, and Burgher's Town is on the east bank. The really old parts of the city are called Bishop's Town.

Mrs. Ma'am

All this historical stuff was lost on my barely adolescent self in 1961. Here I was in Bamberg American School, in eighth grade language arts class minding my own business. I mean, *really* minding my own business. I was pretty good at that. As a student, I was highly compliant, your basic bump-on-a-log. At worst, I may have been gently tapping my pencil on the desk. I wasn't any kind of troublemaker or anything. The nine kids of Sgt. Heath were not troublemakers in school, for the most part. Sgt. Heath of the US Army made it very clear to us that we weren't to be troublemakers—not by threats or anything violent. We just *knew* not to be troublemakers, so we weren't. Mischievous, maybe; troublemakers, never. Well, unless the mischiefs were trouble.

The day I was sitting in language arts class minding my own business, my teacher, Mrs. Miller, asked, "Are you finished with your work, Bob?"

"Yeah," I replied, continuing to mind my own business, tap, tap, tap.

"What?" asked Mrs. Miller with a slight look of incredulousness on her face.

"Yeah, I'm done," said I. No tapping. As a matter of fact, I *was* done. I was just waiting for whatever we were going to do next.

"What did you say?" she demanded of me.

Bamberg American School, 1961

"I said, 'Yeah, I'm done,'" and looked up at her, pencil in my lap, out of sight.

She glared at me, clearly reviled at my very being, and yelled, "Get out!"

I was shocked! Get out? *Get out?* Me? I was minding my own business! Get out? Visions of Dad beating my butt were flashing in my head, but this time I had absolutely no idea why I was in trouble. I mean, *what* did I do wrong?

The only other time in all my school history, to that point, that I'd been sent out of class was second grade in Taiwan. That time, I was goofing around in class and knew I was in the wrong. I really caught it from Dad that time. There was no way I was interested in making him that unhappy again. And this time, I was minding my own business!

How can a teacher just throw a kid out of the room for minding his own business? Isn't there some kind of law about that? I didn't move to get out; I just sat there in shock, looking at her.

She yelled, "I said, Get out!"

By this time, it was apparent that she wasn't in any mood to negotiate the issue, whatever it was, so I got out of my seat and moved quickly to the door. On my way, I kept looking around at my classmates to see if I could pick up some clue as to my sin—nothing! No clues! They looked as shocked as I was. So out the door I went. Where was I supposed to go? This was really a new experience for me. Do I stand by the door? Go to the office? What exactly does "Get out!" mean? I wasn't sure where the office was in any case, so I decided to take my chances and just stand there by the door. All the while, I was thinking that if standing by the door was wrong, I was really going to catch it! Regardless, I just stood there, clueless in Bamberg, reviewing the facts of my case. The facts:

- I was given a worksheet to complete.
- I completed it.
- I was sitting quietly at my desk waiting for the next instructions.
- When asked if I was done, I responded that I was done.

Finally, class was over, and the other kids began coming out the door. I asked a couple of them, "What did she send me out here for? What'd I do?"

Several of the kids shrugged their shoulders and rolled their eyes. Then one of them said, "You didn't say 'ma'am' to her."

I was more shocked than ever. *Ma'am?* Who says, "ma'am" to someone? My Mom and Dad from the Midwest never said that to anyone, nor had I ever been expected or asked to address anyone that way. Well, that's not exactly true—Dad said "sir" to colonels and majors, and "ma'am" if they were lady colonels and majors, but not to just normal people. I was quite baffled by this whole scenario. Surely if Mrs. Miller expected this, she should have told us! I'm sure—I *think* I'm sure—she didn't. I don't know how this got by me. Some of the other kids seemed to know about this ma'am thing, but it was news to me.

Mrs. Miller gave me a note to take home, which I'm sure described in detail my egregious sin for my parents. She didn't say much of anything to me and was actually kind of snippy about it. I was afraid to open my mouth to ask her what was going on.

I gave the note to Mom—not giving up the note in second grade didn't turn out well, so I wasn't repeating that mistake! Well, Mom read the note and calmly said that she would go to see the teacher the next day. That was the absolute last I ever heard of that incident, except that I was instructed by Mom to address Mrs. Miller as "ma'am." I kept waiting to get my butt cut by Dad's belt, but nothing. That always surprised me. Apparently, my parents just agreed I was not in the wrong and quietly corrected it. Sometimes, when it comes to kids, the less said, the better. Mrs. Miller never brought it up again, but I can assure you, she was Mrs. Ma'am to me from that day on! Apparently, she was from Alabama, and that's what they do there.

The Nuclear Threat

My first introduction to the nuclear threat was there, in Mrs. Miller's class. Both the United States and Russia had developed nuclear arms by this time. Both countries were engaged in arms posturing and were very nervous about the other's ability to deliver nuclear warheads to the other side.[93] As a result, Bamberg American School began to have nuclear bomb drills. I remember being a bit unsettled by this, even as a brain-dead middle schooler. We were instructed to get under our desks and to refrain from looking toward the windows at the bright light of the bomb's detonation, should that happen. Upon those instructions, all students, including me, would respond, "Yes, ma'am, Mrs. Miller!"

In retrospect, I'm quite sure that if we could have seen the bright light of the detonation, we might as well have enjoyed looking at it while we could. I don't think the desks or windows would have helped us much. We had these drills frequently throughout our time in Germany.

Forty-five years later, on Mount Charleston outside of Las Vegas, I stopped at an overlook some six thousand feet up and could see a big section of the Mojave Desert. There, I found a placard describing this spot as an observation point for onlookers to see early above-ground nuclear detonations that took place in the Frenchman Flats area of the Mojave during the fifties. I was struck by the fact that people actually came to sightsee nuclear detonations. As it turns out, they didn't really have to go up on Mt. Charleston to see them. They could see them from downtown Las Vegas, a mere sixty-seven miles away. I have often wondered what aftereffects the onlookers may have experienced, being that close to nuclear explosions.

The Sled Race

We lived in a four-story apartment building, and there were lots of them distributed around the housing area. Up the road from our housing area were the officers' housing apartments, which looked the same as ours. Behind a couple of those buildings was a pretty steep, wide hill, with trees at the top; when it snowed, the hill became sled heaven for the area's Brats.

We had a couple of those good old Yankee Clipper sleds with the two red sled rails. The seat was several wooden slats, with a wooden T near the front. You pushed the T to one side or the other to make the sled turn toward the left or right. The brakes were your toes, which you would drag into the snow to stop or slow down. Stopping or slowing down on purpose wasn't a frequent event. We could start our sled up in the trees, which provided a little extra excitement, swerving back and forth to avoid them.

It snowed one weekend, nice and fluffy and deep. It was great snow for all purposes, especially sledding. I managed to get my hands on one of the Yankee Clippers and was happily sledding down the hill, trudging back up, and sledding back down again. I was really having a good time, but as was always the case, I needed some kind of competition to make it really interesting. So I challenged one of my friends to a race to the bottom.

The hill was pretty high and maybe fifty yards long. At the bottom it leveled off a little, ending at the foundation of one of the officers' apartment buildings. We raced down the hill, and whoever won challenged for another go at it. This time, we were racing both for speed and distance. Whoever went farthest and got there first, would be declared the winner.

We slogged up the hill and drew a starting line in the snow. We both picked up our sleds, holding them to one side, and backed up as far as we could to the edge of the trees at the top of the hill. Then, ready, set, GO! We took off toward the starting line, jumped on our sleds on our stomachs, and flew down the hill. I had a slight edge on the other guy as we reached the bottom where it started to level off. I looked over to him, grinning, then, WHAM! Lights out. I woke up looking at the blue sky. The side of my face hurt, and when I touched it with my gloved hand, it stung. I was off to the side of my sled on my back, wondering what happened. I had run right into the back of the apartment building, and apparently, my cheekbone was my sled brake instead of my toes. That hurt! I had a black eye and scraped-up cheekbone for a couple weeks afterward. But, hey, I won!

Another winter sport Rick talks about is when we would water down the sidewalk and driveway with a hose, let it freeze, then get big pieces of cardboard boxes and slide down the ice. We weren't thinking about how much fun those slick driveways might be for the drivers of any cars that might come along ... we were just growing up Army.

CHAPTER 15
HEIDELBERG, GERMANY,
AND THE FINAL BRAT, 1962–1964

D ad had been reassigned to the USA Garrison (3804) in
Heidelberg, which is about 160 miles west of Bamberg in May
of 1962, and we made the move right after school got out. It
is home to the Heidelberg Schloss (castle) and to Germany's oldest
university (founded in 1386). Somehow, Heidelberg had managed to
avoid Allied bombing during WWII, so all its ancient architecture
was intact. The castle, the oldest sections dating back to the eleventh
century, overlooks the town and the Neckar River.[94]

A painting of Heidelberg Castle

The Karl-Theodor Bridge crosses the Neckar River to the castle and has spanned the river since the sixteenth century.[95] It has a twin tower gate and is very impressive. On the two times the castle is lighted each year—when darkness falls, and all the neighboring homes and businesses turn out their lights, and candles are lit in each castle window—the castle appears to be in flames and is absolutely beautiful.

Steve said, "They shot off fireworks; nothing I've ever seen [in the United States] can compare. They had fireworks coming out of the bridge supports and coming out of the castle. It was up on a hill, which made it spectacular. It's why I'm not impressed with fireworks displays here in the US. No one here has the layout for fireworks like that castle."

Heidelberg has a truly ancient history—six hundred thousand years, which is the approximate age of Heidelberg man, whose jawbone was discovered in 1907 at nearby Mauer. It is one of the earliest pieces of evidence of archaic human life in Europe.[96] You would think I would have learned that little piece of information when going to school there, but I didn't. I might have been showing a movie in the coach's class when that was taught, as will be explained later.

The US Army arrived in Heidelberg right after the end of World War II in 1945 and had about 16,000 military and civilian personnel working there[97] when my family arrived. The move allowed Dave to finish high school living at home, and he was very happy with that change.

"In summer of 1962, we transferred from Bamberg to Heidelberg, and that school year I started the eleventh grade at Heidelberg American High School," Dave recalled. "Of my years growing up Army, these were the most fulfilling, though they were not as full of wonder as the years in Taiwan were."

The area where we lived was called Patrick Henry Village, and nearly everything was close by: commissary, P.X., church, bowling lanes, theater, and the elementary school for the younger Brats. Everyone in grades seven through twelve rode the bus to Heidelberg American High School. Rachel, Jim, Steve, and Rick walked to the nearby elementary school.

In addition to being close to those things, another one of the perks of living in Patrick Henry Village was that the Army bakery delivered bread to our door, but it was never fresh. Mom had to wrap it in tinfoil and warm it in the oven to make it as good as fresh bread. That said, we had another source of bread which was even better—delicious German *Brötchen*. A German truck came through our area several days a week with these warm, crusty rolls, and they were really good.

One of the *not*-perks was, anytime we were in a foreign country, we had to mix our milk from a powder, and until this trip, the powder was always skim milk. They called it milk, but it wasn't very good. After a while, drinking the powdered milk was just the milk we had so, oh well, we just got used to it. In Germany we got whole milk powder, and it was somewhat more palatable and reputably better for us growing Brats. Maybe we can say it tasted a little better, but trust me, we were *very* happy to get real milk once we returned to the States!

A Near Miss

Going to school, we rode the bus from Patrick Henry Village to Mark Twain Village, another American housing complex not far away, where Heidelberg American High was located. Mike was in the seventh grade at the time of this close call:

> *The kids on this bus were out of control, and their favorite way of raising Cain was to shoot spit wads. But these weren't any run-of-the-mill paper spit wads; these were made from paper clips, and they hurt like the dickens when you got hit. One day we had a new kid show up at the bus stop, and he got on the bus with us. He didn't say much to anybody and made his way to the back of the bus. Everybody left him alone, and we proceeded to school with several of the kids acting up as usual, until we approached the motor pool. This day, the bus pulled into the motor pool and came to a stop in the middle of the lot. The door opened, and the motor pool sergeant got on the bus—guess who? Dad! The new "kid" got up, went to the front of the bus, and started pointing out the kids that had been causing the problems. Dad then*

proceeded to remove those kids from the bus. Their parents got a call, and they had to come pick them up. In the days leading up to this sting operation, Dad gave no warning or any indication that he knew what was going on. When he got on the bus, he never acknowledged any of our presence. However, I knew that if I had been pointed out, I would have been cooked until well done.

The new kid who got on the bus was actually a young-looking private in Dad's motor pool. This was a pretty clever sting operation, and it worked to settle things down on the bus for a while.

Ch-Ch-Changes

Germany was very different from Japan or Taiwan, needless to say. The Asian people were never rude; Mom found that was not true of the Germans. In one instance, Mom was looking in a pattern book in a very nice store in downtown Heidelberg when a woman tried to rip the book out of her hands. That would never have happened in Asia; they may have wanted the pattern book and might have felt like stabbing her in the back to get it, but they were always polite about it. That said, we did run around outside of our housing area quite a lot, very much like we did in Taiwan, and I never recall any instances in which the German people gave me or any of my siblings or friends any trouble.

I was fourteen when we first moved to Heidelberg, and I completed ninth and tenth grades there. It was during this time that I quit putting Brylcreem in my hair. Billy, a kid from North Carolina, moved into the area, and I thought he was pretty cool without the greasy hair. Girls seemed to think he was pretty cool too. I quit rolling up the short sleeves on my shirts then, too, thanks to Billy's example. The hairstyle and rolled-up sleeves were holdovers from copying my older brother Dan, when he became cool. Being cool was proving to be a moving target ....

At first our family was billeted in a fourth-floor apartment. There were no elevators in any of the buildings. The apartment was designed to be maids' quarters, so there were eight bedrooms. This meant that each of us Brats had our own room for the first and only time ever! Dad decided this would be a good time to have a clean room contest every week, reputedly because I couldn't blame Mike anymore for the mess in the bedroom. Each week, Dad would inspect all the rooms, and guess what? Rachel won every week! All the Brat guys were seriously in belief that there was some gender bias going on here. There was a cash prize at the end of the contest, and of course, Rachel got it.

"I think I frequently won the clean room contest mostly because no one else had ten or twelve dolls they could line up so nicely on the bed," Rachel recalled. "But, boys, remember this: I never once won after I became a teenager!"

Well, once she was a teenager, there was no time when we all had our own rooms anyway, except Rachel. That said, all of us gave all we had to have the absolute cleanest, neatest rooms with the most militarily made beds. I can expect that Dad was pretty proud of that.

We continued our rotation of Brats doing the dinner dishes, which began in Lakewood. Dad, Mom, and those not on K.P. would go for a walk around the village after dinner. The fourth-floor apartment had no good features other than all those bedrooms, and after a few months we moved to a regular apartment.

None of us liked giving up our private rooms, but Dad and Mom were happy when these permanent quarters became available—even though it was on the third floor, and there was still no elevator. Let's face it, stairs to the third floor are better than stairs to the fourth floor. It was great to have two bathrooms for a change, along with a large living and dining room and a nice kitchen. Because Dad was the ranking NCO in the building, we also had access to the attic room above us, which had one small room and a bigger open space. It made a great playroom on rainy days. For several months after our move to the third floor, a young German woman named Petra kept coming to our apartment asking if she could work for us. In return for her work, she would be permitted to have a room on the fourth floor of our building. This young lady really wanted that room, and she kept coming back. Mom and Dad finally let her do the ironing and some babysitting, but she never really earned her free rent as far as Mom was concerned.

Mike, who was thirteen at the time, maintains that, "Since Dad was the ranking NCO, he had the final say on these things. But, in this case, he goofed because she was a spy! She had blond hair, and she was pretty. She also worked as a phone operator on the American military phone system and dated an officer in the military police (MP). She had access to military communications, US police operations, and transportation logistics at the height of the Cold War. She was the spy who lived with us."

No evidence was ever presented to support these claims, or for whom she might be spying, but apparently Mike saw things in Petra the rest of us didn't. However, it could have just been his excuse for spending lots of hours watching her; she was pretty, after all.

Sports
During his junior and senior years at Heidelberg American High School, Dave got into sports, starting out with another go at football. After getting knocked on his tail several times in practice, he decided he was done with football. He then took up cross country and track and field. When he told Dad that he was going to try out for the high jump and hurdles activities, Dave was informed that he was too short to be any good at them. Dave saw this as a challenge and spent many extra hours practicing to be the best he could be. He became so good that he held the school record in both events. Pretty good for a short guy.

I followed Dave's lead in track, attempting high hurdles and the high jump, but being even shorter than he was, it was pretty obvious early on that I wouldn't excel in either of those events. So I went for pole vaulting—not much, if any better there. I was still a pretty short, skinny little guy. I finally wound up running the mile and half mile and usually placed third, fourth, or fifth in both.

I also played in a local football league. On the way to practice every day, I would meet one of my buddies, Mark, and we would practice tackling each other all the way to practice. Mark could really lay a bombshell of a tackle on me. I didn't play much, but in one game I was playing in the defensive backfield and the opposing quarterback launched a nice pass right in my direction. I took a few steps up, snagged the ball, and took off for the goal. Mark, who was also in as a defensive back, ran up in front of me, and yelled, "Follow me, Heath!" I did, and we gained about thirty yards after that interception. I actually got to play defense in a few more games after that, but apparently wasn't as good as the interception made me appear to be. I became closely reacquainted with the bench after that.

Movie, Anyone?

Ninth grade at Heidelberg American High is where I learned that there were ways to get out of class and not get in trouble. One way was to be a library helper and be trained to run the movie projectors. These were reel-to-reel projectors, and they were mounted on a fairly large cart. A library helper who could run the movie projectors was allowed to get out of one class to go to another and run the projector so the teacher there could show a movie. I would get the call, go to the library, roll the projector cart down to the class whose teacher wanted to show a movie, set up the film on the reels, and away it would go. The coaches' classes on Fridays were big movie days, and I got to enjoy lots of movies in the process. It was a highly specialized task, no doubt. It sure was fun missing all those classes, and it's probable that my grades reflected it. You'd have to go to a museum to find a reel-to-reel movie projector today, but I'll bet I could still run it.

Sad News

Near the end of 1962, we received two pieces of bad news from home: Mom's dad passed away the December before Pat arrived. Grampa Archie had been in a wheelchair for eleven years after his stroke and was only sixty-eight years old. Mom, unfortunately, wasn't able to go back to the States for his funeral.

Then, very shortly after that unhappiness, we learned that our cousin Jean Marie was on a plane that went down in the Pacific Ocean the previous summer. She was on her way home for summer break from a convent, where she was studying to be a Catholic nun. Her parents, Gene and Mayme, were stationed in Alaska. When Uncle Gene, Dad's oldest brother and also a lifer in the Army, got his duty assignment in Alaska, their family stopped by to visit us in Lakewood, Washington, on their way there. It was one of very few times we had the opportunity to visit with our cousins Jean Marie, Tim, and Brian and, sadly, our last time to visit with Jean Marie.

Keeping Busy in '63

Shortly after we moved down to our third-floor apartment, in February of '63, Mom, in her words, "started feeling yucky" and went to the doctor. Because the doctor didn't like sauerkraut, which he expressed to Mom, he thought it had to be caused by Mom eating that dreaded German dish. (It does make one wonder where this "medical professional" got his medical degree.) No thanks to him, it wasn't long before Mom knew the real reason for her discomfort: she was on her way to welcoming Brat Nine, Pat, in several months. This occurrence was a bit of a surprise, since it had been six years since Rick came along.

Pregnancy aside, Mom and Dad made some good friends and got involved in lots of activities, as we all did. The countryside was beautiful, and we went on frequent day trips and picnics along the Neckar River in the summers. We caught grasshoppers and threw them in the river and watched the fish come up and get them as they floated along.

"Dad brought some big truck tires, and all of us got in them and rolled down this big grassy hill to a flood plain on one of the picnics," Rick recalled. "I was looking out on the river after rolling down the hill and saw a big barge floating down with this butt-naked kid standing on the front of it. Weird!"

It *was* weird. To us. Experiencing all the differences in how other people lived has always been one of the great benefits all of us Brats express when talking about growing up Army.

Mom and Dad continued their interest in bowling and were in a league on the post with their friends, Alice and Ski. Alice designed their bowling shirts. One of Dad's favorite expressions was "ye gads," and they decided to call their team the "Ye Gads." On the shirts, "GADS" stood for Ginny, Alice, Dick, and Ski. Pretty clever. They were in a mixed league; Mom always had a good handicap, so they were happy to have her on their team.

Lago di Garda! Use Low Gear!

Right after we got out of school for our second summer in Heidelberg, we took a trip to Italy. Mom was five months pregnant with Brat Nine then. This was the only traveling vacation we took while in Europe. While it may seem that we would have traveled more, consider that it took more than just hopping in the car and taking off, especially overnight with seven children. For this trip, we loaded up the 1957 blue and white Ford station wagon, filling the roof rack with a borrowed tent, food, clothes, and camping gear, and we were on the way to Lago di Garda, Italy, a mere 450 or so miles away. The trip took us across the amazing Swiss Alps, and every time we would see a particularly high mountain peak, Dad would say, "There is the Matterhorn." Of course, it didn't take long before we were all saying, "Look, there's the Matterhorn!" In fact, it's pretty unlikely that we would have been able to see the Matterhorn as we crossed from Switzerland into Italy, but none of us, including Dad, had a clue. Our route took us a good two hundred miles west of that huge mountain. Even without the Matterhorn, the trip route was magnificently interesting, and we traveled through countries we had never visited before. We drove south through Garmisch coming out of Germany and into Austria and then Italy. We stopped in a beautiful little town, Oberammergau, Germany, just on the German side of the Alps—it was another incredibly beautiful spot. This was near the end of our first day on the road, and we were all tired and hungry. There was no sign of a camping site, but Dad saw a *Gasthaus* (an inn) nestled among the hills. He stopped and asked the people in the Gasthaus if we could pitch our tent next to it for the night, and they said we could. They might have thought we were all going to grace their Gasthaus for dinner, but we did another cookout by the tent.

Going into Innsbruck, Austria, there is a very long, steep hill, called the Scharnitz Pass, and part of the way down, our brakes gave out. Dave recalled:

> There were signs along the road that encouraged drivers to "use low gear," which apparently went unnoticed by Dad, the motor pool sergeant, during the descent. While we were going down the pass, I was wondering what those steep-incline, bumpy-looking ramps were for that appeared every half-mile or so off to our right. Meanwhile, Dad kept driving and using the brakes on the car to slow us down. Pretty soon, something smelled like it was burning, and Dad realized it was the brakes overheating. He came to that conclusion when the car wouldn't slow down and the brake pedal felt like mush under his foot when he pressed on it with all he had! Then we found out what those steep-inclined ramps were for as we bounced up one of them! They were turnoffs with steep banks at the end of them, and we were able to stop. After quite a few minutes, the brakes cooled enough, and we were able to limp into the next town and get them fixed.

On our way back to Heidelberg from Lago di Garda, at Mom's suggestion, we detoured that pass and went through Switzerland and then back into Germany. This was a longer route home than Dad wanted, but we didn't have any more brake issues.

We camped at Lago di Garda, a large lake not far from Verona, Italy. There was a US Army base near the beautiful, historic city of Verona, and the closest we got to it was the Officers' Club at the Army base to get some ice. I have often wondered as a grown-up why we passed up many opportunities in that area to see the Italian beauty and history. Not too far away from Verona is Venice, which would have been really interesting to visit too. At that time, Mom and Dad weren't all that aware of what a city like Verona or Venice might have had to offer them or their Brats. So we played and splashed around in the water at Lago di Garda—and had a great time doing it. It's a pretty good bet that things like history and historic beauty wouldn't have been nearly as much fun as playing around in the lake and camping to the Heath Platoon!

Steve, Dave, and Mike in Lago di Garda, 1963

Lago di Garda is a big lake, and even though we only saw the part where we camped and played during that week of vacation, the lake and the surrounding area was really beautiful. It wasn't much of a vacation for Mom though, at five months pregnant, trying to keep track of the Brats and keep us fed—and we were always hungry. There was a really nice man at the camp who had a rubber power boat and water skis, and he invited Dad and us to ski. That was the first and last experience that Dad had on skis. He submarined a few times before he gave up, but the older Brats really enjoyed it. Dad was completely exhausted that night, and he snored so loud that we heard some of the other campers the next day wondering who the snoring culprit had been. We didn't rat Dad out.

Steve, who was eight, remembers his first skiing adventure:

Everyone went waterskiing. Finally someone convinced me to try it. All we had were these skis that were twice as long as I was tall. I did go skiing; when the boat started pulling me I went right up; I didn't weigh anything. When we came back around, they told me to let go of the

*rope, so I did, and I coasted and coasted and finally stopped, and then
I finally sank into the water near the shoreline. Those skis were so big.*

For our family, driving over those incredible mountains, camping, skiing, swimming, and cooking out together was a truly great vacation, and one we all remember very fondly.

Summer Work and Play

The week after our return from Italy, Dave felt a need to earn some money and vigorously began looking for a job. He was dating Claudia at the time and believed he needed to expand his dating venues to keep her happy—and that required some income. As I've mentioned, if we wanted money, we had to find a way to earn it. Getting a real job as an American kid in Germany wasn't too easy. A lot of the jobs in our military installations overseas were filled by locals. Getting a job out on the economy might have been available, but not being fluent in German was a pretty major drawback to that option.

In spite of the difficulty of finding one, Dave managed to get a job during that summer in Heidelberg working in a snack bar on the military base. Dave, being the low man on the totem pole, was assigned to busing tables and washing dishes. Every now and then, when the soda jerk was on break, he would fill in for him. He would also stock the walk-in cooler or sweep the floor, all the while earning a whopping fifty cents an hour!

His least favorite job was cleaning the restrooms, especially the ladies room. He was pretty shy around women, and of course, they couldn't come in while he was cleaning. They would stand outside the restroom and ask him how long he was going to be, and then after a while, they would get cranky and yell at him to please hurry up! He would really break out in a sweat to get done when he knew they were getting impatient. Dave didn't regret it when summer was over and he was done with that job! He told us he heard line dancing got its start from the dancing outside the ladies' restroom.

When Dave got his job, I was also feeling the need for some income to support what I hoped would be activities involving girls. I really liked girls and wanted to find some ways to get to know more of them a whole lot better, like taking one on a date to a movie or something. I often went to the PHV Recreation Center on Saturday nights when they had dances, but I wasn't a great dancer like Dan, so my attraction to the girls through that venue was very limited. The Rec. Center is where I first heard the Beatles song "Twist and Shout" and where I learned to do the twist.

I determined that if I had some money, maybe that would help improve girls' interest in me. My friend Peter told me about a job he had just gotten, so I went to see about it and wound up helping him and some other kids put together and deliver the *Patrick Henry Village Newsletter* each week. It turned out that another one of my friends, Joey, was the son of the Army staffer who was assigned to put it out. We had to meet once a week and collate the pages of the newsletter by hand, then fold and stack them. Each of us had to collate and deliver our own, and we were each assigned certain apartment buildings in PHV. We had to go from stairwell to stairwell, apartment to apartment in several buildings to deliver the newsletters. I didn't make much money doing this, but it was certainly more than I had before!

"Ich bin ein Berliner"

In late June of '63, a motorcade sped through Patrick Henry Village. We were all told President Kennedy would be in that motorcade. I was there, as I'm sure most of the family was, but I never saw JFK. I saw a lot of cars, motorcycles, those little flags on the fenders, and all that, but I never saw JFK. But I've always had the thought that I was that close to him, for a very brief second as that motorcade whizzed by. That happened just before his famous speech in Berlin, titled "Ich bin ein Berliner." He really blasted the Russians in that speech on June 26, 1963, over their building of the Berlin Wall.[98] Everybody loved JFK and Jackie. Well, almost everybody.

Some Vivid and Poignant Memories

I also clearly remember experiencing a historic and educational treat one day during lunch not long after JFK breezed through PHV that summer. Our priest, Father McGuire, often came to our apartment for meals. Dad would ask him what he wanted to drink, and he always asked for "Munich tea," which is code for beer. As soon as we finished saying grace, Father would say, "I get first on seconds!"

Anyway, one day Father McGuire brought two young men who had just escaped from East Berlin. The young men spoke very little English, but Father McGuire was able to interpret some, and because we were taking German in school, we understood a little of what they said. Those young men had to swim to West Germany under gunfire to gain their freedom. So many people lost their lives trying to escape Communism during that time. We would hear about the attempts and number of lives lost on the radio on Armed Forces Network nearly every day.

Father McGuire wasn't the only one who would enjoy a little Munich tea. There was another adventure that summer I *vividly* recall. Well, maybe I *fuzzily* recall. It probably goes without saying that we were all still open to new adventures. There was a fence behind our housing area—not a very high one, and there were lots of holes in it. It separated, in a very miniscule way, our complex from the local German folks. There was a large field on the other side, and we could see German kids out there playing soccer. Sometimes, some of us would go over, under, or around the fence and play soccer with them. They were really great about inviting us into the games.

Beyond the field, there was a Hofbräuhaus, which served food and German beer. My friend Peter was aware that there wasn't a minimum drinking age limit in Germany. Peter's mom was from Norway, and they speak a language similar to German. I think this made learning German easy for him, because he was pretty fluent in it.

One Saturday evening near the end of summer, he said, "Bob, let's go over to the Hofbräuhaus and see if they'll sell us a beer."

I said, "What are you talking about?"

"There's a Hofbräuhaus over there; you know, a place where they have food and beer and stuff. Let's go!"

Well, Peter was my good friend, so off we went. This was toward the end of my second summer in Heidelberg, and we were both fifteen years old. We got to the Hofbräuhaus, walked in, sat at the bar, and the bartender asked, "*Was kann ich für Sie bekommen?*" (What can I get for you?)

Peter, without a blink, responded, "*Zwei Biere, bitte!*"

I understood a little but not all the interchange. The next thing I knew, the bartender put two large steins of beer in front of us. So there we sat, two small American fifteen-year-olds, sipping our large beers. It should be clearly understood that I had not consumed alcohol in any quantity other than those single sips Dad would give us in Pittsburgh from time to time. Now, I was drinking a *large* beer. Peter and I yacked with each other and laughed about being able to just walk over to the Hofbräuhaus and grab a beer. No one in the Hofbräuhaus seemed at all concerned about two young Americans sitting there drinking beer. After a while, we finished our beers, Peter paid the guy, and we stumbled home.

I was really stumbling! My head was spinning out of control, and I was very concerned about how I was going to conceal this from Mom and Dad! It's a little blurry, but I remember getting home, forcing myself to walk as straight as I could, spending a good bit of the rest of the evening in the bathroom, then going to bed. The next day, I said to my friend, "Peter, no more beer for me!" He laughed. We remained good friends.

★★★

While Peter and I were off getting hammered at the Hofbräuhaus, twelve-year-old Rachel was getting involved in much more intelligent "grown-up" activities. She had acquired quite a lot of childcare experience with her three younger brothers—skills she very much enjoyed. Rachel had also gotten some childcare practice when we took care of a little infant girl while her parents went to Italy twice, for about a week each time. The baby was under a year old. Rachel loved having that little girl around more than anyone and advanced the development of her babysitting skills while the baby girl was with us.

She got her first babysitting job that second summer in Heidelberg. As a sixth grader, she was quite young to take on that responsibility, but a neighbor-mom asked her just one question: "What would you do if there was a fire?" Rachel's answer: "I would grab the babies and run!" Perfect answer, and she got the job and continued that babysitting gig until we left Germany.

A Different Kind of Sting
Once that adventurous summer ended, we were back in school. In his eighth-grade year, Mike had a couple of unhappy incidents. The first one occurred one morning shortly after school began. We were on the bus headed to school, and apparently the effects of Dad's sting operation of the previous school year had worn off. Mike encountered a painful problem. A boy held a pencil on the seat, sharpened lead pointing up, just as Mike sat down. The lead broke, embedded in Mike's butt, and the kid was laughing his head off. Mike was really ticked off and had a very sore butt all day. Sitting in classes on those hard chairs with a hunk of pencil lead embedded in your butt is tough! Mom managed to get the lead out, and the next morning she handed Mike a note, giving him permission to beat up the kid if that was what he wanted to do. Mike went to school and jumped the kid, teaching him a lesson. Mom never heard anything about it from the school, and Mike never had to answer to anyone at school for it. The kid didn't give Mike anymore pokes in the butt, and hopefully, he didn't do it to any other kids either. These days, I don't think a note from Mom would get a kid out of trouble for beating up another kid, even if he deserved it!

The Gummi Bear Fund Robbery
Mike's second negative incident put an end to what had been a terrific entrepreneurial business in which he had been engaged at school. We spent a good bit of time outside of the American military and dependents' areas. Several of us would often make our way to a small

village between Patrick Henry Village and Heidelberg. They were connected by trolley cars. We would go to the Heidelberg Castle, climb on walls, and just wander around. Mike was often the oldest of the group, which would usually include him, Rachel, Jim, Steve, and Rick. He recalled:

Often, the village was our primary target for a couple of reasons. It was easy to get to, there were cherry trees along the way, and they had a candy shop. The main attractions at the candy shop were the sour sticks and the gummi bears. The sour sticks were a tart hard candy that would pucker you up when you sucked on them. The gummi bears were little bear-shaped gummy candies that came in different flavors. I got in the habit of buying the sour sticks and gummi bears in bulk and carrying them to school in one of Dad's old cigar boxes. I put a serious markup on them and sold out every day. I would put the money I got from the other kids in the cigar box and put it under my desk with my books. Somebody knew it was there, and sadly, I discovered they had ripped off the money I had taken in that day. That was the Gummi Bear Fund Robbery, and it was the last day that I sold candy.

That fall, Steve had an incident that obviously runs in the family, which should be clear by now:

In third grade I had a friend with whom I liked to wrestle. We were about the same size, and our matches typically ended in a draw, but we had lots of fun trying to outdo each other. One day, we're out in front of his apartment wrestling on the grass, and I was getting the best of him. I just about had him pinned when his big brother came up behind me and stuck a dart in my butt!

What's the deal with these Brats constantly sticking or getting stuck by sharp objects, especially darts? The big brother kid was bigger than Steve, so any note from Mom probably wouldn't have persuaded Steve to attempt to beat him up. Steve never mentioned whether he and his friend continued their wrestling matches. One thing that is important regarding the Heath Platoon: we didn't ever go around intentionally doing these kinds of things to other kids. Sometimes things happened when we were playing and being a little (or a lot?) stupid, but we would never intentionally hurt someone else. Well, mostly never.

Brat Nine, Pat Arrives!

When Mom and Pat came home from the hospital in October 1963, Dad had arranged for a message on the big front window, "IT'S A BOY!" and inside the apartment was a banner, "Welcome home, Mom and Baby!"

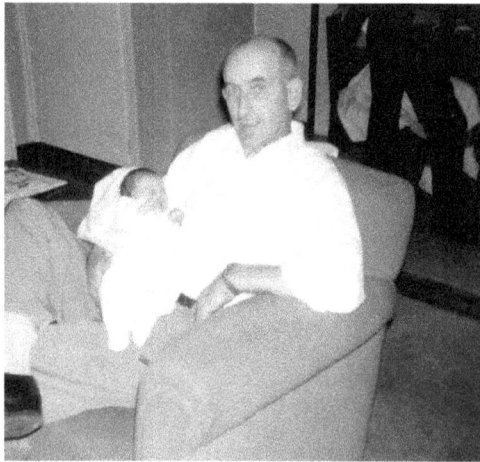

Dad and baby Pat, 1963

Little Pat seldom cried because there was always someone close to hold and comfort him. Rachel said, "We were blessed with Pat. I was praying for a sister, but the moment I laid eyes on Pat, it was all over. A baby brother was okay by me." Rick, who had just turned seven the month before Pat joined us, felt some relief because he was no longer the baby of the Heath Platoon. After Pat was born, Mom was concerned about getting her figure back in shape, and I remember her doing sit-ups in the dining room every morning before we went to school.

That wasn't the only challenge Mom was facing after Pat came along. From our third-floor apartment, we still had to go down lots of flights of stairs to get to our washing machine, which was in the basement. When Pat arrived, a couple of us would carry the dirty clothes and Pat's stroller to the basement, and Mom would come down with Pat, his bottle, and a book. We would hang out down there until the washing was done, get the clothes transferred into the dryer, then carry them back up to the third floor after they dried. As a family, we always got things done.

About a week after the arrival of Pat, it was time to celebrate Halloween by collecting mountains of candy. One of Steve's favorite memories was trick or treating in Germany. Mom would put a big bowl of candy outside the door of the apartment. Because these were so many four-story apartment buildings, we could really collect a bunch of candy quickly. Steve remembers:

We would go up and down the stairwells collecting candy, which would fill up our grocery bags, then back to our apartment where we would dump our candy into the big bowl Mom had put out, and go back out to fill up our bags again. The big bowl at our apartment was for other kids to come and fill up their bags. It was an early form of "re-gifting." Now that I think about it, this was probably going on all over the apartment complex. In the end, everyone ended up with different candy than they began with. Coming back to the States was a real letdown at Halloween because the doors were much farther apart and we never could collect a third of the candy, even with a lot more work.

Another Sad Time
On November 22, 1963, I was running through the buildings as fast as I could to get my newsletter deliveries done when I topped a second-story flight of stairs and a man burst out of an apartment door, nearly running me over. He was shouting, "JFK has been assassinated!" over and over. I just couldn't believe it! I couldn't believe the president of the United States, OUR president, the president who had whizzed through Patrick Henry Village just five months ago, had been assassinated! That was truly a sad day for our country.

"I remember we were driving to a party when we heard about it on the radio," Dave said. "The party was over before it started. These were parts of growing up that I could have done without."

We all agreed with that thought.

A Happy Reunion

Around our last Christmas in Heidelberg, Dan was still serving in the Army in Ethiopia and was able to get some leave time and come to Heidelberg for a visit. On his trip he had a number of delays as he traveled by way of military flights and got stranded in Turkey. He wound up coming from there to Heidelberg by way of train. It was so good to have him home with us again, but he seemed so grown up! He and Pat were born twenty and a half years apart, and Pat was just over two months old when he and his big brother first met. So many times, Mom has remembered Dan walking around the room, holding his youngest little Brat brother, Pat. When it was time for him to head back to Ethiopia, he had some similar problems arranging his transportation, and his leave time was quickly running out. Fortunately, Dad was able to help him make some arrangements, and he got back on time.

High School Prom and Graduation

Heidelberg American High School held their junior/senior prom and senior graduation in the ancient, historically magnificent Heidelberg Castle. That's about as special as those things can get, and Dave was the Heath Brat who was fortunate enough to have had both of those experiences in the spring of 1964. He recalled:

> *When I was a senior, I met my first real love, Claudia. Her Dad was a major, and he was always nice to me. That might have been because I kept his Studebaker station wagon waxed for him. I was a good student, had a nice girlfriend, was captain of the track team, and had a driver's license!*
>
> *Since the venue for the prom was the Heidelberg Castle set high above the Neckar River, guys would take their dates for dinner out on*

the town, [in the] beautiful old city of antiquity. I remember taking Claudia to Perkeo's Restaurant. I had Ox Tail soup (yummier than it sounds!), but the most fun thing about Perkeo's was a large lion mounted up on the wall that would slowly utter in a deep voice, 'Lowwwwwenbrauuuuuuu!' The lion is the mascot of the German beer, Lowenbrau. But, wow, that castle was some place to have a prom! And then there was graduation. At the castle. Awesome! Did you know that there is a 51,500-gallon wine keg in that castle? Of course, it's empty!

Many of the high school kids had cars and would go out partying and so forth. Dave too had his driver's license and was able to borrow the family car every now and then to take Claudia out on a date. His time in Heidelberg, generally, is one of Dave's very favorites.

"Being young in Germany was a great time and a great education," Dave said. "When we left Heidelberg to move back to the States, I left the 'love of my life,' Claudia, behind. Somehow though, I survived, even though I pined quite a while. I saw Claudia two summers later in the Washington, DC, area. She was working at the Pentagon, and I went for a visit. The fire was out. End of that story."

As wonderful as those times were, Dave shared a sad, frightening memory:

One night I went to Dad and gave him my driver's license and told him I didn't want it anymore. My sentiment came from an event I have seen repeated over and over all these years. In my case, a bunch of my friends—seven of them—all piled in a little Volkswagen car and proceeded to drive under a flatbed tractor trailer rig in the middle of the night when they shouldn't have been out partying. Six of the seven died. And worse, the emergency room doctor on duty that night was the father of one of the boys that had been killed. It was an incredibly sad time.

The Heist

One of my last adventures in Heidelberg happened shortly after school was out for the summer of 1964. Peter and I liked to catch the bus to a local swimming pool. Probably the number-one thing that struck me when seeing all the women in their bathing suits was the hairy legs and armpits. We're used to seeing hairy legs and armpits on guys; it's just normal. But it was also the norm for German women to not shave those areas. Apparently, the feminine joy of being expected to shave legs and armpits hadn't managed to make its way across the Atlantic from America yet. I guess that if that's the way it was for us in the States, it wouldn't be a thing at all, but it always seemed odd then. Another thing that seemed unusual to us was that the Germans would put their towels over their bodies to change into and out of their swimsuits right there on the grass next to the pool.

One day Peter and I jumped on the bus on our way to the pool, and some of the other kids from our area got on too. They were going downtown to shop, and one of them, Phillip, invited us to join them, so we did. We were all wandering around downtown Heidelberg, going in and out of stores, looking at things we'd like to buy, but apparently none of us had any money. After we had been doing this for about forty-five minutes, Peter and I both saw Phillip take something off a shelf, look around, then stick it in his pocket and head for the door. As he passed us, he nodded his head toward the door, and we left too.

I looked at Peter and said, "Let's go to the pool."

He said, "Okay."

We waved goodbye to the other guys and took off for the pool. On the way, we talked about how we couldn't believe Phillip would steal something from that store and wondered if the other kids were doing it. We agreed that we wouldn't go anywhere with that crowd again.

The next afternoon, a military policeman came to the door of our apartment, wanting to talk to me. Thankfully, I was the one who answered the door, and I stepped into the hallway and closed the door.

He wanted to know if I was in the store yesterday with some other kids, and I said, "Yes."

He asked if I knew some of the kids had stolen some things, and I said, "I only saw Phillip take something, and that's why me and Peter left and went to the pool."

"Did you take anything?" he asked.

"No, I wouldn't do that."

"Did Peter take anything?"

Again, "No, Peter wouldn't do that either."

The MP then said, "I'll be back if I need any additional information," and left.

I was shaking in my boots when he left and ran over to Peter's apartment. I was really worried the MP would tell Phillip I'd ratted him out. He was bigger than me and could have kicked my butt. The MP had just been to visit Peter with the same questions, and Peter gave him similar answers, but his mom had a lot of questions for both of us. After that incident, I was happier than ever Peter had become my best Heidelberg friend. Neither of us ever heard anything from the MPs after that, but we were both nervous about it for a while. I'm glad the MP didn't ask us anything about drinking beer!

Also early that summer, even though I still had my PHV newsletter delivery gig, I was always on the lookout for other money-making schemes. As was mentioned previously, Mike lost his big gummi-sales venture and was also looking for opportunities. As we are by now aware, we never moved into new quarters that were dirty, and that was great, but moving out was not fun, partly because we had to leave the place just as spotless as we found it, and we knew it would be carefully inspected before we left. We had help with that in Japan and Taiwan with Boysan and Seeny, but we had to do it ourselves in Germany. Mike and I decided we could earn some good money if we became a cleaning crew for families moving out, so we put out the word and got a gig pretty quickly. We scrubbed that place down from top to bottom and really worked hard doing it. I was a bit grossed out scrubbing boogers off the wall next to where a bed was, but that was about the worst of anything nasty we had to deal with. We passed inspection, got paid, and then decided it was too much work. So we took down our Open for Business sign for good. At least for the cleaning business.

That's not to say we were done cleaning, because shortly after that, in July of 1964, Dad received orders to USATC Infantry (3171) at Fort Jackson, South Carolina.

For Dave, "Coming back to the States was the hardest move for me. This time we moved to Columbia, South Carolina, where Dad was stationed at Fort Jackson. Of course, it was easier on Mom because Dad was with us."

Since Japan, this was the only time Dad was able to accompany us on a duty station transfer move. I said my goodbyes to Peter and my other friends, as did all my Brat sibs, and we started packing. Of all of us, Dave was having the most difficult time leaving his friends. For the rest of us, it was just another, "Okay, kids, it's time to move." Since we were leaving, this entailed a thorough cleaning of our apartment, of course.

Dad was due to be at Fort Jackson by August 3, 1964, so when the time to leave Germany came, we went to Frankfurt, which is where our flight would depart. Our good old family friends Les and Naomi were stationed in Frankfurt, so Mom and Dad made plans for us to spend a few days with them. After selling one of our cars and shipping the other one back to the States, Mom was concerned about how we were going to get to Frankfurt. No problem; just sit back and leave everything to the motor pool sergeant. Dad didn't spend all that time working in the motor pool without having some clout, and we had experienced this before. The motor pool sent us a full-sized bus. We all had our own window seat, and there was plenty of room for luggage. Dad didn't even have to drive. Dad's commanding officer came out and said goodbye to us after we were all loaded, and off we went.

After a couple of days with Les and Naomi, we boarded our plane and were off to the States and our next new adventure in life. Our plane landed in New Jersey, and of course, our car and clothes had gone to New York. Since New York wasn't that far away, Dave and Dad traveled there to get our things and transport them to South Carolina. Dad didn't have a lot of leave time, and school in South Carolina was about to begin, so this time we didn't go to Wisconsin and Illinois, but drove straight to Columbia, South Carolina.

PART III:
GROWN-UP ARMY

CHAPTER 16
COLUMBIA, SOUTH CAROLINA, 1964–1968

Pat celebrated his first birthday not long after we got to South Carolina, and he and Dad disappeared right after his birthday dinner. When we saw Brat Nine again, his curls were gone, and he was sporting a good ole Army Brat haircut. Apparently, Sarge's Barber Shop had reopened, and boys in the Heath Platoon didn't parade around with long hair past their first birthday. I can't remember what Pat's reaction was, but I clearly remember our first experience in the Deep South.

We had stopped to get gas as we were closing in on Fort Jackson and jumped out of the car to use the restroom. Posted right on the restroom door was a sign saying, "White Only." This was new to us kids and required some clarification. Although we did get an explanation, it still didn't make any sense to me, as I'm certain was the case among the entire Heath Platoon. Why can't you use the restroom if your skin's not a certain color? This was the first of many cultural differences we experienced living in the South ….

Upon arrival, we were able to get quarters on Fort Jackson, which involved both apartments of a duplex. Getting quarters on the post was a bit of a surprise to Mom and Dad. Right after Dad signed for the quarters, we took off for Brooksville, Florida, the town where Dad's folks had retired from Illinois. We stayed in Florida for a week, and apparently it rained back at our new quarters the entire time. We got back there after dark and discovered one of the bathroom ceilings on the floor.

At that time, Fort Jackson was trying to get funding for new quarters as these were old wooden barracks that had been converted to dependents' quarters. When Dad called billeting about getting the ceiling fixed, they asked if they could send a television crew out to film the damage. They were hoping to use that as additional evidence of the need for the new quarters. Dad was happy to let them, and it wasn't long before the new quarters began to be built.

We were only in military quarters for about four months when Mom and Dad found a home to buy. It was a nice one-story brick duplex close to Fort Jackson. Dad was working on it by making a large opening in the main wall between the two apartments, which gave us four large bedrooms, two baths, two large living rooms, and a nice big kitchen; the other kitchen became our dining room. The extra laundry room was converted into a small bedroom for Rachel. It also had two utility rooms for storage. The yard was nice and big with garden space and had a good-sized vacant lot next door.

Jim said:

> *After we bought our new house, Dad was busy working on it to transform it from a duplex into a single house, so we made a bunch of trips over there and back to our quarters on the base.*
>
> *One day on our way back from the new house, I said, "I can walk to the new house in two hours."*
>
> *Dad said, "No, I don't think so."*
>
> *I replied, "I'll bet I can!"*
>
> *He said, "How much do you want to bet?"*
>
> *Me: "Twenty dollars!"*
>
> *Dad: "If you have twenty dollars to bet on that, I'll take the bet."*
>
> *So I was doing it the next Saturday morning and was taking off at 9:00 in the morning. As I was getting ready to go, Dad told me that I had to take Rick and Steve with me. I'm not sure what that was about, other than stacking the deck, but I said, "Okay," and we took off. As*

soon as we got out of sight of the house, I told Steve and Rick that we were going to jog the rest of the way, and we did. We got to the house and were sitting on the porch for about ten minutes before Mom and Dad got there, right at about 11:00.

"How'd you get here?" Dad asked.

"On foot!" I replied.

"I don't believe it," Dad said. "I'll bet you got somebody to drive you here." He wouldn't give me the twenty dollars. I was really disappointed by that. Later, Mom handed me a twenty-dollar bill and said, "I believe you!"

Trimming Trees and Snow Theft

After we moved into our house off base, Mom said, "We had a next-door neighbor who frequently got drunk, and sometimes when he was in that condition, he liked to trim the branches off his trees with his shotgun." This was obviously very nerve-racking, not just because of the noise his stupid shotgun made, but also because who knows where all those pellets that didn't hit the branches landed? In spite of that, his kids were friends of ours. That would end, at least temporarily, when we had a rare snowfall with any accumulation.

South Carolina tends to have very mild winters. During our first winter, Dad was sitting on the back steps one warm day in his T-shirt and said, "This is where I want to retire." None of us disagreed. During our Christmas break from school, we were running around behind our quarters playing football in shorts and T-shirts with temperatures in the seventies and the sun shining brightly. I don't recall any complaints about missing cold weather and/or snow.

Snow in South Carolina is quite rare and with very little accumulation, but the neighbor kids would come over and try to steal what little bit of snow we had, and we Brats didn't like it. Mom said, "Any need to steal one's neighbor's snow always seemed so funny to me, having been raised in the mountains of snow I experienced growing up in Wisconsin." She remembers snow drifts so deep that they would have to dig a tunnel through the snow at her childhood front door in order to get out of the house. Maybe Grampa Archie could have loaded up his shotgun and used it to blow holes through that snow. Glamich most likely would not have appreciated that technique.

Learning in the South

Mom and Dad enrolled us in Catholic schools. A question in all our minds was, Why? Let's face it: there were still seven Brats in the nest, six of whom were in school. It can be pretty expensive to send kids to private schools, especially six of them. Part of the answer is, given that Catholic families tend to be larger than others, the churches sometimes offered incentives like "pay for two, and the rest can attend for free." The other and more significant part of why we weren't being enrolled in the public schools is this: we were in the Deep South, where racial segregation had been highly dominant in public schools, among other things. We had never attended racially segregated schools either overseas or in the United States. The greatest factor in Mom and Dad's decision was that the US government had just passed the 1964 Civil Rights Act one month prior to our arrival in South Carolina, which said that schools and other institutions could not discriminate based on race or other factors. This, of course, meant African American kids could go to schools that had been otherwise strictly populated with White kids and vice versa.[99]

Why would this be a problem to Mom and Dad, or to the Brats? After all, we had attended schools with kids of many different races, colors, and nationalities for most of our educational lives, and it certainly never mattered to any of us. Mom and Dad were well aware of the fact that it wouldn't matter to us, but they were highly concerned that the integration of kids in schools would likely create lots of strife among the children who did not grow up going to school with people who were not like them. They were absolutely determined that we not get caught up in any of that. So Mike and I went to ninth and eleventh grades, respectively, at Cardinal Newman High School; the other siblings went to St. Peter's Catholic Elementary School.

Catholic school was new to me, even though I had spent many Saturdays while growing up going to catechism, which is kind of a Bible school for kids. Giving up Saturday playtime for catechism wasn't ever one of my favorite activities. We were raised, of course, to be very respectful toward Catholic priests, nuns, and our religion. I was highly surprised and disappointed by the exceptionally disrespectful behavior of several students in my classes.

Thinking about it many years later, the lack of respect those students demonstrated was most likely due to the fact that they had probably attended Catholic schools for the entirety of their education to that point. Because of that, being around priests and nuns wouldn't have felt special to them, like it did to me and probably the rest of the Brats. Hence, they didn't feel the same need to demonstrate the level of respect I felt would be appropriate. To be fair, most of the kids were respectful; it was just a handful that created the issues.

An example of what I witnessed: in English class, Sister Margaret Mary had a little statue of the Mother Mary that she kept on her desk; it was clearly very precious to her. Every day that she wasn't present in the room when our class came in, this kid Joey would grab the statue and hide it somewhere. Sister Margaret Mary would come in, see that the statue was missing and start fussing about where it was and why anyone would take it. Joey and his buddies would stifle their laughter, and I would wonder why they needed to do it. If I had been a better person, I would have filled Sister Margaret Mary in on who was doing it, but I guess I wasn't. That went on all year. There were other classes where the kids did and said things to the nuns or priests that I would call mean. Eleventh grade wasn't one of my happier school years.

There was another incident at the school that sticks with me. I was in the office getting something for one of my teachers, and while standing there, I heard the priest/principal talking with the secretary about a girl who was in several of my classes.

The secretary said to the principal, "We just got word that Jill is pregnant."

The principal said, "She'll have to drop out, or we'll have to expel her. She knows she can't go to school here being pregnant."

The secretary responded, "I'll call her parents and let them know."

Jill was gone the next day and didn't come back the rest of the year. I have thought of this incident many times over the years; it troubled me then and still does. Why should a girl have to give up her education over a pregnancy? Did the guy who got her pregnant have to leave school too? I suspect the answer is no, he didn't. I know this way of dealing with that issue is different today, and we can't change the past. In spite of these negative things, I did pretty well there and made a few friends.

The Bell and Book Covers

Jim was in sixth grade at St. Peter's, and every time he walked down the main hall, he looked at this big bell hanging on the wall. Someone had to pull a chain to make it go *CLANG!* Jim found that chain fascinating and it inspired his curiosity. In his words:

> *How far do you have to pull that chain to make the bell ring? And isn't there a rule somewhere about allowing curious minds to wander the school halls on their way to the bathroom? Especially if it leads them on a path past the bell. That darn chain … just hanging there asking for it, and the bell seemed to be crying out, "I'm useless if I'm not ringing." At least, that's what it cried out to me. How far can you pull the chain before it rings the bell? I have no accurate measurement, but it is slightly less than the distance I pulled it. CLANG went the bell! Zoom went Jim into the bathroom, and every child, nun, priest, and layperson headed for the yard for the fire drill. I had successfully emptied St. Peter's Catholic School with nothing more than curiosity. People say life is a game of inches. I believe the measurement to be smaller. That, and it comes with detention when you are the only suspect and have not yet learned how to lie effectively.*

Rick had his own fun incident there:

> *I was in third grade at St. Peters, and the cover came off my religion book. My teacher/nun instructed me to take the book home and have my parents sign in the book that they knew the cover was torn off. I "forgot" to get that done, and on the bus on the way to school the next morning, I realized that and had to figure out what to do. So, I*

counterfeited Mom's name on the book. The nun didn't buy it, and she got the office to call Rachel to come to the class to verify the signature. Rachel said, "No." I got the nun's ruler smacked on my hand. Dad was required to come get me from school, then I got my butt beaten by Dad.

A Family in Flux

For us, moving to the South in the mid-sixties was an awakening of many things in society we would all have preferred not to know and about which we had much to learn. As we grew into adulthood, we found that there were many things about Southern culture that we appreciated, and other things to which we would never conform. Along the way, not only were we experiencing cultural differences, but also our family dynamics were beginning to see significant changes.

Dan had finished his tour of duty in the Army and, after he was discharged, went to Manitowoc to get Glamich. They drove to South Carolina in his 1955 Ford Sunliner to visit us. Glamich had helped him buy the car before he went into the Army and even made payments on it for him while he was away. A funny sidenote: when they got to South Carolina, Dan was unpacking his suitcase and discovered that his shaving cream had spewed out all over his clothes, and he got really mad about it. When I saw the mess, I inadvertently laughed out loud, which didn't improve Dan's attitude one iota.

After we got to visit with Glamich for a short while, she headed back to Manitowoc. Dan stayed with us and went to work for the Arthur Murray dance studio in Columbia for a year and a half until it went out of business. Apparently, the guy who was running the place was skimming a lot of the income out of the business.

Dave, having graduated from high school in Heidelberg, was a full-time student at the University of South Carolina–Columbia. He worked to offset his college costs and also volunteered to teach the track team that Mike and I were on at Cardinal Newman his great high hurdle and high jump techniques.

Dad helped Dave get his first job in South Carolina at a nearby gas station. One of Dave's primary responsibilities was to do oil changes on cars, which wasn't really in his realm of expertise. You might think that, being the second son of a head sergeant of several motor pools, Dave would have a high level of acumen in the business of changing oil and that sort of stuff. No. When Dad was involved in doing those kinds of things at home, it was typically Dan at his side. Dave had no clue.

He showed up at work the first day, and his boss pointed to a car in the garage and said, "Go ahead and change the oil in that car."

Dave said, "How do I do that?"

Boss: "Take out that bolt right there and empty the old oil, then put new oil in up here."

So Dave got up under the car, removed the bolt, emptied out the fluid, put back in the bolt, then refilled the fluid. Unfortunately, he refilled the transmission fluid.

Boss to Dave: "You're fired."

No tears were shed on Dave's part.

Very shortly afterward, Dave got a job as a cook at the Ponderosa Steak Barn in West Columbia, which was right across the Broad River from the university. He was raking in the big bucks at fifty cents an hour. The waitresses would call out food orders to him, how the steaks were to be cooked, and what other items to put on the plate. He said he could remember as many as fifty orders and always got them right.

Dave was working really hard to pay his tuition and book costs, as well as working hard to keep up with and excel at his school work. One day, a man came to the door of the house with a delivery for Mom. She was puzzled because she hadn't ordered anything. It turned out that Dave had ordered Mom a cedar chest—something he knew Mom had wanted for a very long time. She was really excited and just couldn't thank Dave enough. How he afforded that is hard to imagine, but it certainly speaks to what a big heart he has!

Dave was living with the family that first year and didn't have a car, so he rode the local bus to and from the university. He liked sitting in the back of buses, but when he went to the back of this bus and sat down, he kept hearing, "Only Black people can sit in the back of the bus. What are you doing here?" He found this incredibly disconcerting, along with the "White Only" signs on bathroom doors and over water fountains, among other things.

Another thing about this that is disconcerting is that the Supreme Court, in their 1956 *Browder vs. Gayle* ruling, had determined that laws requiring segregated seating on public transportation were unconstitutional.[100] Either South Carolina wasn't conforming, which was common in Southern states at this time, or those African-American folks sitting in the back didn't know it, unless it was just one of those ongoing culturally racial things we didn't understand.

1965

In Dave's second year of college, he got a room in a house on the university campus. The other students staying in the house were very noisy, and he had a hard time focusing on his school work. Before long he landed a job at a factory making camera parts, earning $1.50 per hour. He worked the night shift from 11 p.m. until 7 a.m., then went back across the river to his 8:00 a.m. class. He had his "lunch" break at around 3:00 in the morning and would pull out his homework and get it done. Some of the workers called him "Professor" when they saw him studying. He worked five days a week on this job.

He was very devoted to his work at the university and put a great deal of effort into it. Toward the end of one semester, he had a research paper due. In preparation for the paper, he had note cards "spread out all over the floor of my room," he said. "The paper was very detailed and so good, the professor wrote on the front page, 'A++, Final Exam Exempt!'" Dave would go to school for three semesters plus summer school, working just one job, then take a semester off and work two jobs to save up enough money to get through three more semesters, then repeat. Financial assistance from Mom and Dad just wasn't available, especially with six Brats in Catholic schools that first year.

Later, in 1967, Dave met Linda. They dated and became "steadies." How he had time to work, study, and date speaks clearly to his ability to focus and do the things that were important to him. Unfortunately, I had not yet found those traits in myself.

Best Buds

Grampa Grump and Gramma Nell came for a short visit in early summer of 1965 from Florida, and sadly, that was the last time we saw Gramma Nell. Just a few weeks after they left, she passed away. Plans were being made to go to the funeral, and Dad's youngest brother Paul was able to get a flight to Charleston, South Carolina. Dad went there to pick him up, and they took a bus to Brooksville, Florida. The rest of the family was waiting for Aunt Pat to come to Columbia by train from Pennsylvania and ride the rest of the way from South Carolina with us. It turned out to be a good thing we were still at home because one of the water heaters in the attic sprang a leak the evening that Dad left to pick up Uncle Paul. If we had not been there to shut off the water, our house would have been badly flooded. Almost déjà vu from the rain that crashed the bathroom ceiling to the floor when we were on Fort Jackson.

Dave drove us to Brooksville in pouring rain with windshield wipers that weren't working. He would reach out the window every now and then and swipe the wipers across. He got us there safely, but every time he rolled his window down to move the wipers, those of us in the back seat got a quick shower. We stayed in Brooksville for a few days until after Gramma Nell's funeral. Aunt Joan and our cousins Peggy Jo and Bootsie were there, which gave us a little time to get to know them. We had only seen them a few times while growing up.

With the loss of Gramma Nell, Grump was a lost soul, and he came up to South Carolina at Thanksgiving that year and spent a week or two with us. Grump and Pat were getting to know each other, and one day Grump was playing with Pat when Pat fell and hit the side of his face on the base of the floor lamp. Grump was really upset at himself, but it wasn't much of a hurt for Pat. Mom said that was when Pat got the dimple in his cheek.

Pat remembers having "vivid memories of holding [Grump's] *giant* hand and walking to the store and him buying me candy … I think we were 'buds.'"

Shiner, Pat, and Mike, 1964

Because Pat was quite a bit younger than everyone else in the family, he may not have been as integrated with all things Heath Platoon. One of those was that there was almost always a dog in the family, wherever on the planet we lived. After we got settled into our house in South Carolina, we got a hound dog puppy. All the fur around one of his eyes was black, so he was named "Shiner." Baby Brat Pat was really frightened of dogs, and he realized that here was a dog that he could be mean to, and it was too little to do anything about it. Mom caught him throwing Shiner off the porch, and she pointed out to him that no matter how much he abused that puppy, the little dog would always love him. She asked him if he thought that was a very nice thing to do. Pat looked down at the ground and mumbled, "No." We never saw him hurt Shiner again; in fact, he and Shiner also became best buds.

Public Schools and Bullies

It would be the early 1970s before the Columbia, South Carolina, area would begin to experience actual integration of schools through required busing, so the potential strife Mom and Dad were concerned about didn't happen.[101] For our second year in South Carolina, we all transferred to the local public schools.

216 Robert R. Heath Sr.

Several of us were at Lower Richland High School: I was a senior, Mike was in tenth grade, Rachel, eighth, and Jim, seventh. Steve was in fifth and Rick, fourth, at Annie B. Burnside Elementary. This was the 1965–1966 school year.

Once we changed over to public schools, we all had some different experiences. According to Rick:

> *Moving to Columbia, civilians were weird people. I got beat up by bullies; they would mess with me on my way to and from school. We were all on our bikes, and they would surround me and give me crap. My lunch got stolen frequently at school. But payback this time was for real. One of the kids put a knife at my throat because I was in "their" sand cave. They took over our sand cave dwellings on the lot next door, so one day I started launching river rocks from the driveway with a sling shot. I was hiding behind the porch on the back of our house. I would shoot one rock and duck behind the steps while watching where it landed. Oh, what joy I had when one of them grabbed the top of his head. I'll bet his head hurt like birth!*

The bullies weren't the only ones feeling the joy of Rick's weapons. He recounts another incident, this one involving a bow and arrow:

> *I was messing around with my toy bow and arrow one day—the arrows had sucker tips and would stick to some of the things they hit. Out of the corner of my eye, I saw Mike [bike] riding in front of the house. He was a moving target, and I didn't have anything else to practice on, so I shot him with one of my arrows. Mike wasn't overly pleased with that and broke my arrow.*

Lesson learned?
Steve kept having cookies stolen out of his lunch box by a really big bully. He told Mom about it, and she said, "I'll make some cookies with red pepper in them, and you can let him steal them!" Steve thought that would be a terrific idea, but Mom never did make those

special cookies. It sure would have been a lot of fun to see the look on that bully's face as he bit into one of them!

One of Jim's experiences with bullies: "I encountered the same bullies as Rick. I got in a fight with one named Ricky and had him down on the ground when his big brother came and kicked me in the ribs until I let his brother go."

None of us spoke "Southern," and there may have been some resentment toward kids whose parents were in the military. While these weren't very happy experiences, we weren't all subjected to these kinds of behaviors.

Steve had "a math teacher who gave tons of homework. I had so much homework that there were times that Mom 'let' Jim do some of it for me. He really wanted to do it for me. That is unheard of in our family—for our parents to let anyone do someone else's homework for them. Looking back at this math teacher, I wonder if my strength in math isn't due in part to the fact that she worked us so hard. I never had a math class after that in which I didn't excel." Sometimes, the hard things in life do make us stronger.

My Senior Year

Lower Richland High School was my ninth and final school in twelve years and the third high school I attended. For military Brats, going to nine different schools is pretty common and a thing to which we just adapt.

When I arrived at school the first morning of my senior year, I made my way about halfway up the bleachers and sat down to wait for the bell to ring, as required. A guy sitting nearby started talking to me, and pretty soon some of his friends joined us. Their names were Duncan, Ronnie, and Buddy. These three guys had gone to school together since first grade and were good friends. I've often wondered why they included me in their group, but they were all really nice, feet-on-the-ground guys, and I have always considered myself incredibly lucky to have been included in their friendships. To this day, we are all good friends.

I joined the football team that year, all five-foot-seven and 130 pounds of me. Not to mention that I hadn't played organized football since about ninth grade. Ronnie was on the team, and he wasn't any bigger than me, so I thought, "Why not?"

Why not? Well, to begin with, I was a small senior with little experience and didn't know the playbook at all. That said, I worked hard in practice and did all I could. The head coach called me "Chicago" because of my lack of a Southern accent. One of the guys told me I wasn't the first "Chicago" on the team.

I remember getting in a game against my former school, Cardinal Newman, for two plays. Two. One other time I was standing up near the sideline, watching the game, and the coach said, "Heath, get your tail back on the bench!" As I sat on the bench watching the rest of the game, I realized that my position on the team was "tailback." The next week I went to the coach's office and quit the team. He didn't seem upset to see me go. There had been one benefit to being this very special kind of tailback—at the end of every game, I had a sparkling clean uniform while those who played most of the game had filthy, sweaty uniforms. It seemed the cheerleaders liked to hug guys with nice, clean uniforms. I didn't mind that attention one little bit.

I joined the track team in the spring and ran the mile and half mile. Duncan, Ronnie, and Brat Mike were also on the team. In every single track meet that year, I finished in either third or fourth place in both events. We had other runners for each of those runs who were a little faster and would almost always get first or second place. Ronnie was one of those guys. Before every single run, he would have to go into the weeds near the track to puke because he would be very nervous. I enjoyed track and ran my heart out to finish as fast as I could, which earned me a varsity letter.

One day, on the weekly Club Day, I was on an extended trip from study hall to the restroom. Since I hadn't joined any clubs, I had study hall and was simply wasting time. Suddenly, several girls came along, and I asked, "Where are you going?"

One of them responded, "To the Thespian Club!"

"Where is that? Can anybody join?" I asked.

"Sure, it's in Mrs. Higgins class."

I hustled back to study hall to let Mrs. Shoolbred know that I was joining the Thespian Club and off I went. I didn't even know what a "thespian" was, but I did know that there were several really good-looking girls who would be there. As it turned out, I enjoyed the club and being in the play *Bye Bye Birdie*, which we did at the end of the year. I remember that when we were performing the play, we weren't getting many laughs from the audience, so the kids in the cast started throwing in some funny ad-libs to spice it up. That worked, and people started laughing. I don't think Mrs. Higgins laughed though.

At the end of the year, the club went to the Thespian Convention at Winthrop College in Rock Hill, South Carolina. The most significant thing that has stuck in my brain about that trip was that I met a nice girl. We began talking and eventually got around to considering going somewhere quieter together. I told her that I needed to ask one of the teachers if it was okay to go. Mr. Saylor said, "Sure, you can go. Would you like to borrow my car?" He handed me his keys and pointed to his beautiful, blue Mustang. So the young lady and I jumped in the 'Stang and looked for a nice, quiet place to park on the college campus. After making out and talking for a while, we realized the convention might be coming to a close, so we made our way back to the auditorium. I returned Mr. Saylor's keys to him, along with a very profuse, "Thank you!" In hindsight, as an adult and educator, I wonder at Mr. Saylor's wisdom in loaning his car to a student to go off somewhere with a girl, but it was an incredibly enjoyable finale to the Thespian Convention for me—really, the Mustang probably even more than the girl!

Late in the school year I found a girlfriend, Janet. She and I eventually went to prom together, but most of our dates were double dates since I didn't have a car at first. I did have a part-time job, so I was finally able to put together enough money to buy a 1953 Ford Fairlane for $300. The body of the car was generally in good shape, but it had a few "quirks." None of the wheels had hubcaps, and each wheel was a different color: black, red, green, and white. There's more: not one of the wheels had more than three lug nuts; they should have had five. Finally, and maybe the bigger issue, was that it didn't have an ignition switch. To start the car, I had to reach under the dashboard by the steering wheel and hook two wires together. Clearly, this was a very high-class car. After I had the car for a couple weeks, I came home from school one day and got in the car to go to my job. I reached down to hook the ignition wires together, and they weren't there; instead, there was an ignition switch with keys! Dad had installed it while I was at school. Wow! The car also had five lug nuts in each wheel. Who's the man? Master Sergeant Heath, of course!

As graduation approached, I decided to apply to the University of South Carolina, where Dave was going, as well as several of my friends. I had no clue what my major might be; Dave was in business school, so I thought I'd follow in his footsteps to start with.

Bob's high school graduation, 1966

For my application, I needed my class rank, so I went to the office to get it. The principal, Mr. Watson, pulled out a rank-ordered list of students in the senior class, counted down the list, and drew a line right above my name. He looked up at me and said, "Bob, it looks like you're at the top of the bottom half of your class: you're sixty-seventh out of 132 students."

TOP of the bottom half of my class! Apparently, I pretty well lived down to Dad's expectations of us in school. I recall one time when we all brought home report cards, and there were lots of Cs. He said, "There's nothing wrong with Cs; Cs are average. The world is mostly average, so that's okay." That could explain partly why I frequently had this note on the bottom of my report cards: "Bob does not work to his potential." I mean, if Dad wasn't worried about it, why should I? I don't recall Mom ever expressing any thoughts about that.

In spite of my lackluster rank in my class, I had really good SAT scores, and I guess the university saw some potential in me because I got accepted, as did several of my friends. High school graduation came along, and afterward, Janet, me, and our parents went to dinner. About halfway through dinner, Dad overheard Janet and me talking about going to different colleges. He looked over at me and said, "Bob, you're not college material, so don't ask me for any money to go to college."

It's not like he whispered it to me; he said it out loud for everyone to hear. I wasn't expecting that and looked over at Janet. She was looking down at her plate and wouldn't make eye contact with me for the rest of dinner. The next weekend, we went to a movie, and when we sat down inside the theater, she looked over at me and said, "You know that I'm going to Winthrop next school year, so I think we should break up." It was tough to watch the movie, and afterward, I took her straight home, said goodbye, and left. Although I wasn't happy about her breaking up with me, one aspect of growing up Army is that I got very used to saying goodbye and not looking back, even though it was never particularly happy.

It should be reiterated that Dad didn't fund anyone's college tuition, so it really wasn't going to make any difference as far as I was concerned. This wasn't because he didn't want to, but was more about not earning that much money in the Army and feeding a large bunch of Brats. There really wasn't much money to spare. The truth is I didn't anticipate getting any help in that department anyway.

Another Heath Is College Bound

Within a few weeks of graduation, I found an apartment near the university. It was about a mile or so from Five Points for fifty dollars a month, and I had two roommates to share the rent.

After moving in, I didn't stay in very close touch with the family, even though they weren't very far away. Mom came to my apartment a couple of times just to check on me and see if I was doing okay. It always surprised me when she showed up, but I was glad to see her. The main reason I didn't stay in touch with the family was that I found a bar in Five Points that I began to frequent while looking for girls, who were plentiful, given the close proximity to the university. You know, we must have our priorities in life ....

Pizza Hut opened their first South Carolina restaurant on Garners Ferry Road in Columbia that summer. I went to work there as they were opening and helped get it set up for business. Ultimately, Dan, Dave, Mike, Jim, and Pat would all work at that Pizza Hut. I continued to work there through my first go at being a college student.

My first semester of college started in the fall of 1966, and I was marginally excited about it. A couple of weeks into my first English class at the university, a girl came in and took her seat near me. The professor immediately addressed her.

"Are you aware that the university's policy is that all female students will wear dresses on campus?"

She was wearing pants and had on a long coat. She said, "Yes, that's why I'm wearing this coat."

Professor: "You will have to leave class. Dress appropriately from here on."

This was one of those many things that came across my consciousness that made absolutely no sense. I was wearing pants, as were all the guys in the class. What was the problem? I have since spoken with others who attended different universities in other parts of the country during that time period that had the same ridiculous policy. I have no doubt that gender-discriminatory policies such as these played a big role in the women's lib movement of the sixties.

My academic performance was so poor that I was put on academic suspension for one semester at the end of my first semester. I guess they really want students to attend most of the classes and do the assignments in order to get a decent grade. I sat out the next semester, then failed to change my habits while I took, and failed, a class during the first summer session of 1967. Hello, twenty-four months' academic suspension!

CHAPTER 17
LOOKING FORWARD TO RETIREMENT
AND AUGUSTA, GEORGIA, 1968–1971

It had taken very little effort on my part to prove Dad correct regarding my being "college material." As I look back, I see that losing Janet, moving into the apartment, my enjoyment of the bar, and chasing girls probably all contributed to my less-than-stellar performance at the university. So I had two "gap" years imposed upon me by the University of South Carolina. During those gap years, I was introduced to Nora by Brat Dan, who was still working at the Arthur Murray dance studio. One of the women he worked with had a younger sister, and she and Dan conspired to get us together. Nora and I dated off and on between fusses with each other, but it seemed we always got back together. Over the course of the next year, many changes were coming in my life and with the family.

One day, Mom and Dad saw an advertisement about a lot for sale on Lake Murray, and they went to take a look at it. The lot was about sixty miles from our house, on the far end of the lake. The first lot they saw didn't interest them, but there was another one that they really liked. According to Mom, "It was a nice, big lot that sloped down to the water. There were lots of tall, beautiful trees, and it was in a cove off the main body of the lake. The lot was on a dead-end dirt road that ran back about two miles from the highway, and this lot was about half way in. Given that Dad's retirement wasn't too far away, we had to have it, which naturally meant that he had to have a boat." After all, retiring and living on a lake required fishing!

They bought an old wooden building from Fort Jackson and had it hauled out to the lake property. Dad tore it apart and built a storage building with the lumber. Rachel became Dad's right-hand girl on that project. She always knew what tool he needed or any other way she could help. Mom and Dad started calling her "Ralph." Rachel said that was when she learned to swing a mean hammer, a skill she hasn't forgotten.

When the building was finished, they had a septic tank installed and hooked into a community well for their water supply. Until then, they had a two-holer outhouse with canvas stretched around it for privacy. A little later they installed a toilet in the building—which affectionately became known as "the purple pot"—privatizing it with the curtains from the two-holer. Then an electric range for cooking and a long table and chairs were added, and they had all the comforts of home. While putting it all together and afterward, they spent lots of time out there, enjoying the warm weather and the lake. Dad got some water skis, and the Brats started skiing.

With the purchase of the lot on Lake Murray, Dad was clearly eyeing retirement, and the family was spending many weekends there. They put up a large tent in addition to the wooden shed they built where they stored the various items they used on the weekends. During blackberry season, Mom and the Brats picked berries, then she cooked out the juice and made jam after they got home. There was a really big blackberry patch not far from their lot, and they were able to pick lots of buckets of really juicy, tasty berries for lots of years. The patch was known to them as "the secret patch." Mom worried some about snakes, but happily never saw one while picking. Even though Dad was not a berry picker, he always had advice for them, suggesting, for example, that setting off firecrackers would scare the snakes. Mom was more afraid of firecrackers than she was of snakes; and by the way, Dad, that would probably start a fire!

Sometimes at the lake on a weekend, they went to mass on Saturday evenings at St. Mark's Catholic Church, which was fifteen miles away in Newberry. Later, after Dad's retirement and they lived at the lake full time, Mom and Dad would become very involved with this church. The older Brats would often come to visit on Sundays, and everybody did lots of fishing, swimming, waterskiing, and just having fun.

Rick was particularly fascinated by fish. He loves fishing and has loved it ever since he discovered it at Lake Murray. "I used to ride my bike down to the pet store to look at the fish," he recalled. "The store clerk told me if I stuck my hand in the piranha tank, he'd give me a fish. Since they are pack hunters and there was only one, I did it. I got my fish." I don't think I would have had the guts to stick my hand in a piranha tank. On Rick's part, it was smart, since he knew stuff about piranhas.

Korea, Christmas, and Vietnam

Dad was promoted to sergeant major (E-9), and not surprisingly, orders soon came for him to go to a new duty station. This time he was off to Korea and was to report in late February 1967. He would be gone until late March of 1968, and the family couldn't go. On a positive note, his assignment to Korea without us provided the only time we ever stayed anywhere for four whole years! Shortly before Dad left, Dan moved back home and was still teaching dance at the Arthur Murray studios.

Mom and Dad as he is promoted to sergeant major, 1967

On Christmas morning that year, Mom was awakened by the song, "Joy to the World," *very loud*! She stumbled out of her bedroom to be blinded by a flash as Dave took her picture, and all of us were standing there grinning. We had bought her a large stereo with a record player and radio and had smuggled it into the house during the night. Those of us who were working at the time had all pitched in, and no one had whispered a word about it. It was a great Christmas surprise for Mom, and she loved it!

Immediately after that Christmas surprise, Dave was drafted into the Army and had to report on January 2, 1968, to basic training at Fort Jackson. He had been working really hard at school and his job, but that would have to be put on hold. At that time, those who were currently enrolled in college wouldn't be drafted. His draft notice came during one of the semesters that he had to work two jobs to earn enough money to continue going to school. Unfortunately, the draft didn't give exceptions for the young folks who had to work their way through college.

When he first got to basic training, and even before he got his military haircut, the drill sergeant had everyone line up and asked, "If you have had any college education, take one step forward!"

Because he had been in college, Dave stepped forward.

The sergeant then said loudly, "HOW MANY OF YOU WOULD LIKE TO BE A LIEUTENANT IN THE UNITED STATES ARMY?"

Dave raised his hand, asking, "Can I ask a question?"

"Ask your question, private!"

Dave: "Do you have to stay in the Army any longer?"

The response: "Yes, private, ten more months!"

Dave immediately and quickly took one step back into the line.

After boot camp, Dave went to radio teletype training for five months, finishing several weeks early, and was promoted to specialist E-4. Following that and realizing there were people in Vietnam still shooting at one another, he signed up for paratrooper training, hoping to drag out being trained as long as possible. He went to Fort Benning, Georgia, for jump training as a paratrooper for one month. Of all his time in the Army, he found this to be the most interesting and fun. After jump training, he was assigned to the 82nd Airborne Division in Fort Bragg, North Carolina. One time when he was home visiting, he was telling me how awesome it was to jump out of an airplane and float to the ground.

Then he said, "Bob, I can probably arrange to get you into an Army uniform so that you can take one of those jumps with me!"

I said, without a second thought, "No, thanks! I do not ever intend to jump out of a perfectly safe airplane!"

For Dave, this was all kind of a game. For example, they had physical training every morning, which he didn't have any interest in doing, so he played the "college card" again and was assigned to be the battalion mail clerk. The other guys would be running around getting physically fit while Dave was taking a nap on the mail room desk. Again, due to the fact that he had been in college for a couple years and had training in radio teletype, he then became the lieutenant colonel's radio operator during jump training and would ride around with him in his Jeep. Play it, Dave!

Every Monday morning, all the battalion soldiers would go to the armory and be issued very heavy M-16 Army rifles to take to the field. Then on Friday, they would return the rifles, and they had to be "white glove clean."

Dave recalled:

> *That was such a pain. You had to wait in line every Friday while the armorer exercised his authority over every man in line, and I wanted to get out of there and get to Columbia to spend the weekend with my fiancé. One weekend, I visited a toy store and saw a plastic M-16 rifle that was four inches shorter than the real thing, and it weighed almost nothing. So here was the plan, and it worked every time: I would go to the armorer to get my M-16 and put it into my locker and take my plastic M-16 and put it in the commander's Jeep along with my radio and ride around with the colonel all week. When we'd come in on Friday afternoon, the fake M-16 goes into my locker; I grab the real M-16 and take it upstairs to the armorer and watch him get*

upset because he couldn't find any fault with it. And then I'm off for my weekend!

Ah, the value of going to college.

Interestingly, two years later, the Army had fake M-16s made for the soldiers to carry out in the field. It seems the locals who lived around Fort Bragg were very fond of M-16 rifles and would sneak on the base and steal them while the soldiers were off somewhere training or jumping out of airplanes.

"One time when we were out in the field, they had scheduled a jump, but whoever was supposed to do it failed to schedule the aircraft for the soldiers to jump out of," Dave said. "So the soldiers were all loaded up into Army trucks, which then drove down a dirt road. The sergeant on each truck dropped the tailgate, and the soldiers would jump off the back of the truck one at a time onto the road." Dave and his fake M-16, however, were riding in the colonel's Jeep and weren't required to jump.

Following jump training Dave got a raise in pay, all the way up to eighty-seven dollars a month! He was also on his way to Vietnam, assigned to the 173rd Airborne Division, nicknamed "the Herd." The war there was really ramping up then. Dave had seen information that this division had earlier been ordered to do a practice jump over a particular mountain in Vietnam, and many of the soldiers involved got hung up by their parachutes in the trees. Many were killed or captured by Viet Cong forces who had dug dozens of caves into the mountain, where they were hiding when the Herd jumped. He wasn't thrilled with being attached to this unit after seeing that information. It isn't clear where Dave got that information, but it was possibly passed down from those who knew soldiers in that unit.

Before heading for 'Nam, Dave was provided thirty days' leave. He arrived in the II Corps, S-2 area in Bong Son, Vietnam, on his birthday in February 1969, about a year after the Tet Offensive had been carried out by the North Vietnamese. Tet began on the night of January 30, 1968, when most people were beginning their observances of the Lunar New Year, a big day for the Vietnamese people. The attacks continued into the next day, involving over 120 attacks on various cities and towns throughout South Vietnam, which included the massacre of several thousand non-military people. The North Vietnamese forces were beaten back by the United States and South Vietnamese, but it had a negative impact on relations between the United States and South Vietnam, which were viewed as not being strong.[102]

Bong Son was very near the South China Sea, about 255 miles south of the Demilitarized Zone and 400 miles northwest of Ho Chi Minh City. Sergeant (E-5) Dave was assigned guard duty the night he arrived in Bong Son. "I was the only one awake or not smoking marijuana. I never understood why guys who were where other people wanted to kill them would want to get high and not have all their senses available. I didn't do dope because I didn't want to be a dope! I saw this large thing moving around by the dumpster, so I aimed my gun and shot it. When I did that, everyone was suddenly awake. It turned out to be an unbelievably huge rat!"

Dave posing with Vietnamese children, 1968

Dave's role as a sergeant during his 7 p.m. to 7 a.m. shifts in the briefing tent of II Corps was to monitor radio information about attacks from the enemy and to call air strikes to those locations. A highly disturbing and surprising incident he observed more than once was when officers would call a strike to a certain area that was not being attacked by the enemy, then board a helicopter and fly near that area so they could take videos of the air attacks. These videos would be sent home for their families to see what air attacks looked like. These appeared to be senseless attacks, done just for the drama of making a movie to send home.

That aside, Dave recalled:

> *[I] received information about an attack and immediately ordered an air strike to that area. We were able to take out fourteen Viet Cong and capture several others due to that strike. It was the only competent assault call that I remember being done during my time there .... The only casualties I witnessed while in Vietnam were when a helicopter carrying six soldiers, including the pilot, took off near my post. As they rose up into the air, probably no more than two hundred feet, the rotary wing came off and left the helicopter to plunge into a rice paddy below, exploding into flames and killing all those aboard. Meanwhile, the rotary wing just kept flying until it was out of sight.*

In briefings prior to going to Vietnam, soldiers were told to never salute an officer in a war zone. The reasoning behind this was that if an enlisted soldier saluted an officer and somewhere nearby was an enemy sniper, this would cause the officer to become an immediate target. It made Dave very annoyed when his sergeant major would tell him and the other enlisted soldiers to salute the officers any time they didn't do so. This particular sergeant major had a number of other traits that Dave and his fellow soldiers found more than a little annoying.

Dave recalled:

> *One day, [while sporting a Hitler-style mustache], I walked past the sergeant major's tent and casually tossed a live tear gas grenade in his tent. Then I quickly went back to my tent and shaved off my Hitler mustache. I was questioned several times about whether I was responsible for the grenade and denied any knowledge. One day not long afterward, I was sent by the sergeant major to get something. When I got there, two guys proceeded to gently "beat me up." They indicated*

that they were happy with my activity regarding the sergeant major,
and I didn't get any kind of hard hits from the guys.

A couple of thoughts: tossing a tear gas grenade in the sergeant major's tent could have led to a serious court martial, Dave. Then, there was paratrooper training: I'm not sure what you might have faced if anyone knew about the fake M-16. I'm just glad that wasn't what you were using on guard duty in 'Nam! Are you *sure* you weren't smoking a little of that weed? Were you really raised by Sergeant Heath as an Army Brat?

While Dave was gone, he was always really prolific about writing to Mom. She kept one letter he wrote on a roll of paper that went on and on. He liked to talk, and at that time, we didn't have cell phones or e-mail. But that didn't keep him from talking, even if it was on paper. He wrote letters daily to his girlfriend, Linda, too. On one occasion, he wrote another of those nonstop letters on a thirty-foot-long roll of paper to her. Just as he wrote lots of them, he was always looking for letters from home, especially when they contained a package from Mom full of her delicious homemade chocolate chip cookies, which by the time they got to him were reduced to small crumbs. He still ate and enjoyed them.

Dad's Back and Mike Graduates

Dad returned home from Korea on March 24, 1968, a little over a month after Dave headed to Vietnam. He was assigned to Fort Gordon, Georgia, near Augusta in April. Fort Gordon was less than two hours' drive from where we were in South Carolina. The house was put on the market, and Mom and Dad went house hunting in Augusta. They found a new four-bedroom, brick house quite close to the base and near schools the rest of the Brats would attend, but they finished out the school year in Columbia.

Very shortly after Dad returned from Korea, and amid the integration of schools, public transportation rights, and many other racial issues raging during this tumultuous decade, another tragically sad day came. On April 4, 1968, Martin Luther King Jr.

was assassinated in Memphis, Tennessee by James Earl Ray, a fugitive from the Missouri State Penitentiary.[103]

Aside from our country's loss of a renowned civil rights icon, Jim (age fourteen) suffered a big disappointment related to that event. He was scheduled to go to Memphis to the Iris Festival with the high school band to perform along with bands from all around the country. The festival was scheduled for the middle of April, and needless to say, it was canceled after MLK's untimely death. Jim had practiced really hard on his clarinet and had been looking forward to this festival for over a year, but never had another opportunity to go.

Mike graduated from Lower Richland High School that year. He played football and ran track in ninth through twelfth grades. He remembers how we all took peanut butter and jelly sandwiches for lunch every day, which were made with Mom's delicious homemade bread. "All the kids wanted to trade something for my PB&Js almost every day, but I would never trade," he recalled.

During his senior year, Mike found a girlfriend and future bride, Martha—or as she told it, she found him. In her words, "During our senior year, I worked really hard to get Mike to talk to me. He mostly just went about his business and didn't talk to anybody. But I liked him and persisted, and finally, I succeeded."

Mike was in the Thespian Club his senior year. At their end-of-year play, Mike played Mac in *Annie Get Your Gun*. The club went to Winthrop College in Rock Hill, South Carolina, to the Thespian Convention, just as I did back in '66. They were to do a play, but none of the members had bothered to learn their lines other than Mike. So when they got on stage, they were just saying whatever came to mind. Mike, who had learned his lines, decided to ad-lib, and he started to just throw out all kinds of funny stuff. Mrs. Higgins was less than impressed with all that. I'm pretty sure Mike never got the keys to Mr. Saylor's Mustang.

Mike and Martha were both in the Beta Club. Generally, membership in a Beta Club requires a higher-level grade point average. It's probable that Mike had a significantly higher class ranking upon graduation than his older Brat brother (me). Mom, Dad, and the remaining Brats, Rachel, Jim, Steve, Rick, and Pat, went to his graduation with the car packed and ready to head for Augusta where Dad had just been stationed. Dad had been there since April, and the rest of the Heath Platoon was headed there immediately after Mike's graduation; *immediately* means they left from Mike's graduation and went straight to their new house in Augusta.

Mike wasn't going with them, having been accepted to USC. He had arranged for an apartment and started putting in forty hours a week at Pizza Hut to pay rent for his apartment and tuition. He wanted to be an electrical engineer. Mom worried about how he managed on his own, straight out of high school. She remembers, "A few years later, his future mother-in-law told me that she knew that Mike was capable of doing anything he put his mind to, so that is very likely how he managed. Any time he called me wanting something, it would be a recipe for my mac and cheese or some other thing I made."

The Move to Augusta

At this point, we were leaving as fast as Mom and Dad brought us into the Heath Platoon: Mike was the fourth to depart. The Heath Platoon of nine had shrunk to five, and Rachel had assumed command as the oldest.

The smaller family—Rachel (age seventeen), Jim (fifteen), Steve (thirteen), Rick (twelve), and Pat (five)—settled in to the new home in Augusta in June 1968, and everyone got enrolled in school that fall, including Brat Pat. They could all walk to school; in fact, they could see the school from the house. Rick was at the same school as Pat, as this was a kindergarten through seventh-grade school. Steve was in ninth grade at the junior high, while Jim was going into tenth grade at Butler High. This was his sixth and final school. As the oldest Brat in the Heath Platoon, Rachel was in eleventh grade at Butler, also her sixth and final school.

Rachel wasn't happy about having to make this move to Augusta, having enjoyed four years in Columbia, South Carolina, and the last three years in the same school. As a result, she had made a lot of good friends that she had to leave behind. In addition, she said, "One of the biggest things I remember from South Carolina is I learned to drive; I believe Bob's Volkswagen stick shift and someone's three-on-the-tree, which equipped me to teach my son Michael many years later how to drive one." She has fond memories of those times, since like the rest of us, Rachel had driving instructions from the motor pool master sergeant. "One of my driving lessons had several of the brothers in the car; I think it was Dave's car, and I hit a bird. My hands came off the steering wheel, and I covered my eyes, screaming. Of course, this caused a great deal of yelling at me from the boys. I often think of that day and get a good laugh. Another day I backed over a small tree, which I was sure grew there after I checked the rearview mirror."

Your first driving mistake, Rach, was letting several of your brothers be in your car while driving!

At Butler, Rachel didn't get involved in any school activities outside of the classroom, but she did get a part-time job at a small hamburger joint. One thing she remembers about that job is saving up her money and buying a really expensive John Romaine purse and that it upset Mom that she would spend so much money on a purse. She fondly remembers spending a lot of time with Mom in the kitchen learning how to bake all her yummy goodies, especially Christmas cookies.

Steve started out at Sego Junior High for eighth and ninth grades: "I had several really good teachers there: math, history, and science. The math teacher had a paddle, and every now and then he'd take a kid out in the hall, give him a couple swats, and bring him back in. He maintained a very orderly class! If you were a good kid, that teacher was really a nice guy and a great teacher."

Given our home discipline methodology, this wasn't such an unusual experience for Steve, especially since he never was invited to the hall for a couple of swats. Steve was one of those quiet students.

One of the funniest things Jim experienced in school happened in his psychology class, when his teacher told her students that she could point out the children in the class who were the only children in their family. Jim was one of those she picked, much to the enjoyment of all those who knew that definitely wasn't so. An only child he was not, being the sixth of nine! Every time he tells that story, we all erupt in heavy laughter! There are several varying sets of traits people have identified as being those of an only child. It would be very interesting to see which of these this teacher was applying to Jim.

Unlike Rachel, Jim was heavily involved in school activities, such as Beta Club, Candela Literary (yearbook staff), Student Counsel Alternate (eleventh grade), Drama Club, and the Junior Boosters Club. He was definitely a busy boy! Although he continued playing the clarinet, he only stayed with it through his first semester due to the band director being what Jim considered to be a very poor teacher with some weird attitudes.

A Return to the Nest

Around the time Dad was transferred to Augusta, Dan moved to Charleston, South Carolina, to manage a new Pizza Hut there. While there, he met Delores, whom he would marry. A year or so after they were married, they moved to Augusta for a while, and he managed the Shoney's nearby. Jim, who was apparently not busy enough with school stuff, went to work there when he was in the eleventh grade.

Before Jim got his license, Dan used to "pick me up at school and drive me to work at Shoney's in his MG Midget," Jim said. "He scared the crap out of me every time. Riding in that MG was as scary as my one ride in one of his home-built airplanes."

Dan at some point took up the hobby of building single-engine airplanes from kits that he would buy, which he would fly and often invite one of us to go along. There are a number of interesting stories about those flights—or *frights*, as some of us would call them. I've always thought it was pretty incredible for him to build a homemade airplane and then fly it. That's kind of vintage Dan though. It reminds me how Dan got his early interest in things mechanical when he was a very young fellow, working with Dad on car engines.

Rebellion

Soon enough, the younger boy Brats really wanted to let their hair grow out—we're talking late sixties and early seventies, after all—but Dad had different, more military-oriented ideas about haircuts. Some of the older Brats who had moved out of the house were growing their hair longer, of course, which inspired an even greater need on the part of those still at home. But living at home? Hair will be short!

Maybe Jim, being one of the older Brats at that point, had an idea he was exempt from the Dad haircut rule. He now had his driver's license, and Dad let him drive his truck to work at Shoney's. His hair was starting to get a bit shaggy, so Dad sent him in the truck to get his hair cut. He came back looking much the same as he had before he left. Dad sent him back twice and made it known there would be no truck keys in his hands until his hair length suited him. Since Jim retained use of the truck, we'll assume that the third run back to the barber took care of things.

Another thing about Dad is that he did not suffer fools. And I think we can safely thank him for how we Brats handled unsavory characters and events in our lives. Our experiences with bullies, for example, may have been related to some negative attitudes natives of those areas had toward military kids. The one additional factor in the South would be that we didn't have the Southern drawl the other kids had, which also set us apart. Maybe even more significant to me is how *none* of us put up with the bullying; we always met it head-on, and that always seemed to put an end to it.

Rick recalled:

> There was this one really big guy in our neighborhood named Jerry, who was a big-time bully and just a bad, mean person. One of our neighbors drove a school bus, which would be parked at his house in the evenings. Steve, Pat, and I caught Jerry trying to tear the stop sign off the bus. He threatened to kick our butts if we told on him. The next day he was sticking firecrackers in a turtle's mouth and lighting them, which was something we didn't like at all. Again, he taunted us and called us names because we protested. He was always pushing people around and mouthing off at them like that. He was doing this to me one day and called me "four eyes." My eyes were crossed from birth, and I was always sensitive about it. When he said that, it really struck a nerve, and I jumped at him in a rage. He took off running with me

right behind him. He was running toward the house on the corner, and between that house and the one next was a bunch of bicycles. He tried to make his way through them and tripped over one, falling down. I jumped over the bikes right on top of him and gave him a hard elbow to the face, and he jumped up and ran off. This guy never bothered me or anybody else that I know of again.

This isn't so much about a bully, but more about some wonderment regarding Shiner. You may recall that as a toddler, Pat was very much afraid of Shiner. Ultimately, Pat overcame his fear and became very attached to him. It turned out, like our many previous dogs, Shiner was just another one of the Brats.

"As a little boy, Shiner just seemed to be larger than life," Pat said. He remembered the boys "playing in the back yard one afternoon when a robin went flying across the yard at about five feet off the ground. Shiner, born a bird dog ... always a bird dog, jumped up and swatted the bird out of the air. Our mouths just dropped ... Shiner, can you believe that? SHINER! We couldn't decide if we were supposed to be mad at him or stricken with awe by him. He was a good dog!"

I think *awe* is the word! But, Pat, Shiner was a bird dog, right? I'll bet he had done that many times before then—you just didn't see it!

Straight A's

For some reason, during this time Dad took a different approach to the kind of grades he wanted the Brats to bring home; prior to Augusta, Dad told us that it was fine to bring home Cs.

Jim recalled:

Dad decided [he wanted us] to ramp up our grades, so he offered us twenty dollars for a straight-A report card. I said, "Okay, I can do that." And I did. Only, one of my As was an A-minus, so Dad wouldn't give me the twenty dollars. Later, Mom quietly handed me a twenty-dollar bill, saying, "This is just between us. You earned this!" I never went for straight A's again, even though this was Mom's second time of covering one of Dad's bets when he reneged on paying me.

The lesson: don't take one of Dad's bets.

Sad News

Shortly after the move to Georgia, Glamich's second husband, who was Grampa Archie's brother, passed away after they had been married only sixteen months. They had really been happy with each other. Bob, Mom, and Pat drove to Wisconsin while Rachel took care of her brothers during Mom's absence. Mom persuaded Glamich to come back to Georgia with us, but she only stayed for a month and then went back on the train. Georgia just wasn't for her, at least not then.

Not too long after that, Glamich went to Florida to help out Grampa Grump, keeping house. Very sadly, she hadn't been there more than a couple months when Grampa Grump passed away. After the funeral, she came back to Augusta with the family and rented a small house not far away, where she seemed happy.

Mom would go to her house for lunch often, and Glamich would come to dinner with the family several times a week. She adopted a stray dog—she never went very long without having a dog around. One day, several months after she was on her own, Mom had a call from the sheriff's department, wanting to know if she was acquainted with a woman named Heath who appeared to be in her mid-fifties. Glamich was in her late sixties, but she always looked young. The officer told Mom the location of the house she had pointed out to him, which was Glamich's.

Mom recalled:

> They had found her, roaming around outside, and she was very disoriented. This was close to Christmas, and we couldn't find a doctor who would take on a new patient at that time. She was really badly disoriented, and we had some very hectic days and nights with her until I was able to get her admitted to the hospital, but they never determined what caused her problem. She was in the psychiatric section for six weeks, and then the doctor wanted to admit her permanently to the mental hospital. I asked him if she wouldn't get better if she came home to the family she loved and who loved her. He said, "That lady will

never get better." I didn't believe him and brought my mom home. She had an appointment with that same doctor two weeks later. He saw her alone first, and then he called me in. His exact words to me were, "I have always felt that if patients went home to the families they loved and who loved them, they would, in most cases, get better." My eyes rolled, and I wondered where he heard that!

Happier News and Bob's Off!

In December 1968, Nora and I got married. I was working with an acquaintance from high school at the same camera manufacturing facility near the Columbia Airport where Dave had worked before he was drafted. Because Vietnam was becoming a bigger and bigger issue, so was the number of guys getting drafted into the Army. Not long before Nora and I married, my friend and I decided to join the Navy Reserves as a hopeful means of avoiding Vietnam. What we signed up for was a six-year commitment. We were to serve two years of reserve duty, then two years active duty followed by two more years of reserves. I volunteered to go to active duty early because I wanted to get on with my life without the active-duty part hanging over my head.

I reported to the Great Lakes Naval Training Command in North Chicago, Illinois, for boot camp at the beginning of January 1969—very, very cold, especially when standing still in long lines for various things, like chow! This was just a week after Nora and I were married.

Following boot camp I was assigned to the Bainbridge Naval Training Center for Basic Electricity and Electronics school in Port Deposit, Maryland, to learn how to be a Fire Control Technician. In this role I would maintain and repair the equipment that aimed and fired weapons, like torpedoes and big guns on ships.

I had a little time between boot camp and BE&E school, which allowed me to go to South Carolina to pick up Nora. At that time I had a 1960 VW Bug. We packed all our belongings into that little car, in addition to another sailor, for our trip to Maryland. It was a tight trip.

Nora and I lived in housing provided by the Navy. It amounted to small mobile homes in a little trailer park on the base. They were all painted yellow, light blue, pink, or light green. We met some other nice, newly married couples in our short time there. Lunchtime at the trailers was quiet, but many of the trailers would be shaking!

Following BE&E school, I was assigned to Charleston Naval Base in South Carolina to the USS *Orion*, a submarine tender. The job of this ship was to service the needs of submarines, particularly the new nuclear-powered ballistic missile subs, as well as the soon-to-be obsolete diesel-powered subs. I was in a shop on the ship that had about ten guys, including the head petty officer. The weapons-firing equipment on the old diesel submarines in 1969 was controlled by very early computers, which were huge, gear-driven pieces of machinery; the computers were not much more advanced on the incoming nuclear subs.

The subs would come into the naval base for retrofitting and repairs, and we would go out to—and under—the sea to calibrate the weapons-firing computer systems. Going under the sea on a cramped diesel submarine was ... interestingly different. As it went down, everything about the entire hull would groan and creak rather loudly. Every inch of the interior had an oily sheen. The cot I slept on was directly on top of a long torpedo, one that could, at any moment, be summoned into the firing tube to be fired out into the sea. How to get a good night's sleep on an old diesel sub? Dream about anything else!

The nuclear subs, on the other hand, were spotlessly clean, very spacious, and we slept in rooms with cots. Going underwater wasn't nearly as creaky as the diesels; much different and better! I have always felt very privileged to have experienced going under the sea and working on both the old diesels and the brand-new nukes. Those experiences didn't last very long though.

Interestingly, command became aware that I had lived in Charleston prior to being assigned there. I had lived there for a while before the Navy, working in the Pizza Hut Brat Dan was managing. I was tapped to be the submarine command commodore's driver for the rest of my time on active duty. I didn't mind that assignment at all—not bad for a guy who was mostly just hoping to avoid Vietnam!

Dave mentioned seeing and shooting at a very large rat in Vietnam. I would wager the rats in Charleston would give them a run for their money. I didn't shoot any, but I did have to dodge one every now and then in the car.

While in Charleston, Nora and I had our first child, Rob. He was born during a torrential rainstorm, and I waded through waist-deep water to get to the hospital during visiting hours. In the waiting room during delivery, I was sitting on a couch reading a magazine. Our good friends Brian and Janet were there with me. Janet was the girlfriend who bailed on me when Dad announced that I wasn't college material. Brian was my former roommate who I had introduced to Janet. Brian was pacing the room like a nervous, soon-to-be father when the nurse came to announce Rob's birth. She went to Brian, and said, "Mr. Heath, your son has been delivered, and he's very healthy!" Brian pointed over to me, and said, "That's Mr. Heath!" I guess having been raised around the birth of six younger siblings allowed me to be pretty calm about it all. We had many laughs over that!

A little over a year after little Rob came along, I was relieved from active duty on December 2, 1970, with a rank of seaman, E-4, and honorably discharged from the reserves in November 1973 after serving the rest of my reserve duty. Joining the Navy as a means to avoid being sent to the war in Vietnam worked out surprisingly well for me. That war was considered a senseless loss of American lives to a majority of Americans, and I was in full agreement with that sentiment. What I could never agree with, however, was the abusive manner in which many people treated the soldiers returning from Vietnam, most of whom were drafted and forced to go there. I believe strongly that those issues spoke very strongly to all military Brats of that time. We respect and honor those who serve the United States in our military, just as we love our country.

Dave's Back from Vietnam

About the time I was heading to boot camp, Dave was returning home from Vietnam. After a rough landing at SeaTac Airport near Seattle, he received his honorable —in-spite-of-tear-gassing-his-sergeant-major —discharge on December 24, 1969. Dave was back in school the following semester, and he and Linda were married on January 10, 1970. Dave had the GI Bill now to help pay for school, and Linda had a good job as a computer programmer. He graduated at the end of the fall semester of 1970 with a bachelor's degree in business administration.

When Dave came home safe and sound, it was a great relief to all of us. That relief was short lived because two weeks after he returned, Dad was on orders to go to Vietnam. Then about two weeks before he was due to leave, Dad came home with a bunch of papers in his hand, let out a whoop, and threw the papers in the air.

"Your orders have been canceled?" Mom asked. Yes, they had been! That was a very happy moment for everyone. The next day, Dad put in for retirement, and no one was in any way disappointed by that move.

As happy as we were about Dave and Dad, we had another great sadness for Uncle Gene and Aunt Mayme. Our cousin Brian served in Vietnam and lost his life there very shortly before he was due to come home. Gene and Mayme had adopted a baby girl about a year before Brian's death, and she may have saved them from complete collapse. As mentioned earlier, they had lost their only daughter, Jean Marie, in a plane crash just a few years prior to the loss of Brian. At that time, his younger brother, Tim, was in the Navy. They are two very strong people.

One More Brat Leaves the Nest

When Rachel graduated from Butler High School in 1970, Dan's wife, Delores, was working at the Pantry Pride grocery store. "After I graduated, I went to work there, making $1.95 an hour," Rachel said. "That's where I met Eddie. He was going to Augusta College and working as a shelf stocker at Pantry Pride. We would go to Shoney's after work on Saturday nights to celebrate the weekend. Eddie and I were married in June of '71."

The boy Brats who were still at home say they never met Eddie. Apparently, Rachel kept him a secret, not wanting her brothers to try to get in the way of her relationship with him. Knowing the Brat boys, that may well have been a very smart tactic on Rachel's part.

Rick remembers visiting Rachel after she moved out though. Apparently, Jim and Rick used to go to the Teen Club on Fort Gordon to troll for girls and dance. Rick found a girlfriend at the Teen Club, but she didn't last long: "My favorite song was 'Tears of a Clown,' Rick said. "This may have been due to the fact that I had what I thought was a girlfriend, Irma. I was fourteen, and she was the sister of Jim's girlfriend. We were at Rachel's apartment one day when Irma said, 'I have a disease, and I'm going to die. It won't be good for us to stay together.' I was heartbroken, sitting in Rachel's apartment crying my eyes out."

Well, Rick, at least Dad didn't run her off at your high school graduation dinner! Besides, you'll have to admit, the "I'm going to die" excuse is a pretty inventive one, but hopefully it wasn't true.

Bob: Still Not College Material?

After completing my active-duty time in the Navy and as a married person with a child, I went back to school at USC with a different attitude and goals, finishing in three-and-a-half years while working full time. I also had the GI Bill to help with the costs of going to school. I had initially determined my major to be in business, modeling after Brat Dave. I dropped that early on due to a serious lack of interest. I earned a degree in English literature, with a minor in history.

USC had a program at that time in which a student could get an undergraduate degree and move straight into a doctoral program, and my goal was to be a college professor. Whatd'ya think about that, Dad? However, sometimes goals have to wait for real life to get out of the way to let them move forward. With a family to support, I needed to get a real job after finishing my undergraduate degree. Not thinking Dad or Mom or anyone else would be interested, I didn't attend my graduation in August 1974. I'm not sure why I thought Dad or Mom wouldn't be interested, unless it was due to the "not college material" comment. You would think that I would have gone and invited them just to get in Dad's face about it. But I didn't. The truth is that Dad was exactly right at the time he said it, and I just needed a few more years to grow up and take on the responsibilities of an adult. They were both there and very proud of me when I graduated with a master's degree in personnel services, then later with a doctorate in educational leadership and policies.

Mike, also uninterested in experiencing Vietnam, signed up for the Air Force National Guard, reporting for duty in January of 1970, midway through his junior year at the University of South Carolina. He went to basic training at Lockland Air Force Base near San Antonio, Texas, then was sent to Keesler Air Force Base in Biloxi, Mississippi, for training in radio repair. He was on active duty for eleven months, then discharged to reserve duty for the remaining portion of his six-year enlistment.

When Mike was released from active duty, he resumed his last three semesters and received his degree in electrical engineering at USC, graduating at the end of 1972. In May of 1971, Mike and Martha had gotten married right after she completed her degree in elementary education. She began teaching third grade at Mill Creek Elementary near Columbia that fall.

Dan, Dave, Bob, Mike, and Rachel had all married while the family was in Augusta. Dan and Delores had a daughter, Tonya, before long. Before Delores and Dan met, she had a young son, Harold, who was welcomed into the family. And Nora and I had brought Robbie into the family. So in addition to Rachel, Mom and Dad had four more daughters: Delores, Linda, Nora, and Martha, and another son, Eddie—along with three grand-Brats.

At long last, retirement was in reach. After Mom and Dad bought the lake property, there never was any doubt as to where they would retire. Retiring didn't happen until July 31, 1971, and Dad had twenty-nine years of service to our country. He was only fifty-one, but ready to go fishing!

CHAPTER 18
GOIN' FISHING, 1971

The full-time move to the lake took place right after Dad's retirement, but Mom and Dad had to get a few things in place to make that happen. One of those was the need for another lot next to the one they had in order to have the space required to put up the size house they needed; luckily, the lot next to theirs was for sale. After securing the second lot, they bought a double-wide mobile home that had three bedrooms and two full baths, which was good for them and the three Brats still home: Steve (age sixteen), Rick (fifteen), and Pat (eight). It took three weeks to get it out to the lot because of nonstop rain. While it was being set up on the sloping lot, one end fell and damaged the mobile home, requiring some repair work. Then the pillars that had to be at specific intervals under the house weren't built correctly by the installers, causing some instability, and the house was quite shaky.

"If one happened to be sitting on the toilet in the back bathroom when the washer was spinning at the other end of the house, one could get a good tail massage," Mom said. "Dad and Dave poured new concrete footings and restacked every one of those pillars, solving the problem."

Mom and Dad put their house in Augusta up for sale, but the sellers' market wasn't very good at the time, so they rented it to an Army captain and his family who were excellent renters, but not for long. Unfortunately, and as one would expect since the captain was in the Army, he got orders to another post and had to leave. It was then rented to an enlisted man and his wife, who bought it soon after they moved in, which was great.

Glamich was needing a good bit of attention at that time, and Mom knew she would be very busy with the move. So just before the move, Rachel accompanied Glamich to Chicago. Mom's brother, Gordon, met them there and picked Glamich up. She couldn't walk at that time, and it was Mom's intention to bring her back after they got settled at the lake. Uncle Gordon put her in a nursing home until they were ready for her to come back to South Carolina. A few months later Mom sent Glamich a flannel nightgown, and she liked it so much that she took it and walked on her own to another section of the facility to show it to a friend. After that, she improved until she could do most things for herself. The following summer, Glamich flew down and stayed with Mom and Dad for about a month; then the next summer she came again and stayed for good. She loved it at the lake, and it was great for the Brats, all who loved her dearly.

Steve, Rick, and Pat were the first of the Heath Platoon to move somewhere without having the thought lurking in the back of their heads about where in the world the next duty station would be. Steve was going into eleventh grade, and Rick was in tenth at Mid-Carolina High School in nearby Prosperity. Pat was in third grade at Prosperity-Rikard Elementary. Another big change for them was that they now were experiencing Dad being around full time, something the Brats had only experienced during those relatively brief times he was on leave between assignments.

The dynamics of family life were a lot different. To begin with, there were only three Brats living at home. Also, when Mom was the main parent home, we ran pretty free and wild around whatever countryside was nearby. Now, with Dad around, the Brats were more accountable as to where they were and what they were doing.

Steve, Rick, and Pat all had to ride the school bus since their schools were a pretty good distance from the lake house. Their bus would only come to the highway end of the dirt road, which was about a mile from the house. On decent days the Brats didn't mind the walk, but on rainy days the road turned to a sloppy mush. On bad weather days, Mom or Dad took them out to the bus stop and picked them up, but that was getting a bit annoying.

"Coming home from school one day, Pat was feeling really bad, and we had to walk all the way from the main road," Steve said. "Rick and I took turns carrying Pat and his books all the way home. The next day, Dad, doing what he does, got the bus to come all the way to the house from then on." Once again, the sergeant came to the rescue!

Mom and Dad: Settling in to Retirement
Dad immediately loved living at the lake, but he and Mom also experienced some wrinkles and changes as they adapted to retired civilian life. He had envisioned this life for several years before he actually retired, and that primarily meant going fishing, which he did nearly every day, at least for a while. Apparently, that retirement dream became boring, and after a year or so, he took several part-time jobs. During those years, he worked in two different grocery stores, a motel, helped a cabinet maker, and installed fireplace inserts—a little bit of everything. Fifty-one is a pretty young age to retire, even after working as hard as he did over the course of his career, and he was finding that it was tough coping with all that free time.

As Mom and Dad were adjusting to their new life on the lake, they were also being happily blessed with new Brat spouses and a growing cadre of grand-Brats. On Mom and Dad's first New Year's Day at the lake, Rachel and Eddie welcomed their first child, Michael, down in Augusta. Michael was the sixth grand-Brat.

Grandchildren continued to come along and got to an age where Mom and Dad felt comfortable having them without their parents. They would invite the boys out for a week and then the girls for a week. The kids always had fun swimming and boating, even turning the john boat over and trying to sink it, which never happened. Most of the grand-Brats learned to water ski, and the girls loved to play house and help Mom bake and then get to lick the beaters. It was a new thing for Mom to have more than one girl in the house, and it was something she enjoyed a great deal. Every one of those grand-girls learned how to bake Mom's goodies.

Our family at the lake, 1975

In addition to all the fun things, these kids really got to know and play with their cousins while growing up. That's something Brats rarely get to do; we certainly didn't. It may help explain why we are all so insistent we gather together frequently. All those grandkids, now grown, still love to get together and reminisce about their fun times together out at the lake.

"The girls liked to get on their Grampa's recliner and did, often," Mom said. "He put a No Parking sign on it. That only encouraged more happy, giggling trespassing. They did love to tease him, and he certainly knew how to tease them. He was always threatening to 'X' them out, which just made them laugh harder."

The area by the water was kind of muddy, so Dad wanted to create a beach area and had a big truckload of sand dumped down there. He didn't bother to level it; the grandkids did that, and it didn't take long. After sliding down that high sand hill many times, they had created a nice sandy beach. The grands weren't the only ones enjoying the sand because it had created a nice nesting place for the lake's large soft-shelled turtles. Mom really enjoyed watching the grands play in the sand, but she also liked watching the turtles come up into the sand to lay their eggs.

Mom recalled:

> *They would dig a small indentation, then lay a few eggs, and shovel sand on top. Almost always, there would be one or more crows nearby just waiting to snatch the eggs as soon as the turtle left. We often ran out to chase the crows away. It was funny to watch though, because the crow would be so close to the turtles who were burying their eggs that it would get a dousing of the sand. Some of the eggs must have survived and hatched because there always was an abundance of turtles. Some days they were lined up, waiting their turns to lay their eggs.*

Meeting New Friends and Staying Active

Something else Mom and Dad appreciated about retirement life on the lake was that they always had good neighbors whom they knew, including most of the folks from the beginning to the end of the road. While Dad was in the service and we were overseas, Mom and Dad would have some good friends, but wouldn't generally know too many of the neighbors. After moving to the lake on that little two-mile dirt road, it was a bit surprising when people would walk or drive by and stop to introduce themselves, tell Mom and Dad where they lived, and offer to help them if they ever needed anything.

Of course, Dad never met a stranger, so that didn't hurt the process of getting to know people. Additionally, this was the rural South, and people have a strong tendency to act that way. When you pass them in your car, even if they don't know you, they'll wave at you. Although they had been at military bases in the South now for seven years, they had only recently become civilians in the rural South, and this behavior is part of that culture.

Mom and several of the neighbor ladies liked to walk the road together almost every day. A fun, or maybe scary thing Mom recalled:

> *I have almost always had neighbors to walk with, and this road can't be beat as a walking track. We got into the habit of walking every day*

except Saturday and Sunday. Sometimes there would be five of us and three dogs. One day, there were four of us and one dog, and that dog had gone foraging in the woods. We were at an area with a high bank, and a deer jumped out onto the road just a few feet ahead of us with the dog at its heels—very scary as we could have been badly injured had we been in its path.

The walkers would come across lots more deer over the years, and it wouldn't be quite as scary as time went on. They dubbed their walking group the "Half-Fast Walkers."

Mom and Dad became very active in the Catholic Church in Newberry. Dad was on the church council for two years, and they both taught the Catholic Youth Organization. Dad taught more than Mom did as he was much more qualified, being a "cradle" Catholic and having had many years of catechism. He taught Pat's confirmation class. Because it was a small congregation, the priests were never there for long, but Mom and Dad became close with some of them, just as they did in Germany.

Besides learning to relax and enjoy the lake, Mom and Dad did some traveling now that they had all the time they needed to explore. Among those trips were several camping jaunts with Rachel and Eddie, who had a small pop-up camper.

"We went to the World's Fair in Knoxville, Tennessee, with Rachel, Eddie, Michael, and Kari," Mom said. "We camped in a very pretty place. As we were pulling into the campsite, Eddie said, 'After we get the camp set up, Rachel and her dad will go around and meet everyone in camp, and her mom and I will sit at the table and talk to each other.' How right he was: one characteristic Rachel got from her dad was that of never meeting a stranger!"

It has been observed that all the Brats have that quality.

The sand, sun, and water at South Carolina's Myrtle Beach also became a go-to destination for Mom and Dad, and they bought a time-share there for one week in June each year. After about four years, they sold it, but kept going down each spring or early summer.

"One year, some of Dick's family met us there—more good memories," Mom said. "Dick's family has really been good about getting together with us since we retired. I feel certain our children will continue to do that too, and that is a very comforting thought."

How right she was about that!

The lake was a big attraction for all the Brats and our growing families in the years after Mom and Dad moved there. This wasn't only because they were at a lake; it was also a "home place" for Mom and Dad where we could go, both to visit them and to be with each other and all our nieces and nephews. As the years went by, the older Brats became more and more involved in work careers and raising their own kids, so there were some quiet weekends with no company, even though there were frequent gatherings on weekends.

South Carolina Snowstorm

Dad's sister Joan and her husband, Lou, started coming down from Illinois every year around Easter. One year, they decided to get away from the harsh winter weather in Illinois, so they came in February and rented a cabin about a mile down the road from Mom and Dad's place. Apparently, they brought the harsh Illinois weather with them: central South Carolina had a hard freeze and a snowstorm with two feet of snow while they were there. Very, very *not* South Carolina-like. Lou had packed the car with some winter things Joan didn't think they would need, and she wanted that space to carry cloth back home. But when the water pipes in their cabin froze, it was fortunate that Lou had brought along a bucket and was able to get water from the lake to flush the toilet. They walked up to Mom and Dad's place: Lou had rubber boots on his feet; Joan's were wrapped in plastic wrap, and she was steaming at Lou because he was rubbing it in that he had packed what they needed, as it turned out. They didn't come in February again; even though hard freezes and big snowstorms aren't exactly the February norm in South Carolina.

Steve remembered that frigid time:

We had a huge snowstorm—shut down the whole state. I was a senior, I think. It was February 9–11, 1973, and we got two feet of snow. They were airlifting people off the interstate. It was called the "Great Southeastern Snowstorm" and apparently affected several Southern states. South Carolina gets very little snow, generally, and just doesn't have the equipment needed to clear roads, like up north …. We didn't have any snow sleds, but couldn't let all this snow go away without having some fun with it. We took some great big skis like the ones I skied on in Italy and nailed two-by-fours across, and we took those skis out to the beginning of the lake road and sledded down that big hill: me, Rick, Pat, and our neighbor Walter. We had a blast!

Pat added:

For brakes, we tied a big rope onto the front cross tie, and on the end of the rope, we tied just a big knot wad. When we wanted to stop, we would throw the rope in front of the sled. The "knot wad" would go under the sled, and believe it or not, the thing would actually slow down. After many successful runs, of course, we got bored. We decided to see how many people we could get on the sled at one time and how much faster it would go. We loaded her down. She went faster. And, and … the lake was there … and that knot wad thingy … How deep was that water, Rick?

"Not just deep, but really cold!" Rick said.

To the three remaining Brats, though, the lake and the woods surrounding them became huge, nature-laden playgrounds.

"We were out on the boat with Dad, Mom, Rick, and Pat, and the boat ran out of gas in the middle, near Blacks Bridge," Steve said. "The marina was halfway across the water, and Dad got out the paddle. It was taking forever, so Rick and I jumped out and grabbed the mooring rope and swam, pulling the boat. We had it going pretty good, and we got to the marina, got some gas, and headed back to the house."

Brats never pass up an opportunity to have some fun!

Speaking of fun—well, to everyone but Dad—during a family gathering one weekend, Pat heard, with great jealousy, the stories of rolling down a big hill inside a great big tractor tire near his hometown, Heidelberg. He said, "I'm not pleased that I missed that …. And I think just about everyone was at the lake that day when we disturbed the neighbors by riding our bikes down the hill and into the lake. The bikes would stop when they hit the water … we just kept going head over heels into the water. We also disturbed Dad by forcing him into the red wagon and pushing him into the lake. He was very angry. I think he threw his soggy hamburger at Bob. I don't think I had ever seen Dad that flustered."

Yeah, Dad didn't think it was so funny, and thanks for the soggy hamburger on my shirt, Pat! Really, it was funny; Dad was the only one who wasn't laughing!

More Brat Fun and Growing Up Not-So Army
Steve, Rick, and Pat really loved living out there. When the weather was warm, they could come home from school and jump in the lake, fish to their hearts' content, and go hiking in the woods.

"Steve and I came home from school with a six-foot-long king snake draped over our shoulders for a picture," Rick said. "Mom was totally cool about it. Not a big deal, it's just a really big snake. That's our mom!"

Steve remembered another Lake Murray snake adventure. "On our way out to the main road to catch the school bus one morning, we saw this hog-nosed snake just sitting on the road," he said. "We poked it with a stick to see if it was alive, and it puked up a bunch of toads, then just laid there and didn't move. We went on to school, and on the way back, we checked that same place for the snake; it was gone, and so were all the toads."

Fun comes in many forms for the Brats!

Steve was in his eighth school of his first twelve years of education, finishing his last two high school years. He excelled while at Mid-Carolina High School. Brat seven graduated from high school in

1973 and went to USC, living on campus. While there, he continued attending the Catholic Church for a while near the Catholic elementary school he attended several years earlier, which was pretty close to the university. As he was sitting in church one Sunday, he was looking around at the pretty girls who were in attendance, and it occurred to him that if he hung around on campus at USC on a Sunday morning, there would be a whole lot more pretty girls wandering around there for him to see. So he was done with church for the time being.

Things at USC got even more interesting for Steve: "Talk about weird things ... I was at USC when kids started 'streaking' on campus. That is, they would run around naked. It was a fad that was taking off around the country in 1974. I saw naked guys hanging from fire escapes; once there was a guy and a girl riding a bike naked through campus. I did not participate!"

Moving from military Brat into the civilian world of the late sixties and seventies was a very significant transition for all of us! Even though I was finishing up my senior year during the spring and summer sessions at USC in 1974, I never witnessed the streaking that was going on, mostly because I lived off campus. I had to agree with Steve about how weird that was though!

Brat eight, Rick, said that moving to the lake instigated some profound life changes for him—changes about himself that he appreciates to this day.

"All it took was hooking a large, large-mouth bass, and I was adapted. Goodbye, city; hello, country forever," he said. "The best days of my younger life were spent there."

Rick completed grades ten through twelve at Mid-Carolina High. He had been taking college prep courses through eleventh grade, planning to be a marine biologist. That is, until he ran into chemistry, a subject in which he didn't excel. The next semester, he switched over to auto and woodworking classes and joined the 4-H Club. He said he also started hanging out with kids who were more connected with country living than the "preppies" with whom he had been friends. Once Rick graduated from high school, he moved to Columbia to the apartment where Jim and Steve were living and got a job. Not too long afterward he met Grace. They later married.

Brat Nine, Pat, was going into third grade at Prosperity-Rikard Elementary School and would go all the way through in the same school district for his last ten years of school. This meant that, aside from just being in the same school district, he also would be in class and school with many of the same friends for all those years. This was a highly unique experience, compared to the rest of us. Along with that, he would finish his last seven years in school and at home as an only child. I can't imagine how that would feel—for Pat or for Mom and Dad.

Pat recalled a very unique experience at the start of school that first year:

> *I was going into the third grade when Dad retired and we moved to Lake Murray. The school practiced ability-grouping of students by placing them in groups: A Group were the brighter students, B Group were students of average ability, and C Group involved those with learning challenges. When Mom signed me up for school, they assigned me to the B Group.*
>
> *When she told this to Dad, he said, "I'll get that straightened out tomorrow!" The next morning, he puts on his dress uniform with its chest full of medals, puts me in the car, and we drive to the school. We walk in, ask to see the principal, and are escorted into her office.*
>
> *Sergeant Major Heath snappily removes his hat, placing it under his left arm, stands at attention, looks the principal in the eye, and says, "I understand you have placed my son in your B Group. I want him placed in the A Group," in a stern voice.*
>
> *The principal says, "I'm sorry, sir, but the A Group is full, and he will have to be in the B Group this year."*
>
> *Sergeant major replies, "He will be in the A Group!" again with the stern voice and still looking the principal in the eye.*
>
> *She then responds, "He will be in the A Group, sir."*
>
> *Dad says, "Thank you, ma'am," replaces his hat, does a sharp about-face, and walks out the door. And I was in the A Group!*

Honestly, up until the sudden comeuppance of Brat Nine, I don't believe Dad ever insisted on a higher-class placement for anyone! Remember his theory that most of the world is average, and Cs are okay on a report card?

Family Support, Help, and Visits

Pat remembers the brothers always having one another's backs:

> *When we first moved to the lake, we had a lot of trouble on the school bus with a few of the kids. On one particularly rough ride home, this guy was giving me a hard time, and Steve stood up to face off the guy. The guy, nicknamed Head, started punching Steve in the head, and the driver pulled the bus over and came back and put a stop to it. Rick had taken all he could from Head, who had been giving all of us a lot of trouble. Head and his older brother, Wyman, got off the bus at Morris's skating rink. Rick and I walked all the way back to the skating rink because Rick had decided that he must confront Head about his attitude problem. Rick walked right up to Head and said something like, "I don't know what your problem is with us, but it's got to stop!"*
>
> *Head nervously tried a diversionary tactic. "What, you brought yo little brotha up here an' now you gon' try an' gang up on me?"*
>
> *Rick said, "Leave my little brother out of this."*
>
> *Wyman chimed in, "Yeah, das 'tween you an' Rick, Head."*
>
> *Rick said, "It's like this, Head. We can shake hands and be friends, or we can fight it out, but the crap is gonna stop right here, right now!"*
>
> *Head thought about it for a minute, held out his hand, and Wyman said, "That's it!"*

And friends they were.

Pat's closest friend, Wayne, spent a great deal of time at the house. For a while they were like shadows of each other. The school bus would let Pat off and wait for him to go in the house and change his clothes, then take him back to the highway so he could go and play with Wayne. That's quite a big change from when the bus wouldn't even come to the house to pick them up.

On the day Pat turned sixteen, he and Wayne and two other boys were planning on going cruising that evening. Dave had come out to visit, and Mom and Dad were planning to celebrate his birthday, so Mom wouldn't let Pat go. Tragically, the boys were in a bad auto accident—the driver was killed; Pat's good friend Wayne was in a coma for several weeks before he died, and the other boy wound up in a wheelchair. This was, no doubt, a very sad event for Pat and Mom and Dad, but they were all so thankful that Pat wasn't involved.

★★★

Getting the house and things around the lot in order was an ongoing process for Dad and Mom. The lot is on a fairly steep slope, and the front of the house—the side facing the lake—is much higher than the back. For about two years, the front door was kept locked because there were no steps. Dad's plan was to build a porch across that side of the mobile home, but he had to determine how to do it and what kind of porch it should be. He nailed a board between two trees down near the water and would spend hours down there thinking and just relaxing, making many of the plans for the house and property. He never did anything halfway, and any project would be right in his mind before he would start working on it. Dad did most of the work but had occasional help from Steve and Rick. He built an enclosed sunroom with lots of windows facing out onto the lake. Even though it was always referred to as a porch, when Rick and Grayce's son Neil was just starting to talk, he would say, "That is not a porch!" It remained a porch regardless. It was a nice, big open space, and we enjoyed years of Thanksgiving dinners on that porch.

"We were so blessed to have found this place to retire," Mom said. "It is so quiet and so relaxing. We can sit at our breakfast table on the porch and watch a Sandhill Crane patiently stalk its breakfast. We can enjoy the songs of birds and the cawing of crows, see the large turtles come up to lay their eggs, and sometimes get a short glimpse of the Pileated Woodpeckers. They never stay long, but that makes it more exciting."

With most of the Brats gone and more flexibility available in what they had time to do, Mom and Dad embarked on some more traveling. In 1976, they went to Wisconsin for Christmas. Dad had an aunt and uncle and several cousins in Phillips, Wisconsin, which is only about twenty miles from where Mom was born. They also wanted Pat to experience some weather like they did growing up, and it was really great that he had the opportunity to meet and visit some aunts, uncles, and cousins he had never seen before. While they were there, Pat had a lot of fun sledding and snowmobiling in the deep Wisconsin snow.

It was so cold that Dad had to attach the car battery to an outlet at night so the car would start the next day. Even in that cold, many of the men and boys wore warm vests over flannel shirts, instead of heavy coats. At night, Dad's uncle put food out near the house to attract deer, and there was a huge old buck who came to get it just at twilight every evening.

One of the things Mom fondly enjoyed was seeing the white poplar forests and the beauty of the northern evergreen trees, which she hadn't seen in many years. She said it with this caveat: "However, I must be clear: there is nothing in the north that is magnetic enough to make me want to live there." She had enough of the deep snow and really cold weather while growing up.

A year or two later, Dad, Mom, and Glamich went to Illinois for Thanksgiving with Joan and Lou. When they got back home, I pronounced, "You can go anyplace you want, anytime you want, except Thanksgiving." Apparently, they hadn't considered that, up until that time, the Heath family Thanksgiving had become a family rule and one of the annual events all the Brats had come to expect and enjoy. Our family has been together every Thanksgiving since. In fact, when Bill asked Dave for Kelli's hand in marriage, Dave had him sign a contract that they would always have Thanksgiving with the family. These events include between forty and fifty family and friends every year. Everyone brings food, and there is always some kind of game or physical activity between the big meal and dessert. Early on we played tag football, then our game became volleyball, and then later it would be mostly the grandkids playing whatever they wanted. We almost always have several friends who are not family in attendance. One year a little boy said, "Mama, this is the best Thanksgiving I have ever had." We all agree with that!

Besides my love for the delicious food at Thanksgiving, my favorite part of it is that when we get together, be it Thanksgiving or family workday, there is always a great deal of laughter and fun. During one of the gatherings, Mom's daughters-in-law mentioned that her sons have many of Dad's traits, some endearing and some not. Mom's response?

"Since I am not sure of the good ones, I will list a couple of the others," she said. He always waited until a meal was ready before he would go to the bathroom or decide he had to make a phone call. One time at a meal, he asked for a slice of bread. It and the butter were right in front of me, so I buttered the bread for him. He held the bread up and said, 'Well, you did it again.' He said I had buttered the bread on the wrong side. It was home-baked bread, and one side had more crust than the other. Our sons agreed with him that the butter should go on the side with the least crust. Believe it or not, this man was fun to live with. If we wanted the little kids to eat their meals, we never put them close to their Grampa. No matter how much their mothers or I would fuss at him, he would keep on playing with the kids."

★★★

Our families would come out to the lake to have lunch or dinner, and just enjoy being with Mom and Dad and whatever other family members were there. Mom and Dad always loved having everyone visit, just as much as we all loved visiting.

Dave's daughter Kelli and her husband, Bill, were out at the lake for dinner one day, and after everyone finished eating, Bill said, "Go ahead, Kelli, tell them."

She said, "Gramma and Grampa, we are going to Romania."

Mom wasn't surprised to hear that, since they had been in Romania for a short time, and she knew that the fate of the children in Romanian orphanages was haunting them.

She said, "It was heartrending to have them leave but I got to thinking of all the times we had told our folks that we were off to a foreign country and we wouldn't see them for three years. I couldn't remember them ever making it harder for us to leave. At least we would be seeing Bill and Kelli every six months."

Kelli and Bill did missionary work in Romania for two years, but they were always home for Thanksgiving.

Dad had been working his part-time jobs for a few years and finally decided retirement should really mean no job, so he quit and took up golf. He went several days a week, and fishing went down the same road as the part-time jobs. Dad was a pretty good golfer and really wanted Mom to get interested in it. She did go out with him a few times, but found she always came home with a sore right arm. She would line up and swing the club at the ball, but the club would hit the ground more often than it hit the ball, and that really hurt! She gave it up pretty early on but kept going with Dad and enjoyed walking around the course with him.

About the only continued connection to the military for them was going to the commissary at Fort Jackson for groceries, a drive of about forty miles. Prices were always good, and the commissary had everything they wanted. Besides that, there may have been a bit of a need to stay connected to the military through those trips. It pretty well took all day to go to the commissary, shop, then drive back home.

Mom's recollection of those trips includes one of the many adjustments they were making to retired life:

> *Dick always insisted on coming with me, and I was not used to that. We would each take a cart at first, but we would stay together. I do not buy canned food if the can is dented; he could not understand that—called it a quirk. When we were checking out, he would throw everything onto the counter, and we would have broken cookies and crackers. By the time we were on our way home, we were not friends. After several trips we decided that he would take a list and would not travel the store with me. When we got to the checkout, he would go get the car while I paid for the groceries.*

The good news is they made the adjustments they needed to make in order to ensure their continued happy retired life.

Finally, Brat Nine was finishing high school. Pat recalled:

I was one of four seniors in the school who qualified to go into the Navy, which I thought I wanted to do. The closer it got to going, the less I wanted to do it; so I didn't. Dad had made it very clear that I would be moving out the day after graduation. Knowing that, tired of butting heads with Dad, and pretty much ready to move on with life, I made arrangements to stay with Jim and Sandy near Columbia for most of my senior year. I drove back and forth to school in Prosperity until graduation. Then I attended USC for a year and worked at the Pizza Hut, like everyone else did (except Rachel). After that, I got a job at the Micalline cultured marble plant in Columbia and worked there for several years. Some years later, one of my oldest cousins, Tonya, who was Dan and Delores's oldest daughter, was having her thirtieth birthday party, and most of the family was attending. In addition to the Heaths being there, some of Delores's family were there, including her unmarried niece Belinda. It had been "set up" to introduce me to Belinda, even though Delores kept telling me that I couldn't hook up with her. Well, we liked each other, got together, and eventually got married. So, the youngest Brat married the niece of the oldest Brat's wife. Someone said that was going to make the universe collapse. We're still waiting for that.

A year or two after Pat's departure from the family nest, Dad was in his early sixties and began having some physical problems. Mom recalled:

Dick started having trouble walking in a straight line, sometimes going around in circles. His doctor suggested that he go to the VA Hospital in Augusta. They did many tests on him, even took X-rays when he was upside down. After several days, his doctor told us that liquid was accumulating on his brain, and she would run a shunt to his pancreas, and that should take care of it. She also told us that this surgery would take very little recuperative time. He had the surgery; Rachel and I held each other's hands, and he came home the next day eager to get to work on home projects that had been accumulating …. Dick had smoked cigarettes since he was a teen, but while he was in the hospital, there was oxygen being used in his room. He could smoke in the waiting room, but he ran out of cigarettes, and I refused to bring him any for fear he would light up in the room. He checked out [of the hospital] on Rachel's birthday, and he gave her and me a most wonderful gift. He said he would not smoke again. He kept his cigarettes in a pocket in his shirt, and for a long time I would see him pat that pocket. During that time, I had terrible nightmares that he was smoking again. When he stopped patting his pocket, my nightmares left.

Dad never smoked another cigarette.

Not Smoking? Let's Hit the Road!

Now, with no Brats at home and after his career in the Army, which required that he and his wife and children be far, far away from their extended family for years at a time, Dad wanted to go on a journey to visit the many places around the country where they had family and friends. Mom was okay with making the trip, although not very anxious for it to be an extended one—and she had been adamant that Dad would have to stop smoking before it could happen. As we all grew up, Dad smoked in our houses and cars, and Mom was done with that. Now that he had quit, the trip was on! Over the winter, they contacted aunts, uncles, cousins, brothers, and friends as they planned a six-week-long trip. Even though Mom wasn't very excited about the length of the trip, she was excited to have the chance to see folks neither of them had seen in a long time.

The big trip began on June 6, 1984, about thirteen years into Dad's retirement. It started off with a nine-day stop in Illinois, visiting relatives and friends they knew growing up, most of whom they hadn't seen in many years. One of those visits was with Mom's brother, Gordon, and his wife, Shirley. Gordon took them to Waupaca to see their old home. They talked about their long walks from there to school in the snow, but Mom noted that it didn't look all that long from the car. While there, they dropped Glamich off in Wisconsin Rapids, where she stayed with her youngest sister as Mom and Dad continued the rest of their journey.

From there, they headed west, stopping at some of the famous sites they passed along the way, to take a break and walk for a while to keep their bodies moving after being in the car for long stretches of time. On the third day they spent the night near Tacoma, Washington, near our Lakewood home (a.k.a. "the castle"). The next day they went to the house and introduced themselves and were invited in by the folks living there, who had bought it from us some twenty-four years earlier. After a nice visit, which included a tour of the house, they visited Dad's youngest brother, Paul, and his family. After catching up with Paul and his crew, they met up with some old friends from Heidelberg, Germany, who lived nearby. Then it was off to Corvallis, Oregon, to spend several days with Dad's younger brother P.J. and his wife Shirley. They had lots of fun camping out in P.J.'s camper on the coast of Oregon and spending time together.

Next, it was farther south into California where they were amazed by the Redwood Forest as they made their way to visit Mom's cousins Mildred and Wayne, whom we all stayed with on our way to and from Taiwan many years before. Following the visit with Mildred and Wayne, the Ford was pointed back east toward home, with several more stops to look at beautiful scenery around Flagstaff, Arizona—the Painted Desert and Petrified Forest to name a couple—along with a few more visits with family and friends. Their main stop on the trip back home was Broken Arrow, Oklahoma, to spend a few days with Steve and Cay, where Steve was in divinity school at Rhema Bible Training College. They really had a great time with them, touring the campus, swimming, and catching up.

Following that sweet stopover, it was onward to Missouri to see old friends from Taiwan, and suddenly, Dad saw a sign for Neosha, Missouri. He hit the brakes, turned the car around, and took off for Neosha, which is where they had their first house after getting married. This was a very special detour and one that both of their hearts told them they had to make. As long as it had been since they were there, Mom and Dad had no trouble finding the house and were happily surprised to see that it was still there. After a long kiss in front of the house, they knocked on the door on the chance someone was home who would let them come in, but no one answered. Oh, well; another long kiss, watering eyes, and back in the car to see Ann and Norman, their longtime friends from Taiwan.

After a nice visit with their friends of twenty-eight years, Mom and Dad were both feeling the need to head for Lake Murray. It had been seven weeks of wonderful catching up with long-time family and friends and seeing parts of the country they had always wanted to visit. They pulled into their driveway after picking up four bags of mail at the post office and saw that Rick had kindly mowed the lawn for their return.

Another Road Trip?

Because our cross-country travels while Dad was in the Army only allowed a specific amount of time to visit grandparents and cousins, there was little, if any, time to make side trips to various sites we noticed that we would have liked to explore. One of the places that stuck in Mom's mind was the Ozarks of Missouri and Arkansas. Dad was always ready to go, no matter where, and the next summer they were off and spent the majority of their time in Arkansas. This time, they only stopped to visit one of Mom's cousins, Parley, whom she had grown up close to but hadn't seen in years. He lived in Mountain Home, Arkansas.

A nearby town had a golf course, and Dad wanted to play a round. They didn't take a golf cart because of their need for some walking exercise after spending several hours in the car. Dad started feeling nauseous and dizzy while they were on the front nine holes and quite a distance from the clubhouse. It was pretty early in the morning but already very hot. Thankfully, another golfer came by in a cart and noticed Dad was in distress and took him to the clubhouse. He sat in the shade and cooled off for a while and was okay after that.

That afternoon they visited cousin Parley's family. It surprised them that the town of Mountain Home was situated in some of the flattest countryside they had seen in Arkansas. The next morning, they went back to the golf course and rented a cart so Dad could play another round with no further problems. Later that day they drove about ninety miles west to Eureka Springs, which was all mountains, with everything built on a hillside. It was really hot outside, and they had rented a small bungalow whose air conditioner didn't work. In spite of that, they had a lot of fun riding on an old-timey train through the mountains and later going to two shows that they both really enjoyed.

"When Dick really enjoyed something, he got into it, heart and soul," Mom said. "I had more fun watching him than I did watching the shows."

About the only thing Mom didn't enjoy was the intensely curvy, winding roads, and she was glad Dad was driving. After ten days full of fun, they arrived back home to find that something had been there, tearing up and scattering paper towels and tissue paper all over the place. Mom's first thought was that it was a mouse, but Dad spotted a young squirrel on one of the countertops and snagged it in a fish net, then released it outside. Squirrels aside, it was another good trip, and they both had a good time.

Getting Sick but a Big Thanks to Delores and Eddie!!

Mom and Dad were still occasionally driving to the commissary at Fort Jackson, and on the way home one day, Dad pulled over and said to Mom, "You will have to drive. I'm seeing double."

After getting home and unloading groceries they went to the optometrist, who sent him to his primary doctor. He took one look in his eyes and immediately recommended he go back to the VA Hospital. During the next several weeks, Dad had a lot of tests, and a double aneurysm was discovered on his brain stem. The VA said that there was nothing they could do for him. Mom asked the doctor if it would be better for him to be in the hospital since they were so far from help. He told her that it wouldn't matter where he was; if there was hemorrhaging, he couldn't be saved. Obviously, this was frightening news to the entire family.

Dan's wife, Delores, started making phone calls, and she didn't stop until she found hope for him. That hope was an experimental procedure called Gamma Knife. At that time, the Gamma Knife was available in Pittsburgh, and Mom was able to get an appointment in July, nearly three months away.

"It was late April, and as relieved as we were to have the July appointment, there were several weeks of anxiety facing us," Mom said. "Dick had to remain quiet and in a fairly dark place. Would he live until he could have the surgery?"

This was a huge concern for the entire family.

Then, Rachel's husband, Eddie, called his aunt who worked at the University of Virginia hospital. Eddie told her about Dad, and she told him that her hospital had recently gotten the Gamma Knife. He passed that on to Mom, and she wasted no time calling there and got an appointment early in May. That was an incredible relief! As a family, we are so grateful for the efforts of Delores and Eddie that saved Dad's life.

Rachel and I went with Mom and Dad to the hospital in Virginia. The next morning, we took him in and were basically told to get lost for a couple of hours, and when we returned, we discovered why. Dad had a metal frame attached to his head, and the surgeon was holding up a drill and squeezing the trigger a couple times. I happened to be looking through the window when he did that, and my knees got a little weak. The frame, or helmet, that was attached to Dad's head focused several small Gamma rays so that they intersected at the specific area being treated. This way, no part of the brain is subject to a high dose of Gamma radiation except for the treatment area. This maximizes damage to the aneurysm, while minimizing the potential for damage elsewhere.

We were allowed to stay in a glassed-in observation area where we could view the procedure. The doctor had some music playing, and we could hear him asking Dad questions from time to time. We could see the big metal helmet attached to Dad's head. The procedure didn't take very long, and Dad spent that night in the hospital. He was released the next morning, and happily for us, he was good ole Dad again, which was really uplifting.

The day after we got home, Dad and I went to the golf course because he was feeling really good and couldn't wait to play some golf. Unfortunately, he didn't have as much energy as he thought, so we didn't play much that day. Even so, he was glad to get out there for a short while. Mostly, it was so great to have him back home and doing well.

Mom recalled:

This was May of 1989. We settled into a fairly normal life. Dick kept his left eye shut as he never got rid of the double vision. We had to make several trips back to the hospital in Virginia for MRIs. There was noticeable shrinkage every time. We went alone the first time, which was a big mistake because we got lost twice. After that, there was one or more of our children with us. Dick had surgery for the double vision, but it didn't help, and they couldn't do any more …. The doctor tried to convince Dick to wear a patch, but he refused. I never thought he was vain, but there was no way we could get him to wear the patch. I kept telling him it would make him look debonair, and I used the same argument later when we wanted him to use a cane. It never worked, so he kept the eye closed; it didn't work for the cane either.

Nevertheless, Mom and Dad were able to settle back into a much more normal life at the lake.

We Love You, Glamich!
Later that year, Glamich moved into an apartment in Newberry. She was excited about it because she hadn't lived on her own in several years. Her apartment had call buttons in case she needed help. Mom had lunch with her frequently during the week, and Glamich usually spent Sunday with them at the lake. In May of the following year, her sister Maxine came for a visit. Early one morning, Maxine called Mom because Glamich had fallen and wasn't getting up. Mom called an ambulance to

take Glamich to the hospital next to her apartment. They determined she had a brain tumor and should be in the hospital in Columbia. She was there for seven weeks, during which she was given radiation treatments for the tumor, then was moved to a nursing home, where she passed away after a week. Dad and Mom were with her during her last night, and Rick, Grayce, and Pat were with her for a while. As precious as our Glamich was to all of us, it was another very sad time.

"After service at her church, attended by family and friends, Mike, Rachel, Dick, and I left for Wisconsin where she was buried next to my dad in Manitowoc," Mom said.

Fifty Years of Matrimony Times Three
Happier times picked up in December 1991, when Dad's brother Gene and his wife, Maymie, celebrated their fiftieth wedding anniversary with a wonderful party in Tampa, Florida. Mom and Dad drove down to join in the celebration. Then in January of '92, Dad's sister Pat and her husband, Phil, celebrated their fiftieth. Mom and Dad flew to Pittsburgh, and Uncle Phil picked them up to take them up to New Castle. Uncle Gene and Aunt Maymie came up from Florida. That part of Pennsylvania was having lots of snow, which kept some of the family from coming. Still, it was another really great party!

Mom and Dad's fiftieth anniversary, 1992

Then, on July 18 of that year, we celebrated Mom and Dad's fiftieth. Most of Dad's siblings and their spouses came from all over the country, and of course, all of us and our kids came. Each of us, with our kids, performed a song that was popular the year each of us was born. Some of the songs were well done; others ... well, they were performed. Unfortunately, Mom's brother and his wife couldn't come, but, as Mom said, "Dick's family has been my family all these years, and I felt in no way deserted."

Two days after the party, Mom, Dad, Aunt Joan, and Uncle Lou went to the beach for several days and enjoyed the warm weather. After they got back home things settled back down to routine stuff. Dad was doing quite a bit better and golfed at least three days a week, but never on Sunday.

An Unfortunate Effect of "Experimental"

In 1992, Dad's neurologist who had done the Gamma Knife surgery, determined he should have it done again, so back to Virginia they went. This time he was in the Gamma dome longer. The need for this second Gamma Knife was also experimental, and Mom—and all of us—wished in retrospect that they had refused to have it done. Dad had been doing really well prior to the second Gamma Knife treatment, but shortly after this one, he sat down in his recliner and didn't want to do anything. His balance got so bad, he gave up golf. Mom tried to get him to stay up and move about, but he would say, "You don't know how I feel."

Mom recalled:

We had two small ponds at the top of the property, and one day I took a nap, and when I got up, he wasn't in his chair or anywhere in the house. I ran out to the road, afraid he had decided to take a walk. When I got to the top of the drive, I noticed some movement at one of the ponds. Somehow, he had fallen into the pond. He said he had been there awhile, waving whenever a car went by. He was on his back, fortunately. I couldn't get him all the way onto his feet but got him sitting up and ran and got our neighbor to help me get him to the house.

The bottom of that pond was covered with small rocks, but other than a few red spots on his back, he was okay. After that, I couldn't leave him alone while I shopped, and he didn't want to come in the store. One day, he agreed to come into Lowe's with me. That is a huge store, and what I wanted was way in the back. They do have those nice carts for folks who have trouble walking. He refused to use one, so I said, "Okay, you take the shopping cart, and I will ride." Somehow, I said the right thing because he decided to ride. He really did enjoy driving around that store. He would holler, "Beep, beep," when he was behind someone, and he used hand signals when he was going to turn. After that one time, he would ride when he was willing to come in the store, and it made shopping much more pleasant. Usually though, he preferred to stay in the car, and he always wanted the windows up. I told him he didn't need to worry about anyone stealing him because they would bring him back. As time went on, Dick decided he would like to take a walk, and he couldn't walk alone. We would walk, hand in hand, and he would hold so tightly that it felt like my bones would break. I would tell him, and he would lighten up for a few minutes, then squeeze really tightly again.

Family Workday and Other Lake Fun

Not too long after Dad's second Gamma Knife, the Brats decided to have a family workday at Mom and Dad's place. There were always quite a few things that needed to be done that Mom couldn't do or didn't have the time or energy to do. After the first one, family workday became an annual event, involving the Brats, spouses, kids, and later grandkids. Mom created a list of things that needed cleaning or repairing, we organized a potluck lunch, and everybody worked, laughed, and had a good time.

One year, my son Rob suggested that we have a fun day. He and his cousins had some great times at the lake while they were growing up, and he felt that we should make sure as many of the kids and grandkids as could, would be there. So on a beautiful July Sunday, we had a fun day. There were four boats and two kayaks. We did some waterskiing, and some of us just sat outside laughing and having fun. It was also a "getting to know everyone" day for Pat's fiancée, Belinda, (Delores's niece), so we all wore name tags.

When Dad was working with the woodburning stove installation company, he installed one on the porch. They used the wood stove on cold days, so a couple of the Brats decided to have some wood-splitting parties. We borrowed a wood splitter from a neighbor for a while, then Eddie and Rachel brought one up from Augusta.

"It brought tears to my eyes to see the guys hug each other and pat each other on the back," Mom said. "We have been so blessed to have most of the family within easy visiting distance."

It should be noted yet again, whether it is Thanksgiving, log-splitting day, or family workday, we work and get things done, but we always have lots of fun doing it!

Knees, Obstinance, Scooters, Fun Therapy, Going Downhill

Mom had been having problems with pretty serious pain in her left knee for a good while. She called Rachel to take her to the doctor where she got a shot in the knee, which helped a lot. After the knee issue, she was becoming concerned that her own overall health was going downhill. Realizing that her health issues plus the care she needed to provide for Dad were wearing her out, she decided that maybe she needed some "Jinny Mae" time. She hired a nice lady, Nancy, to stay with Dad one morning each week, and for the first few weeks, she would run out to the stores and do her errands and hurry back home. After those few weeks of rushing out and back, she recognized that everything was fine and there was no need to hurry, so she would stop for lunch somewhere before coming back home. About that time, one of the ladies from the church invited her to lunch, and when she got there, she found that a dozen or more of her church friends had also come. That was really great therapy for Mom and helped her relax a lot more.

That winter there was another ice storm, which shut down the power to the house for a day. Mom got the wood stove going and piled blankets on the bed. During the night, she noticed that Dad's legs were ice cold. Mom said:

> *I tried to cuddle with him, but he kept throwing out an arm or a leg to keep me away. Dick always liked to cuddle, so I thought this was very strange. The next morning, we were still without power, but the ice had melted enough so I could get to the wood, and I had it fairly warm in here before I woke Dick. The first thing he said to me was, "Can you tell me who that woman was that was in bed with me last night?" I was sad that he didn't know it was me, but I was glad he wouldn't cuddle with someone else, even when he needed the warmth.*

Dad began having problems remembering the names of some of us, especially the grandkids and friends, and sometimes he would ask where Jinny was when Mom was standing right in front of him. I know that was hard on some of the grandkids, even though he couldn't help it. Along with that, he would fall sometimes when he tried to get out of bed. Mom had to call their neighbors a couple of times early in the morning when she wasn't able to help him get up. One morning, he couldn't control his left arm, and his legs wouldn't support him, and Mom quickly got him to the hospital.

He was there for two weeks with a feeding tube, and when that happened, Mom realized that he would have to go into a nursing home. When he was transferred there from the hospital, Rachel was with her. As they were walking down the hall to his room, Rachel turned around, crying. She hugged Mom and let her know she wasn't alone. "I'm here for you," Rachel said. She was and always has been there for Mom. Dad went back and forth between the nursing home and the hospital several times.

During that time, Mom's knee was giving her trouble again, and the doctor recommended that she have surgery, which she did. While she was recuperating, she stayed with Linda and Dave, who took great care of her, as well as frequently taking her to visit Dad.

The Final Salute to a Warrior, Loving Husband, and Great Dad

On the day Dave took Mom back home, Rachel was waiting for them to go visit Dad. Because it was a pretty day, Rachel wanted to get him up into a wheelchair that was fitted with all the paraphernalia that he would need for his tubes and wires. He refused and let them know that he wanted to stay in his bed. His doctor came and told them he was a very sick man and he needed hospice. Mom was okay with anything that would make Dad more comfortable.

The next Tuesday, she had a follow-up with her surgeon in Columbia. Mom recalled:

We got home in the early afternoon, and Dave was on the phone. He told me to sit down and then said, "Dad has left us." There are no words to describe how I felt. The next days are a blur. My children and their families were all here to give me support. My neighbors visited and brought food. Dick's brother Gene came from Florida. Dave did all the calling. The night before the funeral, St. Mark's served a wonderful meal for all of us. At the viewing following the meal, we prayed the rosary, and each of our boys had something to say about their Dad. I don't think Rachel could have talked, but her daughter read an e-mail that had come from Dave's daughter Kelli, who was in Romania. There were so many people and so many flowers.

This is Kelli's email:

On May 14, I brought a new life into the world, Bill's and my first son, Liam. Three days later I received the call I had been dreading—that a life that brought me joy and laughter left the world. My dad became a grampa for the first time, and days later my grampa passed away. One thing I have always said about Grampa is that he lived life to the fullest. He never gave up on himself even in the last months when his body was giving up on him. Yes, we all looked at it as stubbornness, but would he have been Grampa without the stubbornness?

It is a unique and character-building experience to be a grandchild in the Heath family. You learn to laugh at a very young age. Grampa had his own style of showing love and attention to his grandkids. If we didn't know better, we would find his love a bit intimidating! But behind that big bark of his was a tender heart, and we quickly learned of his love. He expected a hug and kiss when we arrived at his house, and if we tried to sneak by him, we'd hear that sergeant voice call out our name. He showed love through his teasing as well.

I remember going to the lake every summer with Kari. She and I would sit in his [recliner] just to tease him. When barking at us wasn't enough, he started putting a No Parking sign in the chair. And don't leave the light on in the hall bathroom because you would have to go back and turn it off—not without a bark from Grampa! Grampa had table manners too. Not typical Southern table manners, but his own set of expectations for all his grandchildren. Rule #1: don't spill Grampa's coffee! And who was the one who always got the seat next to Grampa? Me ... the no-so-graceful one. Every time I would scoot up to the table or back away from the table or just wiggle in my chair, I spilled Grampa's coffee! But how could my gawky teenage body help it? Grampa not only filled his cup to the rim but then he added cream. There was no way around it—coffee would end up on the saucer.

When I was about thirteen, I remember sitting in Grampa's lap and asking for a sip of his beer. He told me when I was twenty-one, we could have a beer together. Well, each year, I talked it up. As soon as I learned the phrase "drink you under the table," I challenged Grampa that I would do just that—drink him under the table. Only I didn't like beer, so we would have to use Baileys Irish Cream. My twenty-first birthday finally came, and I went to the lake to drink Grampa under the table. Gramma decided to join in the fun, so we opened a bottle of Baileys, and we sat at the table and talked. Before long, Grampa was dozing in his recliner, and I was falling asleep in the couch, and where was Gramma? Pouring herself another glass of Baileys and sitting in her chair. So Gramma drank us both under the table!

My favorite memory of Grampa, though, was at Jessica and Kevin's wedding. During the reception, Grampa sat next to the dance floor, and it was easy to see he would like to get out there and dance, if only his body would cooperate. I asked him to dance and he said, "Yes, but you might have to hold your Grampa up!" So we danced. He would lose his balance a bit and holler, "Whoa!" as he held my arms tighter. We didn't stop dancing until the music stopped!

In fact, no matter what life brought his way, Grampa never asked to stop the dance. He embraced his youth with humor, his wife with tenderness and admiration, and his big family with unconditional love. Grampa has set a standard for his family to live life to the last dance— to hold onto life with a stubbornness and to love each other uniquely. Grampa, you will be greatly missed, but you left us a lot with which to remember you.

Dad had full military honors followed by each of his grandchildren and great grandchildren placing a rose on their grampa's coffin.

After Dad's funeral, Rachel stayed with Mom for several days to help her get everything in order. In addition, the Army sent a sergeant out to the house to take her to Fort Jackson to get everything straight regarding finances, Mom's military dependent's ID card, and Army post car stickers.

Mom said:

As Rick phrased it, "Winter, spring, summer, fall, all you have to do is call." And that has been true with him and all his siblings. I have never been left to feel alone, but they let me be alone unless I ask for them. That first year, I spent Memorial Day weekend with Rachel and Eddie at Hilton Head and a long weekend with Rachel, Mike, and Martha in Southport, North Carolina. It is good to know I have so many whom I can turn to at any time …. Because Dick was in the nursing home for several months before he died, it wasn't a strange feeling being here alone, but at times, even two years later, I feel that he is here. He will always be in my heart …. During his Army career, Dick was gone many times; sometimes we all had to stay home and wait for his return. Other times we waited several months for a port call, and we would go to wherever he was. This time I will wait for my port call but not as eagerly as I waited for all the others. I was going through Dick's records, which can be quite interesting, and I hope all our children will take the time to look through them. I came upon a requisition that Dick had put in for our travel overseas. The man who had to approve it wrote in the margin, 'Wow. What a family!'

Growing up Army was, for each and every one of the Brats, an amazing way to grow up. It provided us with incredible adventures and a broad perspective regarding other nationalities and races of people in our world. We loved and respected Dad's work and accomplishments in the Army and the solid sense of right and wrong he instilled in us. He achieved the highest enlisted rank, sergeant major, E-9, in the US Army, as well as many honors, medals, and awards. We are all honored and proud to call him Dad.

Mom would be with us for another fifteen years after Dad passed and was able to remain at her home on the lake until a few weeks following her hundredth birthday when she passed. She lived on her own until her late nineties, and various members of the Heath Platoon and their spouses pitched in to help meet her needs at home. We continued to celebrate our family every Thanksgiving and around Mom's birthday in May with our yearly family workdays. These are celebrations the Heath Platoon have pledged to continue for all time.

Leading up to her hundredth birthday celebration, Mom said to Rachel, "It sounds like this party is going to be quite a shindig; I think I should stick around for that!" And she did, and loved every minute of it. A few weeks later, she passed on and is now with the love of her life, our Dad.

Sometime in her mid-eighties, Mom wanted all of us to join her in walking across the newly completed 2.7-mile-long Ravenel Bridge, which crosses the Cooper River from downtown Charleston to Mount Pleasant, South Carolina. Rachel summed it all up perfectly as we all headed for Charleston to join Mom:

I'm on my way to Charleston, South Carolina, with my daughter and grandson to walk over a bridge. Now, why do I want to do that? It's not the bridge walk that is drawing me there; it is who will be there. My mom, brothers, sisters-in-law, nieces, nephews, great nephews, my daughter, and grandson. Yes, you got it—family! The love of family that Mom and Dad instilled in me, in all of us, still draws us together. The love of family: the greatest gift of all. So thank you, Mom and Dad; we owe it all to you!

ENDNOTES

1 Katie Lange, "'Military Brat': Do You Know Where the Term Comes From?" United States Department of Defense, posted April 12, 2017, https://www.defense.gov/News/Inside-DOD/Blog/Article/2060438/military-brat-do-you-know-where-the-term-comes-from/.

2 "Civilian Conservation Corps and Illinois State Parks," Cultural Resources, Illinois Department of Natural Resources, accessed March 5, 2020, https://www2.illinois.gov/dnr/NaturalResources/cultural/Pages/CCC.aspx.

3 Illinois DNR, "Civilian Conservation Corp."

4 —.

5 Wikipedia, s.v. "Attack on Pearl Harbor," updated January 11, 2023, https://en.wikipedia.org/wiki/Attack_on_Pearl_Harbor.

6 Wikipedia, s.v. "Francis E. Warren Air Force Base," updated October 13, 2022, https://en.wikipedia.org/wiki/Francis_E._Warren_Air_Force_Base.

7 "FDR's 'Day of Infamy' Speech: Crafting a Call to Arms," *Prologue* magazine 33, no. 4 (Winter 2001), https://www.archives.gov/publications/prologue/2001/winter/crafting-day-of-infamy-speech.html#:~:text=Thus%20that%20first%20historic%20sentence,of%20the%20Empire%20of%20Japan.%22.

8 "Dreamland Ballroom," History Harvest, University of Nebraska-Lincoln, accessed June 12, 2020, https://historyharvest.unl.edu/exhibits/show/north_omaha_2011/dreamland-ballroom.

9 "Remembering Operation Torch: Allied Forces Land in North Africa During World War II," American Battle Monuments Commission, posted November 8, 2017, https://www.abmc.gov/news-events/news/remembering-operation-torch-allied-forces-land-north-africa-during-world-war-ii.

10 "Army Morning Reports, 431st AAA AW Battalion, January, 1943–December, 1944," National Archives, Textual Reference Archives II Branch at College Park, MD.

11 National Archives, "Army Morning Reports."

12 Colonel E. Paul Semmens, *The Hammer of Hell*, (self-pub, 1990), accessed at https://skylighters.org/welcome/the-world-at-war/the-hammer-of-hell-the-coming-of-age-of-antiaircraft-artillery-in-world-war-ii.

13 Wikipedia, s.v. "Tunisian Campaign," accessed March 7, 2022, https://en.wikipedia.org/wiki/Tunisian_campaign.

14 Wikipedia, "Tunisian Campaign."

15 —.

16 —.

17 National Archives, "Army Morning Reports."

18 Wikipedia, "Tunisian Campaign."

19 National Archives, "Army Morning Reports."

20 ——.

21 "A People at War, New Roles, the 99th Pursuit Squadron," National Archives and Resources Administration, accessed June 15, 2020, https://www.archives.gov/exhibits/a_people_at_war/new_roles/99th_pursuit_squadron.html.

22 National Archives, "Army Morning Reports."

23 ——.

24 ——.

25 Wikipedia, s.v. "Allied Invasion of Sicily," updated December 26, 2022, https://en.wikipedia.org/wiki/Allied_invasion_of_Sicily.

26 "The Man Who Never Was—The True Story of Operation Mincemeat," Commonwealth War Graves Commission, posted April 8, 2022, https://www.cwgc.org/our-work/blog/the-man-who-never-was-the-true-story-of-operation-mincemeat/.

27 ——.

28 ——.

29 "Liberation: The Sicilian Campaign—1943," Best of Sicily, accessed June 20, 2020, http://www.bestofsicily.com/ww2.htm.

30 National Archives, "Army Morning Reports."

31 ——.

32 ——.

33 Best of Sicily "Liberation."

34 "Allies Invade Italian Mainland," History.com, updated September 1, 2020, https://www.history.com/this-day-in-history/allies-invade-italian-mainland.

35 History.com, "Allies Invade."

36 Best of Sicily "Liberation."

37 National Archives, "Army Morning Reports."

38 ——.

39 ——.

40 ——.

41 Wikipedia, s.v. "Bombing of Cagliari in World War II," updated September 9, 2021, https://en.wikipedia.org/wiki/Bombing_of_Cagliari_in_World_War_II.

42 "Bombing of Cagliari."

43 National Archives, "Army Morning Reports."

44 ——.

45 ——.

46 ——.

47 ——.

48 ——.

49 ——.

50 ——.

51 ——.

52 Wikipedia, s.v. "Italian Occupation of Corsica," Wikipedia, updated July 3, 2022, https://en.wikipedia.org/wiki/Italian_occupation_of_Corsica.

53 Wikipedia, "Italian Occupation."

54 National Archives, "Army Morning Reports."

55 ——.

56 ——.

57 Wikipedia, s.v. "Battle of the Bulge," updated January 2, 2023, https://en.wikipedia.org/wiki/Battle_of_the_Bulge.

58 National Archives, "Army Morning Reports."

59 ——.

60 ——.
61 ——.
62 Wikipedia, "Battle of the Bulge."
63 National Archives, "Army Morning Reports."
64 Wikipedia, s.v. "End of World War II in Europe," updated January 11, 2023, https://en.wikipedia.org/wiki/End_of_World_War_II_in_Europe.
65 Wikipedia, s.v. "Atomic Bombings of Hiroshima and Nagasaki," updated January 4, 2023, https://en.wikipedia.org/wiki/Atomic_bombings_of_Hiroshima_and_Nagasaki.
66 Mieko Endo, "Douglas MacArthur's Occupation of Japan | Building the foundation of US-Japan Relationship" (master's thesis, UM, 2006), https://scholarworks.umt.edu/etd/2104.
67 Wikipedia, s.v. "Japan–United States Relations," updated December 5, 2022, https://en.wikipedia.org/wiki/Japan%E2%80%93United_States_relations.
68 Endo, "Occupation of Japan."
69 ——.
70 ——.
71 *Encyclopedia Britannica Online*, s.v. "Mount Fuji," updated October 6, 2022, https://www.britannica.com/place/Mount-Fuji.
72 William Wetherall, "Kishine Barracks and the 106th General Hospital: Life and Death in the Vietnam War Medical Communications Zone in Japan," Wetherall.org (blog), updated May 10, 2022, http://www.wetherall.org/kishine/Wetherall_2015_Kishine_Barracks.html.
73 "Yokohama American School History," American Overseas Schools Historical Society, accessed February 12, 2021, https://aoshs.org/collections/school-histories/as/jp/895/.
74 "The 1949 Ford," Ford Motor Company, accessed June 15, 2020, https://corporate.ford.com/articles/history/the-1949-ford.html.
75 Owen Rust, "The Economic Effects of the Cold War: Conservatism Plus Deficit Spending," TheCollector, posted December 1, 2021, https://www.thecollector.com/economic-effects-cold-war-conservatism-deficit-spending/.
76 Wikipedia, s.v. "Truman Doctrine," accessed April 14, 2021, https://en.wikipedia.org/wiki/Truman_Doctrine.
77 ——.
78 Wikipedia, s.v. "Spanish Formosa," updated November 22, 2022, https://en.wikipedia.org/wiki/Spanish_Formosa.
79 Wikipedia, s.v. "Taiwan Under Japanese Rule," updated January 9, 2023, https://en.wikipedia.org/wiki/Taiwan_under_Japanese_rule.
80 "The Chinese Revolution of 1949," Office of the Historian, Foreign Service Institute, United States Department of State, accessed June 15, 2020, https://history.state.gov/milestones/1945-1952/chinese-rev.
81 "The Taiwan Straits Crisis: 1954–55 and 1958," Office of the Historian, Foreign Service Institute, United States Department of State, accessed June 15, 2020, https://history.state.gov/milestones/1953-1960/taiwan-strait-crises.
82 Wikipedia, s.v. "Taipei American School," updated December 17, 2022, https://en.wikipedia.org/wiki/Taipei_American_School.
83 US Dept. of State, "Chinese Revolution."
84 Wikipedia, s.v. "Foot Binding," accessed March 20, 2022, https://en.wikipedia.org/wiki/Foot_binding.
85 "History of Fireworks," American Pyrotechnics Association, accessed January 3, 2023, https://www.americanpyro.com/history-of-fireworks.
86 Wikipedia, s.v. "May 24 Incident," updated September 5, 2022, https://en.wikipedia.org/wiki/May_24_incident.
87 ——.
88 Noah Buchan, "Dem Bones, Dem Bones," *Taipei Times*, September 17, 2006, https://www.taipeitimes.com/News/feat/archives/2006/09/17/2003328096.

89 "Cold War History," History.com, updated December 6, 2022, https://www.history.com/topics/cold-war/cold-war-history.

90 "Berlin Wall," History.com, updated March 31, 2021, https://www.history.com/topics/cold-war/berlin-wall.

91 Wikipedia, s.v. "Kagnew Station," updated December 16, 2021, https://en.wikipedia.org/wiki/Kagnew_Station.

92 History, "Cold War History."

93 History, "Berlin Wall."

94 Wikipedia, s.v. "Heidelberg," updated January 10, 2023, https://en.wikipedia.org/wiki/Heidelberg.

95 ——.

96 ——.

97 "USAG Heidelberg Army Base in Heidelberg, Germany," MilitaryBases.com, accessed September 4, 2020, https://militarybases.com/overseas/germany/heidelberg/.

98 "John F. Kennedy: Ich bin ein Berliner" American Rhetoric Online Speech Bank, updated September 9, 2022, https://www.americanrhetoric.com/speeches/jfkberliner.html.

99 James H. Billington, ed., "Epilogue" in *The Civil Rights Act of 1964: A Long Struggle for Freedom*, published online with an exhibition of the same title, organized and presented at the Library of Congress, September 10, 2014–January 2, 2016, accessed online September 4, 2020, https://www.loc.gov/exhibits/civil-rights-act/epilogue.html.

100 Wikipedia, s.v. "Browder vs. Gayle," updated December 20, 2022, https://en.wikipedia.org/wiki/Browder_v._Gayle.

101 Roy Reed, "Columbia, S.C., Follows Nixon's Ideas on Integration," *New York Times*, September 2, 1970, https://www.nytimes.com/1970/09/02/archives/columbia-sc-follows-nixons-ideas-on-integration.html.

102 "Tet Offensive," History.com, updated December 12, 2022, https://www.history.com/topics/vietnam-war/tet-offensive.

103 Wikipedia, s.v. "Assassination of Martin Luther King Jr.," updated December 19, 2022, https://en.wikipedia.org/wiki/Assassination_of_Martin_Luther_King_Jr.

BIBLIOGRAPHY

American Battle Monuments Commission. "Remembering Operation Torch: Allied Forces Land in North Africa During World War II." Posted November 8, 2017. https://www.abmc.gov/news-events/news/remembering-operation-torch-allied-forces-land-north-africa-during-world-war-ii.

American Overseas Schools Historical Society. "Yokohama American School History." Accessed March 17, 2019. https://aoshs.org/collections/school-histories/as/jp/895/.

American Pyrotechnics Association. "History of Fireworks." Accessed January 3, 2023. https:// www.americanpyro.com/history-of-fireworks.

American Rhetoric Online Speech Bank. "John F. Kennedy: Ich bin ein Berliner." Updated September 9, 2022. https:// www.americanrhetoric.com/speeches/jfkberliner.html.

Best of Sicily. "Liberation: The Sicilian Campaign—1943." Accessed June 20, 2020. http:// www.bestofsicily.com/ww2.htm.

Buchan, Noah. "Dem Bones, Dem Bones." *Taipei Times*, September 17, 2006. https:// www.taipeitimes.com/News/feat/archives/2006/09/17/2003328096.

Endo, Mieko. "Douglas MacArthur's Occupation of Japan: Building the foundation of US-Japan Relationship." Master's thesis, UM, 2006. https://scholarworks.umt.edu/etd/2104.

Billington, James H. ed. "Epilogue." In The Civil Rights Act of 1964: A Long Struggle for Freedom. Published online with an exhibition of the same title, organized and presented at the at the Library of Congress, September 10, 2014–January 2, 2016. Accessed online September 4, 2020. https://www.loc.gov/exhibits/civil-rights-act/epilogue.html.

Commonwealth War Graves Commission. "The Man Who Never Was—The True Story of Operation Mincemeat." Posted April 8, 2022. https://www.cwgc.org/our-work/blog/the-man-who-never-was-the-true-story-of-operation-mincemeat/.

Ford Motor Company. "The 1949 Ford." Accessed June 15, 2020. https://corporate.ford.com/articles/history/the-1949-ford.html.

History.com. "Allies Invade Italian Mainland." Updated September 1, 2020. https://www.history.com/this-day-in-history/allies-invade-italian-mainland.

———. "Berlin Wall." Updated March 31, 2021. https://www.history.com/topics/cold-war/berlin-wall.

———. "Cold War History." Updated December 6, 2022. https://www.history.com/topics/cold-war/cold-war-history.

———. "Tet Offensive." Updated December 12, 2022. https://www.history.com/topics/vietnam-war/tet-offensive.

Illinois Department of Natural Resources. "Civilian Conservation Corps and Illinois State Parks." Accessed March 5, 2020. https://www2.illinois.gov/dnr/NaturalResources/cultural/Pages/CCC.aspx.

Lange, Katie. "'Military Brat': Do You Know Where the Term Comes From?" United States Department of Defense. Posted April 12, 2017. https://www.defense.gov/News/Inside-DOD/Blog/Article/2060438/military-brat-do-you-know-where-the-term-comes-from/.

MilitaryBases.com. "USAG Heidelberg Army Base in Heidelberg, Germany." Accessed September 4, 2020. https://militarybases.com/overseas/germany/heidelberg/.

National Archives and Resources Administration. "A People at War, New Roles, the 99th Pursuit Squadron." Accessed October 1, 2019. https://www.archives.gov/exhibits/a_people_at_war/new_roles/99th_pursuit_squadron.html.

National Archives, Textual Reference Archives II. "United States Army Morning Reports, 431st AAA AW Battalion, January, 1943–December, 1944." College Park, Maryland.

Prologue staff. "FDR's 'Day of Infamy' Speech Crafting a Call to Arms." *Prologue* magazine 33, no. 4 (Winter 2001). https://www.archives.gov/publications/prologue/2001/winter/crafting-day-of-infamy-speech.html#:~:text=Thus%20that%20first%20historic%20sentence,of%20the%20Empire%20of%20Japan.%22.

Reed, Roy. "Columbia, South Carolina Follows Nixon's Ideas on Integration." *New York Times*, September 2, 1970. https://www.nytimes.com/1970/09/02/archives/columbia-sc-follows-nixons-ideas-on-integration.html.

Rust, Owen. "The Economic Effects of the Cold War: Conservatism Plus Deficit Spending." TheCollector. Posted December 1, 2021. https://www.thecollector.com/economic-effects-cold-war-conservatism-deficit-spending/.

Semmens, E. Paul. The Hammer of Hell. Self-published, 1990. Accessed online at https://skylighters.org/welcome/the-world-at-war/the-hammer-of-hell-the-coming-of-age-of-antiaircraft-artillery-in-world-war-ii.

United States Department of State. "The Chinese Revolution of 1949." Office of the Historian, Foreign Service Institute. Accessed June 15, 2020. https://history.state.gov/milestones/1945-1952/chinese-rev.

———. "The Taiwan Straits Crisis: 1954–5 and 1958." Office of the Historian, Foreign Service Institute, Accessed June 15, 2020. https://history.state.gov/milestones/1953-1960/taiwan-strait-crises.

University of Nebraska–Lincoln. "Dreamland Ballroom." History Harvest. Accessed June 12, 2020. https://historyharvest.unl.edu/exhibits/show/north_omaha_2011/dreamland-ballroom.

Wetherall, William. "Kishine Barracks and the 106th General Hospital, Life and Death in the Vietnam War Medical Communications Zone in Japan." Wetherall.org. Updated May 10, 2022. http://www.wetherall.org/kishine/Wetherall_2015_Kishine_Barracks.html.

www.ingramcontent.com/pod-product-compliance
Lightning Source LLC
Chambersburg PA
CBHW022005080426
42733CB00007B/480